UP IN THE CHEAP SEATS

ii

PRAISE FOR

UP IN THE CHEAP SEATS

"If you've ever been a theater-obsessed teenager, this book is for you. If you're a theater-obsessed adult of a certain age this book will bring back many sweet memories and remind you of why you became a theater-obsessed teenager. An utterly charming and thoroughly entertaining memoir that draws back the curtain on many famous and infamous Broadway shows of the sixties and seventies, all through the eyes and thanks to the chutzpah of a budding actor and critic who never met a stage doorman he couldn't schmooze. It also pays beautiful tribute to four unique actors who should never be forgotten—Julie Harris, Maureen Stapleton, Joe Maher, and John McMartin. For that alone it is worth the price of admission."

- Nathan Lane

"As a theatre-buff, I've read countless books about Broadway, but Ron Fassler's *Up in the Cheap Seats* is unique among them all. It demands to be in theatre departments worldwide. I can't think of a single comparison, as it is from the perspective of a passionate theatre-goer who just happens to be a child! It's so good, I relished every word and tried to read it as s-l-o-w-l-y as possible, simply because I didn't want it to end! I intend to buy several copies as gifts, as it is one of my all-time faves, right along with William Goldman's *The Season*."

- Mark Hamill

"I deeply enjoyed *Up in the Cheap Seats*. The combination of Ron Fassler's personal, resonant story, along with the interviews and history of the shows make for a fascinating and very entertaining book."

- Michael Feinstein

"Love of the theatre, from an early age (and it's almost always from an early age) is a hard thing to make clear to people who don't have that particular affliction. It has a texture of its own, a sensation all its own, and attempts later in life to shake it off have been known to make people inexplicably sad. What is this thing called this kind of love? How do you evoke it? I don't know. But Ron Fassler does. If you want to understand your theatre-crazy friends, or understand yourself if you are such a one, read this beautiful and joyous book.

- Austin Pendleton

"I don't think I've ever read a book about the theatre that was as good natured, funny, and moving. A coming of age non-narcissistic love letter to some well deserving theatre legends."

- Emanuel Azenberg

"What a delightful book! I also grew up in New York City with the same kind of infatuations as Ron Fassler (I too loved Robert Preston). And just as he did, I wrote rather unconvincing reviews of everything I saw, offering very, very strong opinions. I devoured *Up in the Cheap Seats* with great glee."

- André Bishop

"For those of us whose hearts belong to the theatre, this is uninterrupted bliss. From the evocative cover to the delicious story inside, it is a funny and moving journey of a lifetime of theatre going. At 14, Ron had the eyes and ears of the toughest *New York Times* drama critic, along with the gift for expressing his opinions. Luckily for us, he wrote them all down. A gorgeous, brilliant book to be cherished."

- Swoosie Kurtz

"It is my great honor to be included in the pages of Ron Fassler's wonderful book, *Up In The Cheap Seats*. Not only does he manage to capture the essence of the historical aspects of latter twentieth century theater, he inspires us with what it means to be a lover of the stage, its practitioners, and its traditions. I'm thrilled and proud to be a part of it. Thank you Ron, for giving us a memorable and lasting legacy."

- Stacy Keach

"What a wise and wonderful book! It brought back many memories for me of the glory days of Broadway. Delightful.
-   Robert Morse

"Ron Fassler was going to the theatre and seeing shows just as I was beginning my career in New York. His exuberant memories took me back to a golden time. After reading the introduction, I didn't think it could get more moving or thrilling, but I was mistaken. Lumps in my throat, tears in my eyes, gasps of recognition, and cheers and laughter. I felt a visceral response about the theatre in ways I hadn't in a long time, and for that I say thank you."
-   Maureen Anderman

"Jesus, the first chapter alone and I was 😢   It is soooo great!"
-   John Benjamin Hickey

"I just loved *Up in the Cheap Seats*. In terms of MY growing up—it's exactly the kind of book that I would have DEVOURED when I was a teen. I would have curled up with it and never wanted it to end! Because it teaches you so much—about theatre and about the people you most revere, and makes you feel like you too could be part of it all. How wonderful that through this book, people young and old will find a doorway into this beautiful and fascinating world."
-   Winnie Holzman

"Thanks to Ron Fassler, we can now all participate in his story. Part history, part memoir, part reviews and all heart, all from a precocious, insightful kid who is now a talented, insightful adult. It is a must-read, must-own, must-cherish volume for all theatre fans, scholars and students. In the words of my Tony Awards writing partners Neil Patrick Harris and Lin-Manuel Miranda, 'We were that kid.'"
-   Dave Boone

UP IN THE
CHEAP
SEATS

A Historical Memoir of Broadway

RON FASSLER

Illustrations by Jeff York

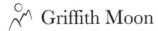 Griffith Moon

Published by Griffith Moon
Santa Monica, California
www.GriffithMoon.com

ISBN: 978-0-9993153-9-2
Library of Congress Control Number: 2018931145

Printed in the United States of America
First Printing, 2017

PHOTOGRAPHIC CREDITS
Photofest: 39, 63, 119, 138, 159, 199
Gerry Goodstein, photographer: 93
Fred Lombardi, photographer: 147
Photo by Martha Swope © The New York Public Library: 107
Courtesy of Joe Davis: 22
Courtesy of Timothy Jerome: 147
Author's Photos: 9, 85, 104, 173, 192

Those were the good old days.
And I hate to say that, and I will not say it
... but I said it.

Harold Prince
in conversation with the author,
April 2013

While I was doing Man of La Mancha, *I used to take the train from my home in Tuxedo Park into the city each day. And I made it a policy while on the commute not to read a book or to do any writing, but to take that time to create either a little boy or a little girl in my mind. If it was a boy, he was someone I imagined riding a bike and having a paper route. I'd give him a name and a family and I would picture him having saved his money to buy a ticket to come see* La Mancha. *And if it was a girl, she would be someone who came with the savings she made from selling Girl Scout cookies. And when I would get to the theatre I would pick out a seat, usually the front row of the balcony, and put a piece of tape on the wooden seat arm. And I would picture that little boy or girl in that seat and sing the entire show to that child. Then, during the actual performance, I would always find a moment or two and make sure I sent what I was doing to exactly that spot—and do it for them.*

- Actor Richard Kiley
(1922-1999)
as told to Peter MacKenzie

CONTENTS

Robert Preston in his signature role as
Professor Harold Hill in *The Music Man*.

THE GENESIS

I Do! I Do! – October 11, 1967

I was ten and a half when, out of the kindness of her heart, my Aunt Helen took me to see my first Broadway show. And not just any Broadway show: it was one starring my idol, Robert Preston. I Do! I Do! was the first two-character Broadway musical, and co-starring with Preston was none other than Mary Martin.

It's impossible to express what this gift meant to a child obsessed with the musical theatre: "The Music Man" and "Peter Pan" together for the first time on Broadway. In truth, it was beyond imagining. These legends of the stage—with five Tony Awards between them—would be all there was to see. No chorus or even much in the way of scenery or costumes. Simply two of the finest pros in the business with sterling reputations doing what they do best.

But how had a fifth-grader from a somewhat normal (though not really) middle-class family in Great Neck, Long Island, come to possess such a strong pull for the theatre?

Oddly enough, it began with a film. In 1962, at the age of five, I came with my family into "The City" (Manhattan) for my first visit to Radio City Music Hall. There, at what was then the premier movie palace in the world, in all its Art Deco splendor, I saw The Music Man starring Robert Preston.

As "Professor" Harold Hill—the role he'd created in the Broadway production five years earlier—Preston's charismatic performance was the real deal. Playing a con man posing as a band leader (who couldn't read a word of music), he wriggled his way into the hearts of the corn-fed populace of composer Meredith Willson's fictitious River City, Iowa.

I was so mesmerized by Preston up on the Music Hall's enormous screen that I have no memory of the Rockettes kick-lining in the pre-stage show. I was right around the same age as young Ronny Howard, who in the film lisped and sang the role of Winthrop Paroo, and was captivated by "Technirama" and "Technicolor." It was a thrill to share the experience with the 6,000 applauding people surrounding me in the Music Hall. Not only did that afternoon hook me on musicals for the rest of my life, it hooked me on the idea of becoming an actor.

I was awestruck (and star-struck) by Preston's career-defining performance. I now had an actor to follow, much in the way some kids follow a sports star. It wasn't long before I was poring over Sunday's Arts & Leisure section in the New York Times hoping for word he might return to Broadway in something new. All those ads for upcoming shows were so inviting and mysterious and wonderful. And in my heart of hearts, I knew it was more than just wanting to see Preston. It was more like wanting to be him.

I picked my idol wisely, for the more I learned about Preston, the more I discovered how admired he was within the profession. He was an "actor's actor," with a versatility that knew no bounds. In his book The Season, published in 1969, author William Goldman summed it up perfectly: "Preston is probably the most sought-after performer on Broadway. This is because he can do it all: drama; comedy, both light and dark; and, of course, musicals." [1]

One night my dad's best friend saw Preston in a theatre district restaurant, and in the sort of move that would never have occurred to my dad, he went over to Preston's table and asked if he'd sign an autograph made out to me, explaining, "I know a seven-year-old kid who worships you."

Naturally I still have it.

"For Ronnie, All my Best, Robert Preston."

Like my dad's friend, my great-aunt Helen understood what Preston meant to me. An independent woman, she lived on her own in New York City her whole life, maintaining an apartment on the Upper West Side well into her nineties. She looked out for my five siblings and me like her own children in thoughtful ways that never occurred to my parents. I loved her a lot. And when she announced that she was taking me to see Robert Preston in a Broadway musical, I loved her all the more. Even though it was nearly fifty years ago, I can recall everything about my first time walking with her through the theatre district. Shubert Alley, the famous thoroughfare between 44th and 45th Streets, made my heart sing with its gallery of oversized posters, the same as today. They were larger than any I'd ever seen. Then again, *everything* seemed oversized that night: the noisy crowded sidewalks; giant pretzels for sale from vendors on every corner; horse-drawn carriages accompanied by the clomping of hooves.

Taking in 45th Street, with more theatres on it than any other, was eye-popping. My familiarity with Broadway marquees up to this point were the ones that flashed during the opening credits for the popular ABC sitcom of the day, *That Girl*, starring Marlo Thomas as aspiring actress Ann Marie. I never missed that sequence, not only because I shared Ann's look of awe when she stared up at the marquees, but because the cuts were edited in such a rapid fashion that I was forever trying to decipher the titles. *

Finally, we arrived at our destination: the 46th Street Theatre (renamed in 1990 for composer Richard Rodgers, it is where *Hamilton* resides today). Walking into its crowded lobby, surrounded by a crush of people, I was hit by the smell of cigarette smoke that swirled overhead in large clouds, a buzz of electricity coursing through me.

There was a grand staircase leading upstairs—not my destination this night. I wouldn't ascend those heights for some time to come. Our seats were in the orchestra, and Aunt Helen handed me a single ticket, explaining that there weren't two available together and that she would sit a few rows back. I was going to sit alone in the seat closest to the stage. Don't you just love her?

---

* Long before the days of a pause button, it can now be revealed the titles were *The Star-Spangled Girl, Cactus Flower, Cabaret* and *Philadelphia, Here I Come!*

The plot of *I Do! I Do!* is simplicity itself. Based on Dutch novelist and playwright Jan DeHartog's *The Fourposter*, a Tony-winner for Best Play in 1952, it covers the life of a couple's fifty-year marriage. In its musical version, written by Tom Jones and Harvey Schmidt, it remained true to its source—a seriously old-fashioned take on marriage. Critics quibbled (not unmerited in such a politically radical year as 1966), but audiences made up their own minds and turned it into a decisive hit.

The crucial casting of Agnes and Michael determines whether any production will succeed or fail. With Martin and Preston, a score tailored to their needs, and with a full orchestra the likes of which is rarely heard nowadays, the production was charm personified. From the moment it began, with Martin stage left and Preston stage right singing their thoughts aloud on their wedding day, the audience related, rapt participants in all that followed.

I was one of them. And from the seventh row of the orchestra, I couldn't escape a feeling that all eyes in the house were focused on me from the moment I sat down. It was as if everyone was murmuring, "Welcome to the theatre, kid. Having a good time?"

Before the curtain rose, my level of excitement was soaring. It wouldn't be long before I saw Preston in person. Having memorized the record album, I knew it was he who sang the first line of the show.

When the lights came up on Preston and Martin in front of me, I rubbed my eyes. Accustomed to movies, this 3-D aspect took some adjustment. I had to take off my glasses and look outside the window of the lenses. Yup—it was them all right. In an instant I was thoroughly engaged by their singing and dancing. Much to my joy, the songs I'd imagined in my head were being staged in exceedingly clever ways—nothing like how I had pictured them.

The first act flew by. When I turned to look back at my aunt at intermission, I found her emphatically pointing at me. I discovered why when we met up in the lobby.

Aunt Helen grinned at me. "Do you have any idea who's sitting in front of you?"

"You mean the lady with the big hair?"

Exactly. The lady with the big hair. Lady Bird Johnson—then First Lady of the United States—and I was seated directly behind her. All those eyes I thought were on me before the show weren't for the boy in seat G 112, but for the woman in F 112.

With Lady Bird meaning more to Aunt Helen than she did to me, I was asked to switch seats for Act II. Of course I said yes, and when Aunt Helen squeezed herself in between the two large secret service agents, one of them asked after me. "Where's that little boy who knows the lyrics to all the songs?"

This was the cue my aunt was waiting for. She unleashed everything in her arsenal with these guys in order to gain the permission necessary to allow me backstage to meet Preston. Giving it her best shot, she pulled out all the skills she'd honed over fifty years as a top saleslady at Bergdorf Goodman on Fifth Avenue.

"My nephew is Robert Preston's number one fan!" she cried. Only this time there was no sale. The First Lady had every intention of visiting her fellow Texan Mary Martin, and securing the backstage area made any other guests impossible.

I wanted the show to never finish. Even after the final curtain, I waited until almost every other audience member had left before I would even consider leaving the theatre. It then dawned on me that I should grab some extra *Playbills* as souvenirs, so I knelt down and began scooping up discarded ones off the floor in my aisle.

After a minute or so, I encountered a pair of feet and looked up.

An usher was standing over me, arms crossed.

"What are you doing?" she asked. I didn't know if I'd been caught at something illegal.

I froze, then stammered, "I wanted some extra programs to pass out at school for Show and Tell."

The woman smiled at me, reached under a seat, and produced a stack of twenty-five *Playbills* neatly tied up in string.

"Here," she said.

I was floored. This lovely usher had recognized a kindred spirit. It would be the first of many kindnesses that lured me into this enchanted world, the sort of generosity abundant among "people of the theatre."

The next day when I gave out the *Playbills* to my fellow fifth graders, instead of reactions of awe or jealousy, they looked at me like an alien who crash-landed from another planet.

That evening, I got a special treat from my father when he returned home from work.

Ordinarily the first thing he would do was hand over the evening edition of the *New York Post*, having already read it on the train. But that night, before I could grab it out of
his hands, he held it up without saying a word and pointed to a photo on the front page:
Lady Bird, Mary Martin and Preston in Martin's dressing room.

I taped the clipping (along with my ticket stub) over my desk, where it remained for years. The clipping has long since disintegrated. I still have the ticket stub.

* * * *

My fascination with Preston continued for years. And after college, when I began living and working pretty steadily as an actor in New York, I always held out hope that I would meet and perhaps have a meaningful conversation with him. So when it was announced that he was being inducted into the Theatre Hall of Fame at a morning ceremony in the Gershwin Theatre rotunda, I knew I had to be there.

This was the chance I'd been waiting for. I was *not* throwing away my shot.

One problem: The event was by invitation only, and I had no invitation.

So what to do? Simple. I got dressed in a suit and tie and arrived at the Gershwin thirty minutes before the ceremony started.

I summoned all my courage and approached the official-looking young woman at the entrance who had a list of the invitees on a clipboard. I walked up and said, "Hello, how *are* you?" and breezed right past her. Sometimes acting as if you belong is enough.

Among the inductees that day were Edward Albee, Garson Kanin, Kim Stanley and James Earl Jones—an impressive group—each to be introduced by someone with a personal connection. Bernadette Peters did the honors for Preston, her *Mack & Mabel* co-star. He made a delightful speech, asking to be remembered for his flops as well as his hits, saying with a laugh, "I left the greatest performance of my life in Philadelphia in a musical called *We Take the Town*." *

---

* *We Take the Town* closed out of town in 1962. It had Preston playing the Mexican revolutionary Pancho Villa—in a musical, no less. As Nathan Lane once said, "Can you imagine that accent?" But the few who saw Preston, like Harold Prince, reported to me that Preston was "spectacular." John Cullum, who was in the cast, told me, "Bob never really recovered from that show's failure. He really was incredible in it. I pointed out once he was hitting a particular note and I didn't know how he was doing it. He stopped me cold and said, 'I don't know either—and let's not talk about it."

At the conclusion of the small and intimate gathering, people began to scatter and there was Preston collecting the overcoat he'd flung over a chair (it was that informal).

I timidly approached and extended my hand, a million thoughts flooding my brain.

"Mr. Preston ... congratulations," was all I was able to get out.

He whipped around and in that voice, as familiar to me as my own, boomed, "Why, thank you!"

He shook my hand and looked me straight in the eye.

I was inches away from him. He wasn't that tall (5'10", although in interviews he claimed to be 6'1"). He had a huge head and his grin seemed to occupy his whole face. He held my hand firmly and I completely froze. I had nothing left to give.

"Congratulations." It was all I could manage to say.

Someone shouted "Bob!"

His attention diverted, he let go of my hand, embraced his friend, and that was it. Our meeting was over.

* * * *

Two years after my brief encounter with Preston, I was living in Los Angeles and attended what was then a rare showing of the 1960 broadcast of *Peter Pan* on a movie screen, with the added bonus of an introduction by its star, Mary Martin, live onstage.

It was an emotional night, but I had no idea what else was in store when I came home to an answering machine blinking with a dozen messages. Friends and family had been calling in all evening, everyone asking the same question: How was I dealing with the death of Robert Preston?

Unaware that he had been ill, I was not prepared for this. It didn't seem real. And how strange to get this news right after seeing Mary Martin in person for the first time since that night at *I Do! I Do!*

I couldn't believe Preston was gone forever at the age of sixty-eight from lung cancer. If not for his being a constant smoker, perhaps he might have lived as long as his father, who died at age ninety-seven, nine years after his son. It seemed impossible that a life force such as Preston's could suddenly cease to exist. My mind raced at the thought of never seeing him perform again—his energy so different from any other actor in his class.

When it all sank in, I broke down and cried. I knew where the tears came from, too. I was grieving the loss of a dream—a fantasy, really—that I'd had since childhood: That one day I might work with Preston and become colleagues … *chums* even.

While I was still processing it all, my then-fiancé, Margaret Nagle, sat me down the next day in the kitchen of our tiny one-bedroom apartment and convinced me to write down everything I was experiencing.

In a short time, I composed a personal appreciation of Preston's work as an actor, tying it together with the Lady Bird story, my ever-so-brief meeting with him, and other details that made for what I hoped was an effective piece.

I submitted it to *Playbill* and was surprised and pleased when they decided to run it in a few months' time.

After it was published, a friend suggested I send a copy to Preston's widow, Catherine, his wife of forty-seven years. Tracking down her address in Santa Barbara, I wrote a quick note to accompany the article and popped it in my corner mailbox.

Two days later, I received a large padded envelope in the mail with the return address "Preston." Due to its size, I knew it had to contain more than a written response. I opened it and read Mrs. Preston's note first:

> *"Thank you for sending me your lovely piece in Playbill. I found it quite touching. I feel Robert understood your few words in their fullest sense. As one actor to another, the meaning was all there.*

I thought that was so sweet, only it couldn't begin to match what she sent along with it.

> *"It occurred to me you should have a picture that has hung in Robert's study for years—taken backstage the night you and Lady Bird saw 'I Do.'*
> *I hope you love being an actor. Be a good one.*
> *All my best wishes,*

This is what she sent me:

Mary Martin, Lady Bird Johnson & Robert Preston

Since I mailed my note on Wednesday and got Mrs. Preston's response on Friday, I have to conclude she removed the photo from the study wall, took it out of its frame, and went directly to the post office. Talk about an irresistible impulse! Her heartfelt generosity remains one of the most meaningful gifts anyone has ever sent my way.

Saddened as I was by Preston's death, by doing something positive with what I was feeling, I ended up being entrusted with a piece of memorabilia that Preston had kept for his lifetime. It commemorates the first time I ever went to the theatre. It doesn't get more personal than that.

That night at *I Do! I Do!* was the first of many remarkable nights (and afternoons) that I've spent going to the theatre. This book is dedicated to the four years between 1969 and 1973, from ages twelve to sixteen, when caught up in a whirlwind of passion, I saw 200 Broadway shows. Those were the days when fifty to sixty shows came in a season, and I was able to see almost every one of them at an average ticket price of $3.

How do I know exactly how many I saw? Because I numbered every one of them when I came home after each show and wrote my reviews (see Chapter 12: "The Critic").

With my visits backstage, I met some of the greatest actors of this or any other time. Sometimes it required a bit of ingenuity, such as when I was barred by the stage doorman from meeting Henry Fonda after his performance in a 1969 revival of Thornton Wilder's *Our Town*. Told he wasn't seeing any visitors, I knew it was a lie when I spied a group heading up the stairs to his dressing room. Seizing the moment, I slipped in unnoticed ... among a pack of nuns.

Lucky thing I was wearing a black coat.

In writing this book, I have been aided by the generosity of over a hundred theatre artists who sat for interviews with me, the majority of them directly connected to the shows of my youth. Their insightful and personal reflections made this a pleasure to research and write.

A lot has changed since I began my weekly theatregoing—some for good and some for bad. And though cries persist that the theatre is "never what it used to be," I remain an optimist about its future. For as long as artists of every kind are willing to feed the appetites of hungry audiences, there will always be live theatre to nourish us and keep the stories coming.

Now on with the show.

CHAPTER 1

The Hit

Fiddler on the Roof - December 21, 1968

A year went by after Aunt Helen introduced me to the lights of Broadway. In poker terms I was "all in." I couldn't wait for the chance to see another show. I would have happily depended on the kindness of strangers.

I didn't have to ... thanks to Mrs. Leboff.

The Leboffs lived up the street from me in Great Neck. Their sons, David and Kenny, were friends, and Mrs. Leboff had invited me along to see *Fiddler on the Roof* for David's birthday. At a pre-Christmas matinee, we climbed what felt like hundreds of stairs to the fourth to last row in the rear mezzanine, then foreign territory to me. When I reached the top, I was concerned about how far away things looked. I was seemingly a mile from the stage. Once the show began and the actor playing Tevye (Harry Goz) made his entrance, I was delighted how easy it was to see and hear him (and this in the days before a tiny microphone was attached to the skull of each and every performer).

Due to the cast recording, I knew all the songs by heart. But this was my first exposure to the world of Sholem Aleichem who, writing in Yiddish from his native Russia, had first introduced the character of Tevye in the late 1800s. I was thoroughly taken with the deft combination of humor and sorrow of the play's storylines, as well as the vibrant physical production, directed and choreographed by Jerome Robbins. *

At intermission I blurted out to Mrs. Leboff, "These are *great* seats! How much did they cost?" Smiling, she handed over the ticket stub. $3.60 didn't seem at all unreasonable, though for a little perspective, in 1968 it cost only seventy-five cents for a child like me (under twelve, that is) to see a first-run film. This ticket, at roughly five

---

* Jerome Robbins (1918-1998) was a true innovator in the worlds of theatre and dance. Among the many Broadway musicals he directed and choreographed were *West Side Story* and *Gypsy*, and his ballets *Fancy Free* and *Afternoon of a Faun* set a new standard of originality and excellence.

times the cost of a movie, was still an extravagance.

Then Mrs. Leboff informed me that the seats behind us—the last two rows in the theatre—were a significant eighty cents less, costing just $2.80.

Now I *knew* I could make the numbers work for me!

At the time I was earning around $12 a week on my paper route. As a respectable wage-earner, I convinced myself on the spot that I was plenty mature to handle coming into Manhattan without adult supervision.

Besides the cost of the ticket, I could afford the train fare, subway tokens (yes, tokens), and lunch. And if David and Kenny came along there would be safety in numbers. As each second ticked by, my scheme became more of a reality.

"Do you want to see some more shows?" I asked them. They answered with a non-committal shrug (which I took for an enthusiastic yes) and I swept into action. I wrote down the titles of what was playing: *Cabaret, Hello, Dolly!, Mame, Hair* and *Promises, Promises*—all up and running in their original productions. And even if most of the first set of actors were out of these casts, this guy Harry Goz playing Tevye was pretty good, right?

When *Fiddler* was over (and to this day I don't know why), I announced to David and Kenny we were going backstage. I guess it seemed a logical extension of our good time that afternoon and so, within minutes, the three of us were standing in the Majestic Theatre's star dressing room, where Harry Goz looked up at us quizzically from his perch on a sofa. He couldn't have been more welcoming. He dutifully signed my program—the first actor who ever did that for me—and so I remember his kindness.

A dozen years later, near the start of my acting career, leave it to the theatre gods to put me in a commercial audition waiting room seated next to—who else? Harry Goz.

There we were. Two actors killing time, waiting to be called in. I introduced myself and told him he had provided a memorable experience with his portrayal of Tevye and was nice to a little boy who knocked on his dressing room door. I could tell he was touched by this. So was I.

Neither of us got the job.

Harry Goz did get a commercial that I'm sure helped pay for his children's college tuitions: he was the Apple in the Fruit of the Loom underwear commercials for many years, alongside future Academy Award-winner F. Murray Abraham.

And what if on this same trip backstage, I had decided to visit some of the other actors' dressing rooms?

It would have been fun to report I had met Bette Midler long before she was famous, as it was she who played Tevye's eldest daughter, Tzeitel, at this Saturday matinee.

Midler joined the Broadway company as Rivka, one of Anatevka's townspeople, in 1966. It was her first professional job in New York after arriving at age twenty-one from Hawaii, where she was born and raised.

When she got the chance to audition as a replacement for Tzeitel, she told me what happened when we spoke in 2015: "Someone in the company suggested it wasn't such a good idea for me to try out for it. That Jerome Robbins didn't like Jewish women and would never cast me in a supporting role like Tzeitel. And worse, he might not like finding out that I was in the ensemble. I could risk losing the job I had."

"Did that make you rethink the audition?" I asked.

With a characteristic wave of her hand, she said, "Naahh, I sang 'Matchmaker' and he gave me the part."

In its early stages, *Fiddler* received a major contribution by way of its prolific producer, Harold (Hal) Prince. It was he who convinced Joseph Stein (book), Jerry Bock (music) and Sheldon Harnick (lyrics) that it would be worth the wait of more than a year for the availability of Jerome Robbins to direct and choreograph. In the opinions of all involved, it was Robbins who guided the musical from a show that might have been very good to one for the ages.

"We knew from the beginning that Jerry was obsessed," recalled Harnick. "He said the reason he accepted the invitation to direct it, was that when he was six his family went to Poland—the area where they all came from—and he said even at the age of six, he remembers it as being a very moving experience. Now, he said, he has the chance to put that culture back onstage, to bring it back to life. And that is exactly what he did." [1]

Set in a Jewish community the likes of which no one had ever seen on Broadway before—and certainly not in a musical—was risky. "People told us we were brave to be doing a very specifically Jewish show," he said. "I used to tell them I spent three years in World War II in the army fighting Hitler. Maybe that was brave: this was just Broadway." [2]

It was odd that even with Jews being voracious theatergoers, from a producer's standpoint, anything overtly Jewish was shied away from. Jews, who in large numbers helped make the long runs possible for such non-Jewish musicals as *Oklahoma!* and *My Fair Lady*, had no hit show to claim for their own prior to *Fiddler*. The entire social strata of New York Jews deeply loved the American musical and supported it as a kind of lifeline. They treated Jewish composers like Irving Berlin, Jerome Kern and the Gershwins as their own—buying records and sheet music to expose and nurture their children through example, to keep alive the tradition of going to the theatre.

In its early tryout in Detroit, *Fiddler* got off to a rough start, though things improved at its next stop, Washington, D.C. Word of mouth began to spread, though this didn't stop nerves from fraying, as Sheldon Harnick describes: "Out of town during the intermission, I went to the men's room, and there were two very well-dressed men standing peeing. I heard one say, 'If I'd known this was about Jews, I wouldn't have come.'" [3]

On the other hand, Harnick tells another story that happened early on: "I was standing next to Hal Prince when some lady ran for the telephone. She called her husband and said, 'Harry, you should have given up your card game tonight. This is a very wonderful show. You won't believe it. In the middle of everything there's a pogrom!' Except she said it in Yiddish, so I had to translate it for Hal." [4]

Eventually, audiences of all kinds came to embrace *Fiddler*. Still, it dispirited the show's creators when its initial reviews didn't jibe with what its sold-out crowds were so clearly enjoying. Adjectives such as "magnificent" were reserved for Mostel's performance, less so for the show that surrounded him. Of the major newspaper critics, two were outright raves, with the others finding flaws of one kind or another to nitpick.

It didn't matter. Nothing would stand in the way of *Fiddler*'s success and its multiple awards, or take away from the singular triumph of Zero Mostel. This multi-faceted actor received the reviews of his career when the show opened in September of 1964. Richard Watts in the *New York Post* perhaps best expressed the critical consensus: "Mr. Mostel's Tevye is one of the most glowing creations in the history of the musical theatre." [5]

It was Jerome Robbins who was responsible for Mostel playing Tevye, convinced that he was the only actor who could project the outsized personality (and authenticity) that would take the role of Tevye to another level—and he was right. Though they hated one another personally, Robbins and Mostel found common ground in their love for Sholem Aleichem.

But love and discipline are not mutually exclusive. In 2013, Sheldon Harnick and I discussed Mostel and fifty years had in no way dimmed his memories:

> Sheldon Harnick: *He made life miserable for every actor I've ever met.*
>
> Ron Fassler: *Zero certainly had a bad reputation. Renowned as he was for being undisciplined onstage, from all I've read, he really brought his A-game when* Fiddler *was recorded, didn't he?*
>
> SH: *Oh, on that day he was something else! He did "If I Were a Rich Man" in one take—then he wouldn't let any of the other actors forget it.*

If all agreed Mostel was brilliant, it was unfortunate that his brilliance could be turned on and off on a whim. The stories of how he broke character are legion: how he bored easily, how the natural clown in him (which the audience ate up with a spoon) came out in moments that sometimes worked and often did not. According to Joseph Stein, "There were times when we who had created the show felt uncomfortable going to the theatre, because we never knew what the hell we would see." [6]

Mostel's antics drove most of the cast up the wall as well. They didn't know what to expect—which Zero would be Tevye tonight?

Austin Pendleton, who created the part of Motel the tailor, was perhaps the sole actor who didn't feel the way that many in the company did. When I asked him about Mostel's outrageous stunts, Pendleton explained his somewhat different take on all of it:

> *Zero was capable of just about anything onstage. One night, he fell on me when I told him I wanted to marry his daughter. He took a long pause and collapsed his whole weight into my arms. He was so big and I was so small, and he was lying on top of me, and the audience was beside themselves.*
>
> *I was yelling, but they were screaming so loud who could hear me? And besides, Zero was so big you couldn't even see me.*

"Get up, Zero. I can't breathe, I can't breathe."

He had his face down into the floor and said, "Shut up! I'm in my part!"

He would do literally anything onstage and it drove some of the actors crazy. But it didn't drive me crazy.

RF: *I read that you said he helped to free you up as an actor.*

AP: *He was my liberator.*

RF: *So Zero taught you acting could be fun and not so serious?*

AP*: Yes, and yet his work was also profoundly serious, though he would follow any impulse. And there were nights he would do absolutely outrageous and, I guess, inappropriate things. But they weirdly had to do with the show. There was a strange kind of poetry to it.*

I was totally gone with him. He was irresistible.

Not all found him so appealing. At the 1965 Tony Awards, after what was a victorious night for all involved (*Fiddler* won nine of its ten nominations), Mostel took to the stage for his inevitable Leading Actor honor and couldn't help himself. He brought up the subject on everyone's minds, by stepping up to the mic and saying, "Since no one else has thanked me, I will thank me."

With Mostel's contract set to expire before the end of *Fiddler*'s first year, and as the sole producer in charge, Prince took a firm and courageous stand that life was too short to continue with him. Box-office draw that Mostel was, Prince gambled that by this point in its run, *Fiddler* itself was the star of the show. He would be proven correct when it would go on to a record-breaking eight-year-run, most of the time with no star names as Tevye.

As for me, I didn't care whether Zero was in the show. I was too busy being entertained and meeting Tevye for the first time. Discovering how the dairyman and his wife and five daughters dealt with a new world that upended their traditions and intensified their religious persecution riveted me.

It also brought up feelings of my own Jewishness in ways that caught me somewhat off-guard. I was diligently attending Hebrew school at the time and struggling with what it meant to be Jewish. My older brother had been bar mitzvah'd two years earlier, but everything about temple

Austin Pendleton and Zero Mostel as Motel and Tevye
in *Fiddler on the Roof.*

and Old Testament studies felt foreign to me.

As Jews, my parents did the bare minimum. They never spoke to us about what it meant to be Jewish or knew enough Hebrew to recite the proper blessings when lighting the menorah at Hanukkah. That ritual was particularly weird as my mother preferred to use an electric menorah. I know that screwing in a bulb may be the modern equivalent of lighting a candle, but it definitely took away some of the magic.

And in full disclosure, we didn't get any presents at Hanukkah. With six kids, my mother drew the line at spreading gift-giving over eight nights.

So we opened our presents all at once—on Christmas morning.

Don't ask.

Leave it to the power of the theatre (my temple, after all) to make me sit up and take notice of my Judaism as the storytelling in *Fiddler* struck me as both deep and true. Later, I discovered that Joseph Stein did a lot more than merely translate the works and that he took liberties and made broad changes to Aleichem's stories.

"Joe had to invent material—particularly the malaprops and the whole style of speech for Tevye—out of his own imagination," said Harnick. "His reward for that was that many of the critics said, 'Well, you know, how could he go wrong with that wonderful Sholem Aleichem material?'" [7]

Stein gets the tone of the stories right while also creating a core structure with stronger plotting, particularly with regard to the ending.

Aleichem had Anatevka's citizens evicted, the same as in the musical. Wisely, Stein chose to give the audience something in the way of hope by letting us know that at least Tevye (and what is left of his family) are on their way to America, which promises the audience a sense of relief that they will make it there and thrive. It is not for nothing that former *New York Times* theatre critic Frank Rich wrote that the ending "was one of the most moving final curtains of the American musical theatre." [8]

When Harvey Fierstein succeeded Alfred Molina in the 2004 Broadway revival, it was a role he sought personally. *Fiddler* had great meaning for him. He saw it as a child and felt a connection to the characters onstage in a way he never had before:

The curtain went up on a stage full of Jews, and it was shock-

ing to me. I felt a part of that world. Remember, this was a time when many American Jews were changing their names, fixing their noses ... They knew they were Jewish, but felt they couldn't be Jewish."[9]

Fierstein also articulately stated his own personal take on Tevye in this way:

> *There's always been this sort of theory that Tevye is an every-man, and that he just happens to be the guy in town who tells you these stories. But I don't believe that. To me he is the one God chose to survive. He is the only person in that village who could come up with that dream. He is the only one who loves his children so that he is willing to bend that far to breaking to accept them.*
>
> *And what that allows, and what his imagination allows, and what his capacity for love allows, is for him to go from a life of fundamentalism (because this is a fundamentalist life) to a modern life.*
>
> *He survives to go to America. And he survives in America.* [10]

Seven years after *Fiddler* opened, it was set to become the longest running musical in Broadway history. A few months before the date was announced, I did the necessary math and figured out in advance when it would be (July 21, 1971) and bought a ticket.

It was an amazing night. When the curtain call ended, the festivities did not. To commemorate the number of performances, 2,845 balloons dropped. Zero Mostel was there, hogging the limelight. When the speeches ended the audience was invited onstage, where there were free hot dogs from Nathan's Famous, my favorite.

When I met with Prince in 2013, I reminded him of the Nathan's catering, and his response was "Really? We had Nathan's? Well, how about that?"

Not satisfied with just this milestone, less than a year later, Prince broke the all-time record for a Broadway show when *Fiddler* surpassed the run of *Life With Father*, which had held the top spot for twenty-five years.

There was a reason for the endurance of *Fiddler*, which had as much to do with its creative team being on the same page as with the passionate desire of all involved to get it right. Jerry Bock said, "I felt if we had to write fifty more songs, they were still inside me. I had tapped a source that would not run dry, and I think that came from having nourished it without being able to express it all my life." [11]

Bock's words hold particular resonance for me since *Fiddler* has nurtured me close to all my life, from the earliest stages of my theatregoing to my beginnings as a professional actor.

I was nineteen when I was cast in *Fiddler* (as Motel Kamzoil) in my third consecutive summer at the Priscilla Beach Theatre in Plymouth, Massachusetts. Although I didn't know it then, these would prove to be the waning days of summer stock, a once-thriving institution devoted to churning out shows on a weekly or bi-weekly basis (mostly in non-air-conditioned venues).

The group in which I took part was made up of college students from the Boston area. Our playhouse was the real thing—originally a working farm built in 1875, its rustic barn had been transformed into a theatre in the 1930s.

In its glory days, the Priscilla Beach Theatre attracted glamorous film stars like Gloria Swanson and Veronica Lake, who appeared there alongside youthful apprentices such as future Academy Award-winners Paul Newman and Estelle Parsons. Adding some late luster to its roster, Rob Reiner and Albert Brooks who, during a summer off from Beverly Hills High in the mid-1960s, made the trek to Plymouth. By the time I showed up on its run-down campus in 1974, even at ninety-nine years old, the worn-out barn somehow retained its magical allure.

When I drove off its campus at the end of the summer of 1976, I thought it was for the last time. So I couldn't have been more surprised when I received an email from Bob Malone nearly forty years later informing me he was personally staking a fortune into restoring the barn-theatre. After a dozen years of being out of commission (a nice word for condemned), he wanted to know if I would be interested in returning to direct the inaugural production.

It didn't take long to refresh my memory that this same Bob Malone was a longtime resident of the town who lived down the road from the theatre and, as a young boy, sold sodas at intermission.

Would I be interested in returning? What could possibly keep me away? Bob sweetened the pot by allowing me the choice of any musical I wanted to direct (providing it was one he could sell).

So I chose *Fiddler,* which I think I had been waiting my whole life to direct without really knowing it. Although I enjoy a cheery musical as much as anyone, when it comes to devoting time and energy into directing, it's best when "there's meat on them bones." Not only is *Fiddler* that show, but six of its ten leads call for young actors (which was all I had to work with).

In addition, there was the obvious temptation to come full circle, since it was the last big musical I did there. And widening that circle, I would be bringing my twenty-five-year-old son Jeremy along to play Perchik, the young revolutionary.

Choosing *Fiddler* didn't mean I was foolish enough to consider such an undertaking without someone in mind for Tevye. To offer one more completion of the circle, I was able to allow a young actor to take on a part that, if he wasn't born to play, was at least born into playing.

Herschel Bernardi was the third Tevye (after Mostel and Luther Adler). He was, in Sheldon Harnick's opinion, "the best of them. He was disciplined, he had a wonderful musical sense, he was a terrific actor, he was paternal, he had a good sense of comedy… I thought he was the best." [12]

That opinion is shared by Jason Alexander. No stranger to the role of Tevye, Alexander performed some of the best *Fiddler* songs in the musical revue *Jerome Robbins' Broadway* (for which he won a Tony). In 2016, he spoke with me of his memories of seeing *Fiddler*—his very first Broadway show:

> *I had to have been something like four years old, because I saw Zero in it, and he didn't play it past 1965. Then on return visits I saw almost everyone who played it on Broadway in its original run: Harry Goz, Paul Lipson, Jerry Jarrett and Jan Peerce. I even saw Theodore Bikel in New Jersey at the Paper Mill Playhouse. But my absolute favorite was Herschel Bernardi.*
>
> *There was a "haimish" quality about Bernardi [Yiddish for cozy and homey]. I just believed the essential goodness, kindness and warmth of his Tevye and remember so clearly when he had*

to cast off Chava and he says, "No, no, no!" More than any of the other actors who played that, he was the one that rose above everybody else. I'm not an easy cry, but I was in tears watching him do that. He was ripping his heart out of his body to achieve that moment.

Bernardi would go on to play Tevye more than a thousand times in a twenty-year span all over the world, returning to Broadway one final time in the summer of 1981 and receiving a Tony nomination for his performance.

But there were more Tevyes in the Bernardi family. Berel, Herschel's father, played the role long before there were fiddlers on any roofs, when in the 1920s he appeared in a Yiddish theatre play titled *Tevye the Dairyman* in lower Manhattan. "Not on Second Avenue," Herschel said. "My parents never got to Second Avenue. Never got to 'their' Broadway." [13]

For the Bernardi family, it would seem all roads lead to Tevye, as it was Herschel's son, Michael, whom I asked to play the part in Plymouth.

For this thirty-year-old actor, playing Tevye was the fulfillment of a lifelong dream. He was not only following in his father's but his grandfather's shoes as well. Boots, actually.

For when Michael took those same boots his father wore as Tevye to be fitted at a shop in Los Angeles, he mentioned their history to the cobbler. Examining the boots more closely, the cobbler informed him that it was *his* father who had made them for Michael's father.

Again, circles.

Michael Bernardi and Katy Corbus in Fiddler on the Roof, *Priscilla Beach Theatre, (2015)*

Before rehearsals began, I let Bette Midler know I would be directing Michael as Tevye, as she had played opposite his father over the course of her Broadway tenure. She was delighted to hear it and had this reminiscence of the elder Bernardi:

> *I loved Heshy [Herschel]. He was so good as Tevye—a wonderful actor. My favorite memory of doing* Fiddler *was that between the matinee and evening performances, Heshy would order in a steak dinner from Frankie & Johnnie's. The smell of that steak would waft through the theatre and I would think, "Now that's a star!"*

Though Herschel Bernardi passed away in 1986 when Michael was two years old, the connection of son to father is a profound one. For Michael, playing Tevye honored his family's history and gave him the opportunity to continue their memory in the name of "tradition."

On his opening night, Michael was interviewed for an article in the *Boston Globe* and spoke of some of his discoveries while playing Tevye: "It's amazing the power of theater that can unite two men who only knew each other for two years, unite a father and son from beyond the grave. I mean ultimately it's not about me. It's about my father, my grandfather, the Jewish people, all displaced people." [14]

Plymouth audiences came out in force to support the comeback of the once forlorn Priscilla Beach Theatre. An eyesore for decades, its new incarnation was as pristine and fresh as its new coat of red paint.

The show sold out every night, even with added performances to accommodate the demand. *Fiddler* turned out to be a perfect choice for a community excited and ready to reconnect with its roots, even if its Jewish population was close to zero (and I don't mean Mostel).

Personally, a most meaningful encounter occurred when, after one evening's performance, I spotted an elderly woman on the arm of the young actor Philip Feldman, who played Motel.

He introduced me to his grandmother, Cecile, who took my hand in hers.

"You know, we were forced out of Antwerp, my family and I," she told me. "We had no time to pack. I wore three sets of clothing and we just walked away from our home."

With the citizens of Anatevka having done the exact same thing moments before in the final break of their communal circle, I was deeply moved looking into this beautiful woman's eyes as she leaned on her cane, speaking her words with simplicity and no embroidering of the facts. It became so clear to me what a gift this show is, not only for those fortunate enough to work on it and present it, but for how it provides its audience an exchange of ideas and feelings to be shared together.

As Harvey Fierstein puts it: "The day the boys finished writing it and put it up on the stage, it was part of our culture." [15]

Over the years, *Fiddler's* record-breaking Broadway run has been eclipsed by more than a dozen musicals, some doubling—even tripling it—in total performances. Commenting on *Fiddler's* status in 1979 when it was still the record-holder, Hal Prince, in his memoir, *Contradictions,* wrote: "I don't think a show will run longer than *Fiddler's* 3,242 performances on Broadway." [16]

And today what currently holds the long-run title?

By far and away *The Phantom of the Opera* with more than 12,000 performances—twenty-eight-years—and counting.

And directed by who? Hal Prince, of course.

While *Phantom* continues its phenomenal run, any ideas for reviving it remain far and in the future. As for *Fiddler,* in conjunction with its 50th anniversary, it returned to Broadway for a fifth time in December 2015, opening to excellent reviews and a year's run.

And who was cast as Mordcha the Innkeeper (as well as an understudy for Tevye)? None other than Michael Bernardi in his Broadway debut. And in late August of 2016, he achieved what only a handful of actors have done: playing the same role on a Broadway stage as his father when he went on as Tevye to a delighted house filled with friends and family (of which I consider myself both).

In a *New York Times* article on this milestone, Michael spoke of the journey that got him to the stage that afternoon: "The stories of Sholem Aleichem, and *Fiddler on the Roof,* have put food on my family's table for generations. Even if I never sang one note of *Fiddler,* this show is responsible for my survival—it's responsible for my life." [17]

Circles indeed.

And why not let the last word on the endurance of *Fiddler on the Roof* come from Herschel Bernardi?

"*Fiddler* is immortal, it's an immortal show. The sun will never set on *Fiddler.* Never." [18]

CHAPTER 2

The Street

Times Square 1969 - 73

My going to the theatre as a teenager made it possible to take charge of my own destiny as well as providing a means of escape from a home where chaos reigned. And where did I go to escape? Times Square in the late 1960s and early '70s.

For a kid not yet twelve and looking to the religion of the arts for comfort, little about New York City screamed "sanctuary." The theatre was there, but so were pornographic peep shows, prostitutes, pimps and drug dealers.

To give a clear picture of how crummy the city was when I was hanging out at its epicenter, check out films like *The French Connection* and *Serpico* from 1971 and 1973, or worse, *Midnight Cowboy*, which really scraped the bottom off the shoe of the neighborhood's degradation. Shot in 1968, it comes closest to documenting the time when I was roaming about on my own. Not a pretty sight ... or a safe one.

Journalist James Wolcott humorously described this era (and area) when he wrote of that "stretch of Forty-fourth Street in Times Square where one tended to pick up the pace just in case it became necessary to race for survival." [1]

And from what exactly was I escaping?

Well, to call my home a madhouse isn't too much of an exaggeration.

For starters, a TV blared constantly because my mother thought it wasn't good for it to be turned on and off. So it accompanied everything we did from the time we awoke, providing atmospheric background all day long, then straight through dinner and well beyond bedtime.

At age seven, when I had my first sleepover at a friend's house (in what was a normal home), the silence after 10 p.m. terrified me. My parents were called to pick me up so I could return to my safe and noisy womb.

Six kids, with just a thirteen-year spread between us, had a wear and tear on my mother's good graces that slowly wore away to exhaustion. One day she decided that folding laundry was a waste of time, so instead of putting it in the drawers of our dressers she left it all out on a sofa by the washing machine in our downstairs playroom. Every morning before school we would file in and gather up our clothes for the day to get dressed.

The house was tiny with apartment-sized rooms shared by eight people. It was both claustrophobic and a zoo. And any sort of traditional parenting held no sway. My folks' method is best described as "benign neglect."

My mother grew up having to follow stringent rules so she raised us with none. I often felt like Mowgli in *The Jungle Book*: a sincere human being raised among wolves.

How many typical suburban homes could claim its own graffiti wall—*inside* the house?

It started off innocently enough with my littlest brother and one crayon. But instead of removing what he drew on the wall leading to my parents' bedroom, we all contributed more to it. Soon visitors were writing on it, and then before we knew it, the whole wall was covered in graffiti.

I wondered why other families didn't have graffiti walls in their homes. It wasn't until years later that I discovered it was not proper decorum.

That's the way it was on Valley View Road, and I didn't know any different. It was puzzling watching the TV sitcoms of my youth—shows like *Father Knows Best, Leave It to Beaver* and *The Brady Bunch*—as those families all seemed so weird to me. Why did none of the children ever fight? I don't mean argue or be mad about something—I mean fight— with their fists. Didn't Chip and Ernie on *My Three Sons* punch each other every once in a while?

And what was it with the parents always having answers to their kids' problems? Mine never did. I don't mean they had the wrong answers, I mean they didn't have *any* answers. If I asked something of my father, he would say, "Ask your mother." The same went for the reverse. It was enough to make my head hurt.

The sitcoms I related to were *The Addams Family* and *The Munsters*.

Now *those* were some lifestyles that rang true to me.

Luckily, something clicked in my head at some point that told me I needed to escape the anarchy that was my household, if only for a few hours in a given week. Heading into Manhattan every Saturday provided that necessary getaway, and the money I made from my paper route made these weekly visits to the theatre feasible. It was important that I adhere to a strict budget, which is what I did:

Theatre ticket: $3.
Train fare (round trip): $4.
Subway fare (round trip): $0.60.
Lunch (usually at Nathan's): $2.00.
Soda at intermission: $0.25.
Variety: $0.75.
Total: $10.60 a week.

Insanely cheap. The requisite copy of *Variety* was a classy touch and I loved checking the weekly grosses of my favorite shows.

I would come in from Great Neck on the Long Island Rail Road where the twenty-five-minute train ride would end its run at Penn Station/34th Street. Then, because the adult I first consulted told me to, I diligently hopped the subway one stop to 42nd Street. It worked like a charm for maybe a year or so until in a head-slapping moment it came to me that it was an eight-block walk!

I was happy after that to save the thirty cents each way.

The better question is why my parents allowed me at age eleven to go into Manhattan by myself at all. It wasn't like I was some paradigm of maturity. I recently asked my 88-year-old mother whether she ever worried about me. With her usual bluntness, she replied, "What was there to worry about?"

Ignorance is bliss.

There were times I would see two plays in a day, matinee and evening, and not return home until 11:00 o'clock at night. With sometimes as many as four hours to kill between shows, I figured out spots that were safe and allowed me uninterrupted periods of undiluted pleasure. Mainly, the Sam Goody record store (yes, records) on West 49th Street and the Drama Book Shop on West 52nd.

Being on a tight budget, I was forever in search of any bargain that
could be had in the Times Square district. If I was thirsty at intermission,
there was no way I was ever going to buy an orange drink from the con-
cession at the outrageous price of $2.50. Early on, I discovered a handy
soda machine inside a parking garage (only recently demolished) next to
the Imperial Theatre. With eleven theatres on 45th Street, as well as five
on 44th and three on 46th, there was ample time given the fifteen-min-
ute intermissions, to walk over and grab a Pepsi for twenty-five cents. I
would have preferred if the machine dispensed Cokes, but beggars can't
be choosers.

Further north, if I was at any of the theatres between 49th and 53rd
Streets, an arcade on the corner of Broadway and 52nd was the spot to
hustle to at intermission, where you could find the best hot peanuts and
cashews in the city. Scoping out these sites was all part of my master plan
to make this stretch of Broadway my own.

All that was later. In early 1969, before my twelfth birthday, when
I first walked the streets of Manhattan unaccompanied by a grown-up,
everything was new to me. I felt an awe that was almost overwhelming.
Did I even take in that it was seedy? Sure, but so what? So was my house.

Unbeknownst to me, the area had been steadily getting more and
more depressed for some time. Many of the great legitimate theatres
were closing, either converted into movie houses (some for triple X-rated
films) or destroyed. It was a sad time for those who remembered many of
these architectural gems in their glory days.

It's hard to picture how dark it was back then what with the wattage
in Times Square now dialed up past "eleven." Novelist Jonathan Safran
Foer has asked the question, "Is there really anyone, besides Rudy Gi-
uliani, who prefers the new Times Square?"

Not the late Shirley Herz, a press agent who was honored with a special Tony in 2009 for her sixty-five years of service to the theatre. Herz,
a grande dame in the best sense of the term, was one who openly pined
for "the bad old days" of Times Square right up until her death in 2013.
"It was fun," she told *New York Post* columnist Michael Riedel. "I knew
the names of all the hookers on Eighth Avenue. I used to leave my car in
front of a cheap electronics store on 42nd Street. Didn't have to lock it.
The guys in the store looked after it." [2]

There are those today who share the preference Herz had for the roughness of 42nd Street as opposed to its current "Disneyfication." Nostalgia often makes for an overly-romantic vision of the past, but the ugliness that makes up what Times Square looks like today is indisputable. The garish neon and massive skyscrapers squeezed in over the last few years give it the appearance of downtown Tokyo rather than midtown Manhattan. Yet a statistic published in a *New York Magazine* article in 2015 states that "this transformation between 42nd and 47th Streets, 0.1% of New York's land mass, represents 11% of the city's economic activity, generating $110 billion annually." [3]

Somebody is doing something right.

Back in the early 1970s at the height of my theatregoing years, the danger of patrons being mugged once out on the streets after a show in the darkness of Times Square was for real. There was no question the neighborhood had a decidedly haunted and desolate look. Of course, I wasn't aware of any of this because I was having too much fun and took no note when Walter Kerr wrote: "Broadway was like a ghost town the streets of which were so silent you could put your ear to the ground and hear only the subway." [4]

He was right. It was not uncommon for some of the most in-demand theatres to stand empty for months at a time. Pre-made signage was slapped up on darkened marquees inviting patrons to "SEE A BROADWAY SHOW!" This was seemingly wiser than leaving up for months on end flop titles that ran one night like *A Place for Polly* and *Let Me Hear You Smile*, but it couldn't help add to the overall gloom and lack of luster.

In the first four years of the 1970s, when I was handing over my hard-earned paper route money, there were an astounding seventeen shows that closed in one night (eight of which I managed to see during previews). At one point, ten shows closed in a two-week period. With the high cost of mounting shows today, statistics like these would set off alarms of death-knell proportions for modern Broadway.

But sometimes a ray of sunshine poked through the dark clouds, courtesy of creative producers with a talent for smart publicity. When a well-received revival of *A Funny Thing Happened on the Way to the Forum* began to see its box office dip in the summer of 1972, a special Fourth of July event was announced in an effort to boost sales. For that matinee, every seat in the house would be given away for free starting at noon that day. To top it off, they would be handed out in front of the theatre by the show's stars, Phil Silvers and Larry Blyden.

By July, I had already seen this production 1 ½ times (I snuck into the second act one day when another show I was seeing proved a waste of time—yes, at fourteen I was *that* discerning). When I arrived at the theatre with my brother Allen in tow, we hoped to be among the 1,500 lucky souls to secure tickets. Without even thinking that there would be thousands of others with the same idea, we arrived way too late to get in.

But another teenager (this one from New Jersey) had better luck than we did.

"I was sixteen years old and showed up for the giveaway," recalled Nathan Lane. "Every ticket was being handed out for free—which would never happen today—and I was the last one to get in. They closed the door after me. And with everyone there for free we went berserk when Phil Silvers came out. What a day that was! I thought he was phenomenal. I'm so glad I got to see him." And when cast as Pseudolus in a Broadway revival of *Forum* over twenty years later, like Silvers—and the role's originator Zero Mostel before him—he won a Tony for his performance.

In talking with Nathan Lane about our mutual theatregoing days, we shared the same memories of hyper-vigilance, always on the lookout for winos, druggies, beggars and muggers. With Times Square constantly teeming with people, being cushioned by the masses was a help in never feeling too alone or afraid. However, whenever wandering outside its boundaries, an immediate sense would creep in that I wasn't in Kansas anymore. This would explain why I rarely saw anything Off-Broadway during those years. I never once made the trip to Joseph Papp's Public Theatre, which began presenting exciting new plays in 1967, two years before I began my regular theatregoing. I couldn't bring myself to go. It was too scary.

Interviewing writer and critic John Lahr for this book, we hit on the subject of my missing out on so much that was happening at the time.

"Don't be hard on yourself," Lahr said. "It *was* dangerous to go below 14th Street."

As to any real danger, I was lucky that things stayed quiet and uneventful—for a time. That is, until one sunny spring afternoon when I came in with my friend Josh, who had steadily become someone I could count on to see nearly anything, be it good or bad. We had arrived without benefit of purchasing tickets ahead of time, which was rare, so we needed to head over to the theatre and make sure our choice of show wasn't sold out.

The Playhouse Theatre was one I had never been to before, located on what was then considered the wrong side of 8th Avenue, west of Broadway: a filthy and dangerous hood called "Hell's Kitchen." The Playhouse was offering the classic dramas, *A Doll's House* and *Hedda Gabler* in rep, and this seemed a great way to start my introduction to Norway's father of modern drama, Henrik Ibsen. So feeling it was worth the risk, Josh and I set off to see *A Doll's House*. It was broad daylight. What could possibly go wrong?

Call it bad timing, but as soon as we ventured into this uncharted territory, two guys came out of nowhere and started up a conversation with us. Josh and I speed-walked as fast as we could, only they stuck to us like shadows, pestering us with questions—and trust me, they weren't asking about Henrik Ibsen.

It was Josh who realized something was up and sent me a silent signal that going to the box office and flashing cash wasn't such a great idea. We U-turned, and now with Ibsen the furthest thing from our minds, tried to get these would-be muggers off our tails. I came up with the not-so-brilliant notion of going to the Drama Book Shop, where I thought we could browse until our followers got so bored they would leave.

Only there was one little flaw in the plan: the sole access to the store was by way of a tiny elevator. As our pursuers kept up their endless jabber, Josh and I were so distracted that we didn't realize our mistake until it was too late.

Unintentionally sealing our doom, the long and empty lobby gave the guys the opportunity they had been seeking for the last half-hour. Staying close on our heels and with the elevator doors opening instantly and conveniently, like lambs to the slaughter, they quickly shoved us inside.

The first thing one of them did was pull the $20 Timex watch off my wrist. I shouted "Hey!" and he punched me in the chest. It didn't hurt, but it shut me up.

He demanded my wallet and seeing there was no cash inside, threw it back at me. I emptied my pockets handing over what little I had. All told, they probably took both of us for $25 combined, if that. They ran off and the elevator doors closed.

As the car headed up the five flights, the silence was broken by Josh starting to laugh. What was funny to him had been terrifying for me. Even if our getting mugged was safely over, I felt violated. And to make matters worse—for some deranged reason—I thought they were coming back.

"For what?" Josh asked, incredulously. "They *got* everything!"

His logic did nothing for my irrational fear they would be waiting for us, lurking around the corner, once we were back out on the street. So there was a lot more browsing than usual at the bookstore that afternoon as we had no show to see.

When I arrived home, I remember my younger siblings asking me if this meant I would stop going into the city every weekend. That hadn't crossed my mind, though it didn't take long for me to conclude I wasn't about to let anything stand in the way of my seeing shows.

I mean, if I did that, then the terrorists would win.

Eleven years later, long after my aborted visit to the Playhouse, I found myself employed there in Scottish playwright John Byrne's *Slab Boys*. I had the underpaid privilege of understudying five actors: Kevin Bacon, Sean Penn, Val Kilmer, Jackie Earle Haley and Brian Benben. Full confession: this was due more to its producers being tight with a buck and not hiring more understudies than to any great talent on my part.

Challenging as that may have been, I was more concerned with having to travel west on 48th Street for the first time in ten years, as by no means had things been cleaned up in any demonstrable way. I decided that if these guys were brave enough, then dammit, so was I (though I kept an eye out for my two muggers of yesteryear).

Slab Boys opened to unenthusiastic reviews and stuck around for six weeks (hey—longest run of anything I've ever been involved with). It was also the last show to play the theatre in its incarnation as the Playhouse. Its owner, Jack Lawrence, briefly named it after himself (which takes more than a little *chutzpah*), booked a few quick flops into it over the next four years, then sold it.

There's an apartment building there now.

And today, with the gentrification of Manhattan extending in all directions and every spot of land more and more valuable with each growing day, real estate agents are now apt to refer to the neighborhood of Hell's Kitchen as Midtown West or Clinton, its original designation.

Obviously not named for Bill or Hillary, but DeWitt Clinton, a former Governor of New York in the early 1800s.

There's a park that bears the Clinton name on 52nd Street between 11th and 12th where people roller blade and parents push their babies in strollers.

I hear it's a beautiful park.

Still a little too far west for me.

CHAPTER 3

The Drama

The Great White Hope - March 8, 1969

“**M**r. Earl Jones, please.”

With that gaffe, a combination of arrogance and a teenager's ignorance, I stepped through the stage door of the Alvin Theatre on West 52nd Street minutes after the curtain came down on Howard Sackler's *The Great White Hope*. Nothing was going to keep me from meeting its star, James Earl Jones, who had just given a performance that had sent shock waves through my system.

What in the world did the doorman make of me and my sixteen-year-old brother Allen—hippie-types with hair down to our shoulders? Did he think we knew James Earl Jones? Or did the actor have a policy to let anybody backstage who wanted to meet him? Or was my pushiness simply too precocious and irresistible?

Whatever the reason, Allen and I were instructed to cross the stage to where the star's dressing room was located.

It's impossible to forget this particular rite of passage: my first time on a Broadway stage.

And to top it off, this was my baptism by fire to the world of drama on Broadway. *The Great White Hope* was the first straight play I had ever seen. Up until then my diet consisted of musicals. Sure, there was some terrific acting in *Hello, Dolly!* and *Fiddler on the Roof,* but *this*? This was theatre of a different animal: intense, visceral and raw.

As boxer Jack Jefferson, Jones possessed physical and vocal qualities like no actor I had ever seen. And now, from center stage, I stood looking up to the second to last row of the balcony where I had been sitting. It afforded me Jones's perspective—and Alice's. I had stepped Through the Looking Glass.

I could have stood there forever if not for my brother's insistent tugging at my arm, which broke the spell. It was thrilling and a little scary—the enormity of it—plus the sense of history I brought with me that afternoon.

At twelve I was already aware this was the same stage where Henry Fonda performed *Mr. Roberts* for two and a half years and where Ethel Merman made her Broadway debut, stopping the show cold on opening night of the Gershwins' *Girl Crazy* singing "I Got Rhythm." Both alive at the time (and actively working), it wasn't Fonda and Merman's ghosts I was communing with, but their still-pulsating presences.

Off into the wings, my brother and I entered an anteroom next to the star dressing room where we joined a small group of all ages and ethnicities. There we waited, mainly in silence, for Mr. Jones.

Most theatres today no longer accommodate stars in this manner, what with backstage space at a premium. The large dressing room at the Majestic, where Harry Goz had greeted me after *Fiddler on the Roof,* now houses costumes (for future reference: if you are heading backstage to see "the Phantom," he's one flight up).

I was delighted to learn from Bryan Cranston when he was playing in Robert Schenkkan's *All the Way* at the Neil Simon (as the Alvin was renamed in 1983), he had the same arrangement as Jones. "I had the anteroom set up for guests," Cranston told me, "and I was very aware of the legends that used the same space as me, and all those historic years and shows that were staged there."

When Jones entered the anteroom (all six-foot-two inches of him to my five-foot-whatever) he appeared as if seven feet tall. Dressed in a white terrycloth bathrobe with half-glasses perched on the end of his nose, he spoke with a gentle and soft voice, nothing like the explosive bass that had just shaken the rafters fifteen minutes before.

I could hardly believe it was the same person. His bald head, shaved expressly for the role, was beaded with perspiration, and he was smoking a thin, black cigar. When I mentioned this to him more than forty-five years later, Jones said, "Ah, yes ... my Tiparillo."

He went around the room exchanging pleasantries, finally landing on me.

"And what is your name?" Jones asked in his low and resonating voice.

"Ronnie," I croaked.

He looked me up and down and asked, "How old are you?"

Hesitatingly, I said, "Eleven."

I was twelve. My birthday had been four days earlier, but Jones frightened that fact right out of my head. I couldn't remember how old I was.

When I told this story to Jones's co-star, Jane Alexander, she laughed and shared something similar with me—how a certain backstage visitor at *The Great White Hope* nearly caused her to forget her own name:

> *I opened the door and there was Sidney Poitier.*
> *"Miss Alexander, I wanted to say how much I enjoyed your performance."*
> *Words wouldn't come. I stood there in total silence.*
> *And that was our entire meeting.*

When Allen and I were back out on the street, our autographed programs clutched in our fists, there was acknowledgement that this was a first between us. I had impressed my brother with what he told me were "my balls." I don't think I mentioned anything to him about a plan to go backstage that afternoon. This was just part of the experience as far as I was concerned. I didn't feel it was my right or anything. It seemed to be allowed, so why not go for it?

Four years younger than my brother, this trip to the theatre held an interior motive, as I was always seeking ways to bond with him. The reason I chose this play was because it was about a boxer, so I gambled that might resonate with Allen, who loved sports the way I loved theatre. As it turned out, the play had a lasting effect on him that had nothing to do with a sports connection. It was his first drama too, and it's hard to come up with anything more dramatic, in the best sense of the word, than *The Great White Hope*.

The play, as Walter Kerr astutely wrote in the *New York Times*, is "about a man who is afraid of nothing written by a man who is not afraid of the theater." [1] Based loosely on the life of Jack Johnson (Jefferson in the play), it tells the story of the first black heavyweight champion of the world and of the devastating and overt prejudice that prevented his rightful place in the pantheon. The play stunned audiences more accustomed to less in-your-face fare, at a new top ticket price of $9.50 for a straight play. A relentless depiction of American racism, its premiere at the Arena Stage Theatre in Washington, D.C. had been five months before the assassination of Martin Luther King. If ever a play was a bellwether, this was it.

Jane Alexander: *It's always easier to look back at something and see the patterns. But we were right in it. And when you lived in Washington, as our company did—I mean, those were the times when the streets were burning sometimes at night. There were curfews. We all had to be in at a certain time, and if you were under a certain age, you had to be in by nine o'clock. We were aware of all those things, and then we were at the seat of a very complicated situation in Vietnam. We were in the cauldron.* [2]

Zelda Fichandler (one of the founders of the Arena Stage): *It had a horrendous impact on Washington. I mean, when the lights came up in December 1967 on a black man and a white woman in bed in Washington, D.C., you could hear, audibly, the intake of breath. That intake of breath is what rode northward.* [3]

Jane Alexander: *Most of my life I had never been exposed to prejudice. My father is a bone surgeon, and color is not very relevant to a man's bones. I have no unusual feeling as an actress about kissing Jimmy and getting to bed with him. If I were in love with him in life and he asked me, I'd marry him. Color means nothing. And then, too, Jimmy Jones is a great human being. He never makes anything of his color, either.* [4]

Staged originally in the round in the Arena's 800-seat theatre, *The Great White Hope* was a behemoth. Boasting a cast of 63 performing 247 parts, and comprised of 21 scenes set on 5 continents, it was easily the largest cast of a straight play New York had seen in twenty-five years (or since) in an independent commercial production.

James Earl Jones was well aware that playing the boxer held the potential to change his world forever: "I knew immediately that this was a role I had to play … a role of a lifetime." [5] All his previous work on and Off-Broadway, as well as small parts in big films (*Dr. Strangelove* and *The*

Comedians), had only served to move his career in a lateral direction.

James Earl Jones as Jack Jefferson
The Great White Hope (1968)

All that changed with *The Great White Hope*. "As I was leaving the theatre," wrote Clive Barnes in the *New York Times*, "Mr. Jones was receiving a standing ovation of the kind that makes Broadway history. ... If anyone deserves to become that occasional thing, a star overnight, then Mr. Jones deserves no less." [6]

Overnight indeed. It was thirteen years from his Broadway debut in a minor role in Dore Shary's *Sunrise at Campobello*. As Jack Jefferson, critics were unanimous in their praise: "The performance of James Earl Jones is literally out of this world" [7] and "[It] catapults the actor into theatrical immortality," [8] are but two samples that reflected all the others. Jones's newfound stardom in the theatre made it possible for nearly fifty additional years of steady film and television work. Along the way he has won two Tonys, three Emmys and an honorary Academy Award in 2012. Not to mention his voluminous voice work, including the announcer declaring, "This is CNN" off and on for over thirty years and the voice behind the mask of Darth Vader in the *Star Wars* franchise.

There is no stopping "the force" that is James Earl Jones. At eighty-four-years-old, he recently appeared in a revival of D. L. Coburn's *The Gin Game*, opposite Cicely Tyson, marking his sixth Broadway show in the last ten years alone.

Whenever I see an actor like Jones onstage, I wonder if a perfectionist such as he would consider it their best effort on any given day. Sometimes after a show, blinded by a brilliant performance and wandering the streets with tears in my eyes, I wonder if it's possible that same actor threw something across the dressing room the minute the curtain came down, angry at how he had stunk up the joint. And on days when I would overthink this, I would use Jones as the prime example whenever I put out the question: If what I saw was Jones *not* giving what he considered a hundred percent, then what would a hundred percent have been like?

While researching this chapter, I came across a passage in Jones's autobiography on *The Great White Hope* that shed some light on this: "The play was physically and psychologically exhausting, and after the first six months, I began to feel that in a week's time, we might get four of eight performances right. I wanted to get every performance right." [9]

As I saw Jones close to six months from his opening night, it's possible I could have been there at one of the "four of eight" a week he confessed might not have been up to his high standards. Again, it strained credibility that he had more to give on that Saturday afternoon.

Not one to dwell, Jones took a pragmatic approach to this question. "That's what rehearsal and preparation are all about. You set the form and you try and meet the form every night. Sometimes you do and sometimes you don't. Sometimes you exceed it."

I told Jones the effect his performance had on me personally, and his response was honest and heartfelt. "Thank you for being in that audience. They were wonderful audiences. I would occasionally, I'm afraid, misbehave when I was tired. And I would snap back at people who would cough too much or disturb me, you know? I was very selfish."

Digging deeper, I discovered that what Jones may have once considered selfish, his co-star, Jane Alexander, believes was more an act of self-defense:

> *The audience changed from virtually all white audiences in the beginning of the run to 80% to 90% black by the year's end. And their perception of the play was diametrically opposed.*
>
> *By the end of the year the audience really hated "whitey"— that was me. I represented all the forces that were against him, although I loved him.*
>
> *So they cheered when I died. And this was very difficult for Jimmy to take, because first of all he loved me as the character, and second of all he felt that the audience did not fully understand what the love relationship was about if they could cheer my death. So that made it real difficult for him particularly.*
>
> *It was easier for me, except I was lying there dead, sometimes for five to ten minutes, while Jimmy dealt with the audience's response. He would stop and he would talk to them. He would be very angry. And it was a huge emotional commitment for him as well, and Jimmy never gives less than a hundred percent, so he was truly sobbing.* [10]

Tony-winning actor John Glover, a young hopeful of twenty-five and new to New York, described for me the time he found himself in the audience of *The Great White Hope* at one such performance:

> *I remember when Jones was beating her with a towel, he was so angry at her, and it was right before the end, and there were a bunch of black kids up in the balcony who started screaming and cheering! And within a minute, he went down to the footlights and went, "SHUT THE FUCK UP OR I'M GONNA COME UP THERE!"*
>
> *And you could hear a pin drop.*
>
> *Then he went on with the scene.*

For Jane Alexander it was a noticeable debut in a career that hovers at the fifty-year mark on the New York stage. She won a Tony for *The Great*

White Hope, one of seven she has been nominated for overall. Jones won as well. His second Tony came eighteen years later for August Wilson's *Fences*. However, director Edwin Sherin, in a glaring oversight, was not even nominated for *The Great White Hope*. As the force behind the play since its inception, Sherin's guidance was invaluable in shaping Howard Sackler's script into something viewable in one sitting.

Zelda Fichandler: "The whole theatre was against doing it. It was fragmented. You couldn't tell what it was—it was literary." [11]

When Sherin gave it to Jane Alexander to read early on, she was surprised by how thick it was and how long it took for her to read. "It ends so peculiarly," I told Ed, and he responded by telling me, "Jane, that was only the first act." [12]

I asked Jones about the physical transformation necessary to play Jefferson. It was easy for him to recall his rigorous training, as well as how a small part of that change manifested itself:

> *I had weight to lose and hair to lose; a lot of adjustments to make. I knew I would never look like a boxer because I don't have the upper body and the biceps for a boxer or the chest muscles. But I knew I could get in better shape than I was. I felt I was fairly young then and capable, but as the rehearsals began, so did my training.*
>
> *I was assigned Bill Terry, an ex-fighter. He was my trainer and he'd get me up at 6:00 o'clock every morning before rehearsals and do what a boxer does. You hit the road, jogging, and you come back to the gym and drink some lemon juice and you go to work on the bags and so on.*
>
> *Then about two weeks into the rehearsal process, I decided to shave my head to see what that would feel like. And I did and I came into rehearsals and the lady playing my mom in the play, Jefferson's mother, said to me, "Oh, and we'd like you to know that we really liked Mr. Jones, but we welcome you." And I said, "Thank you."*
>
> *She didn't recognize me. And we'd been rehearsing together for a month. With the hair gone I was another person. I thought, "Well that's impressive!"*

Whether or not he wanted it, a certain leadership role was foisted upon Jones as the star in the play's company of sixty-three. Being the lead onstage often requires taking on that responsibility offstage as well, which can prove complicated, as Jones explains:

> *I knew there was an "us," but I didn't have time to look back at them. I knew as the leader I had to keep pushing and keep my eyes focused in front of me. And what was in front of me was the play and it being a black cast. And when racial issues would pop up in the society and they would reverberate backstage, I didn't have time for it.*
>
> *I think that sort of set the tone for the rest of my career as to how I deal with social events as contrasted to the events of the play. They must not bleed into each other too much. A writer has written a play and he has created a whole universe and it doesn't include the shit going on now around us.*
>
> *It might be about the shit, but it doesn't include the shit.*

Beautifully put.

* * * *

Born in rural Mississippi, Jones had a childhood far from the bright lights of the big city. Nothing strange in that, considering many actors are drawn to a life in the theatre from even greater distances and tougher personal obstacles.

Jones's major stumbling block, not an easy one when your sight is set on becoming an actor, was that he stuttered as a child, causing him painful shyness and anxiety.

At age twenty-two, and unsure of any kind of career path, Jones connected with the father he never knew. Jones was in the army and met up with his father in New York before going into active duty. In the intervening years, Robert Earl Jones had become a fairly successful actor and this meeting marked Jones's introduction by his father to the world of the theatre. Jones shared with me the changes it brought about for him in more ways than one:

I did not know my father. I came to get to know him better, and he took me on what I called "a grand tour" in 1953.

*One night he took me to see an opera—*Tosca*—with Leontyne Price. I didn't know what that was about. A lot of clapping and singing. I didn't know the ritual.*

The next night he took me to Swan Lake. *I liked that better, oddly enough, not that I had any aspirations to being a dancer. But I liked the movement and I liked the beauty of the bodies.*

And the next night he took me to see Pal Joey—*and—ba-boom!—that got me. Not that I thought I could ever match that kind of energy, the song and dance, never could I do that.*

But I loved it! I loved the lights, I loved the warmth of the world on the stage. And I said, "That's a nice place to be."

"Ba boom!" That really says it all, doesn't it?

But there's more, as Jones continues:

The last night of the "grand tour" was Arthur Miller's The Crucible.

Contrast to the warm lights of Pal Joey, *this was cold. A cold play, but I thought what a great way for a writer to make a statement without political words. He was talking about another time. I thought that was a great way for him to comment.*

My father was a staunch leftist. And he said that was Arthur's way of striking back at the House Un-American Activities Committee.

It's important to add that Jones's father's staunch leftism secured him a spot on the blacklist, curtailing his career as it did so many others. When I mentioned that they must have had quite a conversation after seeing *The Crucible*, Jones laughed warmly.

"We did," he said. "We had a lot of them."

Seeing *The Great White Hope* in the theatre remains with me to this day. It contained moments that made the hair on the back of my neck stand up, when I would feel flushed and my eyes filled up with tears. I cry in a movie theatre, but never once have the hairs on the back of my neck gone up while watching a film. It's simply not the same as when it's happening live in front of you.

Critic Walter Kerr stated it best:

> *Of all the time-space arts, drama is the one that digs deepest, finds profundity oftenest. Film can skim a surface brilliantly; but its work is essentially lateral, horizontal, a stone skipped on water. Drama stands still, puts a spade to the earth, and works downward until—at its best—it hits rock bottom.* [13]

Writing like that leaves no mystery why Kerr is one of only two critics to have a Broadway theatre named for him.

And the Kerr in me was slowly taking shape in these early days of my theatregoing. For whatever reason, I possessed the discipline of putting pen to paper when I returned home each Saturday after a matinee to file my reviews.

Yes, I wrote reviews. It's why recalling the 200 plays and musicals I saw in this four-year time span is even possible. They are all written up on my "Play Evaluation Sheets!" (note the exclamation point), numbered and stored in the same two loose-leaf binders I first put them in more than forty years ago.

From the ages of twelve to sixteen, I diligently wrote them down, forever working to expand my vocabulary in the secret hope that one day they would show how erudite I was for a Long Island teenager. They are by and large criminally overwritten and loaded with grammar and spelling errors. They are also, more often than not, unintentionally hilarious. Proof being my review of *Hello, Dolly!*, which I called "gripping."

So when it came time to do a write-up of *The Great White Hope*, only my sixth show, it was early enough that my penchant for hyperbole was in full gear, and I have to confess, it contains the absolute favorite line I ever wrote.

For the full flavor and effect, here it is. And as the main character in Robert Anderson's *Tea and Sympathy* says as the curtain falls, "Years from now, when you talk about this, and you will, be kind."

PLAY # 6

PLAY EVALUATION SHEET!

PLAY The Great White Hope

STARS James Earl Jones and Jane Alexander

DIRECTOR Edwin Sherin

AUTHOR(S) Howard Sackler

MUSIC

LYRICS

SEAT 14

PRICE $ 3.60

DAY I SAW IT March 8, 1969 (SAT, MATI)

THEATRE Alvin

PLOT - The story of the 1st black heavyweight champion of
the world, Jack Johnson. It tells about his being
the center of prejudice and his having a white girlfriend.
            (REVIEW)
This play is definatly one of the better dramas ever
written. With crisp, witty, sometimes bitter dialoge.
It's never so boring. James Earl Jones, with this
performance becomes one of the better, or best, actors
in the business. His performance is so powerful, and
takes such talent and strength it is magnificent!!!!!!!
Jane Alexander gives a fine performance as the tormented
girlfriend. Also excellent in supporting performances
are Lou Gibert as his manager, and Marlene Warfield
as his first negro wife. But Jones's performance
is so magnificent it will appaul you!

The last line is the one to which I referred as my favorite. "Jones's performance is so magnificent it will appaul you!"

My incorrect and improperly spelled use of "appall," a genuine attempt to pay James Earl Jones a compliment without quite pulling it off, has produced a few laughs over the years whenever I showed it to anyone. So I was eagerly looking forward to the opportunity to quote this to Jones himself in the days before we were to speak. I played the scene over and over in my head, safe in the knowledge I was going to engage his *basso profondo* in a belly laugh, and how entertained he would be.

But instead, after speaking it aloud, I was met with silence. Repeating it again, in the likelihood I wasn't heard clearly, I over-emphasized it: "Appall you."

Finally, he spoke up:

> JEJ: *(softly, repeating)* *"It will appall you."*
> RF: *(laughing, nervously)* *"It will appall you."*
> JEJ: *That's a great word.*
> RF: *I think I misused it.*
> JEJ: *No … no. My wife used to ask me, "Did you get a lot of action when you were doing that role."*
> *I said "No. Women were afraid of me."*
> *I got no Stage Door Janes. I got no sort of come-ons from women like Denzel will get … or will always get. Denzel gets panties thrown at him onstage while doing a Shakespeare play (laughing).*
> *But that didn't happen to me in that play, especially because he was scary. He put people on notice.*
> *No, appall is apt.*

I couldn't believe it. After all these years waiting to say this to him, I got a very different response than the one I imagined. Having long thought my childhood review inappropriate, it was instead revealed to have a whole new meaning.

I guess I was more incisive than I knew.

Thanks, Mr. Earl Jones.

CHAPTER 4

The Favorite

Julie Harris

A ctress Julie Harris (1925-2013), in a 2005 interview with the *Washington Post*, stated what her work as an actress meant to her:

"I found God in the theatre." [1]

The metaphor befits her as the theatre was her religion.

"God comes to us in the theater in the way we communicate with each other … It's a way of expressing our humanity." [2]

"You want to slip into this consciousness so that you make the person that you're trying to be come alive and that's sort of an act of faith. And you don't want it to be false. My soul prays for it to be correct, to be truthful, so it is a sort of prayer inside me that I will be true to that." [3]

It was one of her esteemed directors, Harold Clurman, who described her as "a nun whose church was the stage." [4]

So it was on the occasion of seeing my 26th show that I first saw Julie Harris's name in lights. It also marked the first time I saw an actress billed alone above the title of a play. There is no doubt my theatrical education would have been incomplete without seeing this luminescent actress live onstage, and I happily did so many times.

Though she made numerous appearances in films and on television, the theatre is where Harris lived. It was the air she breathed and her devotion to it was limitless and passionate.

In 2001, her career was cut short by a stroke, that is if "cut short" is the appropriate term when she had been working steadily in the theatre for fifty-two years. Living beyond her impairment another dozen years meant we were deprived of a number of great parts she might have played.

When I saw Harris in *Forty Carats*, a slight but extremely successful comedy, in the summer of 1969, I had no idea she was already a living legend who had recently won an unprecedented third Tony for Leading Actress in a Play. Occasionally I would stumble upon Harris on some mundane TV fare like *Tarzan* or *Bonanza*, hardly hinting at her status as theatrical royalty.

And though she positively glowed in *Forty Carats* as a woman of a certain age indulging in a May-December romance, this first introduction to her talents didn't display anywhere near the depths of what she could realize with better material, as I would find out soon enough. The Tony that Harris won for *Forty Carats* was more likely for who she was offstage than for what she did onstage. As she herself confessed: "I considered that a kind of a bright, funny, charming play but not remarkable. That I would win a Tony took me by surprise." [5]

By *Forty Carats*, Harris had already been charming audiences and critics for close to twenty-five years. Since her Broadway debut at age nineteen in the short-lived comedy *It's a Gift*, what follows statistically is a stunner: 21 Broadway shows over the next 21 years.

That's not a typo. Check it out. I did—twice.

During this period, she also found the time to tour the country in an assortment of roles including Blanche DuBois in *A Streetcar Named Desire*. When you also take into account her healthy output of feature films and television work during this same time span, it is an astonishing workload.

There was a price, however, to pay for such devotion to her craft. Harris was married and divorced three times, and there were periods when her absences created inevitable tensions while caring for her only child, Peter. In an interview she confessed, "My husbands were good men ... my work really isn't conducive to family life, but most professions have restrictions if you're really dedicated to what you're doing." [6]

And it was that very dedication which set her apart from all others. "Julie Harris wasn't simply one of the great American actors of the 20th century," wrote *Los Angeles Times* theatre critic Charles McNulty after her death. "She represented to those in her profession a reverential ideal." [7]

True, though Harris never took that too seriously, verified by a story her friend Anne Jackson would tell. "We were at an audition for some show. I was waiting my turn when Julie came out, slammed the door behind her, and announced to everyone: 'If I had tits I could rule the world.'" [8]

For whatever reasons, Harris undervalued her appeal, commenting that "pictures make me look like a twelve-year-old boy who flunked his body-building course." [9]

But I have to differ.

At twelve-years-old, waiting for Harris outside the stage door after *Forty Carats*, I wasn't prepared for the effect she would have on me. Looking directly into her piercing blue eyes and delicate features dazzled me. She looked infinitely more glamorous close up than from the last row of the balcony. Her infectious smile was only matched by the musicality of her speaking voice.

Turning her attention to me, she looked deep into my eyes and purred, "You have such beautiful hair."

With that, she ran her fingers through it—and I was a goner.

I wasn't alone. When Elia Kazan, no less an authority on actresses, as well as great beauties, cast Harris opposite James Dean in *East of Eden*, the head of the studio, Jack Warner, wished he'd taken a prettier girl. In his autobiography, Kazan wrote: "I thought Julie beautiful; as a performer she found in each moment what was dearest and most moving. She also had the most affecting voice I've ever heard in an actress; it conveyed tenderness and humor simultaneously." [10]

Not everyone shared that opinion. Walter Kerr, who wrote love letters to actors better than almost anyone, for some reason practiced tough love with Harris. Criticizing her physical attributes for not fitting his personal old-fashioned guidelines for beauty, he wrote: "Miss Harris's initial problem, I would say, was not her nose but everything ... her features lacked emphasis ... her voice was a small, rustling, warm but intractably girlish one-note: raise it a decibel and it scratched." [11]

Truly, beauty is in the eye (and ear, apparently) of the beholder.

In a 1991 *New York Times* interview, Harris revealed with honesty and good humor how she felt about her looks. When asked what she considered her only regret, Harris replied, "That I was not a great beauty ... it would have been w-o-o-nderful ... I would have liked to be just like Cher ... if I could have looked like Cher and also been able to act well, that's everything." [12]

Julie Harris as Ann Stanley in *Forty Carats*.

Born in Grosse Pointe, Michigan, an affluent Detroit suburb, her father was an investment banker and her mother a nurse. She attended finishing schools, but didn't have much interest in dating and coming-out parties.

In love with the theatre from a young age, Harris was indulged by her parents, who took her to every play that passed through Detroit. "When the great stars of the theatre had success in New York," Harris recalled, "they took it on tour. You didn't see a substitute for them. You saw the actor or actress who had made the show a success. It was thrilling." [13]

This explains Harris's lifelong commitment to "the road," stemming from those feelings of wonder when seeing stars of whom she daydreamed as a child, live onstage in her own community.

Stephen Root was a part of this now nearly forgotten tradition when, beginning in 1988, he toured the country with Harris and Brock Peters in Alfred Uhry's three-hander, *Driving Miss Daisy*:

> *When we went out with* Miss Daisy, *for what turned out to be two years on the road, Julie was sixty-three years old and worried about whether she was old enough for the role. Of course, that proved not to be an issue.*
>
> *Julie had this wonderful thing she would have us all do before the curtain. We would gather together and she would raise her arm straight up, her hand in a fist, and we would all follow and repeat the gesture. It was our way of connecting as one in solidarity before going out onstage. I just loved that.*
>
> *She was so much a theatre person to her very core that when our first year was up, she immediately signed up for another. Brock and I felt we had no other choice: if she was going, we were going. It was as simple as that.*
>
> *I wouldn't have traded that experience for anything in the world.*

After being accepted at the age of nineteen to the Yale School of Drama, Harris landed an audition right away for the aforementioned *It's a Gift*, which resulted in her Broadway debut. When it closed six weeks later, she returned to New Haven, though there really was no going back. She never got beyond her freshman year at Yale, or any other school.

Five years (and ten Broadway shows) later, Harris found the stardom she had been waiting for as Frankie Addams in Carson McCullers's adaptation of her own best-selling novel, *The Member of the Wedding*. Playing a girl of twelve, the twenty-four-year-old Harris was a revelation to anyone who saw her.

In 2002, Charlie Rose entertained Dames Judi Dench and Maggie Smith on his PBS broadcast. When asked if they had ever seen a performance that made them think, "Oh my God, I could never do that," it was Dench who quickly blurted out, "Julie Harris in *The Member of the Wedding*."

Smith, nodded in agreement. "Wonderful. I feel the same way." [14]

Playing a broad range of roles over the years made it difficult to come up with a "Julie Harris type." In response to an interviewer, Harris once said, "I think they mean a cross between Frankie Addams and Joan of Arc. Sensitive, a little rebellious … odd."

The interviewer followed up: "Fragile, on the edge, with a strong inner life?"

Harris's reply was a simple, "Yes." [15]

Her stage work would continue with as much variety as volume. Following her young tomboy in *Wedding*, she switched things up with *I Am a Camera* (based on Christopher Isherwood's *Berlin Stories*—the vehicle that served as the basis for the musical *Cabaret*), creating what is now the iconic role of Sally Bowles and winning her first Leading Actress Tony. This was her first of five in that category, still a record, plus a sixth for Special Achievement.

Over the next few years, Broadway productions featured her as everything from an Irish nurse in the earnest drama *Little Moon of Alban* to a parlor maid in the French farce *A Shot in the Dark*. She even made her musical comedy debut in the somewhat less than entertaining *Skyscraper*, with a score by James Van Heusen and Sammy Cahn.

For anyone curious as to what Julie Harris sounded like as a singer, an original cast album was recorded for posterity. Critics, heretofore incapable of writing her a bad review, worked overtime to find favorable adjectives to describe her singing powers. "Agreeable" and "enthusiastic" are two examples, while a third relied on that old standby, "She seems to be having a fine time."

Walter Kerr, though not saying anything nasty, stated what would prove prophetic: "[Miss] Harris has never appeared in a musical and may never again." [16]

And yet did it matter that she couldn't really sing? Not to composer Van Heusen, who stated for the record emphatically: "For me that broad can do no wrong. I want her to sing my songs." [17]

Harris's respect for acting moved her to mentor young people throughout her career. Urged to put her thoughts on the profession into a book, she sat for a series of dialogues with her friend Barry Tarshis. In 1971, these were published in *Julie Harris Talks to Young Actors*.

A primer for the acting novice, it bears Harris's distinct sunny personality and optimism. Her beliefs on what it takes to be a success, emphasizing hard work and determination, are pleasant, but provide little detail concerning her process. I suspect it's doubtful she could have done so even if she wanted. There are many actors who can wax philosophic about their craft, although there are just as many who cannot.

Learning how to become a great actor was something I was curious about from the time I first discovered what great acting was. If I were to register a guess that would have been sometime in the mid-1960s when I was around eight or nine. One evening I was watching NBC's *Saturday Night at the Movies* and saw Richard Burton and Peter O'Toole in *Becket*—and I was hypnotized.

It would be years before I fully understood and appreciated the subtle underplaying Burton brought to the film's title role, but the thrillingly over-the-top performance by O'Toole as King Henry II has (for better or worse) stayed with me forever.

With each passing year of my adolescence, the question of how actors and actresses became great artists consumed me so I read every biography and autobiography I could get my hands on. I was particularly taken with books I had read on Spencer Tracy and Paul Muni, two very different actors who captivated me with their screen performances. And it was during this period of influence that something caught my attention in the *Great Neck Record*, our town's local newspaper. It was an advertisement with a photo of a handsome middle-aged woman announcing auditions for her acting school—The Ruth S. Klinger Theatre Workshop.

I was intrigued, and what really caught my eye was that a full year's tuition scholarship would be awarded to some "outstanding student."

Scholarship! I liked the sound of that, especially as going for free was my sole option. There was no way I would ever get my parents to spring for acting lessons.

This was exciting, and all I had to do was make myself that "outstanding student."

From the instructions it appeared something called a "monologue" was required.

A monologue? I looked the word up and upon discovering it was a speech, my next thought was, "How hard could that be?"

So I wrote one—seriously.

I didn't even think to pull a speech from an existing play. What possessed me at eleven to think I knew enough about what to write, let alone *how* to write it, I'll never know. I didn't ask anyone's advice. I just did it.

Finding a subject suitably stageworthy wasn't easy, though another of my passions equal to that of the theatre seemed a good idea: my love of old movies. This gave me the thread of the speech as it would involve my going on a tear about how much I missed the great films of yesteryear.

But coming from the mouth of a kid? That didn't make sense.

Which is why I decided to embody a middle-aged man, dressing for the audition in a cardigan with a coffee cup in my right hand and a newspaper tucked under my left arm.

As my character built his tirade with a litany of how current stars couldn't hold a candle to the ones of old, I built to a climax by shouting out the last line for a topper: "Whatever happened to Nigel Bruce?" *

I'm proud to say this got a laugh out of Ruth S. Klinger herself that was music to my ears. She clutched the arm of the woman seated beside her and repeated the line, "Nigel Bruce!" I remember this so specifically (and nothing else of the speech whatsoever) because it was the first time in anything close to a professional audition that I got *exactly* the response I intended.

I won the scholarship and studied at the workshop for two years. It was a good learning experience and served as my introduction to elements of the teachings of Konstantin Stanislavski, the founder of the Moscow Art Theatre, whose ideology boiled down to finding the emotional truth in a character—a radical concept for European theatre in the late nineteenth century. The paths to arriving at these truths would

---

* Nigel Bruce (1895-1953) was a British actor, famous as a bumbling Dr. Watson, a role he played mostly opposite Basil Rathbone's Sherlock Holmes in 14 films and in some 200 radio broadcasts.

become controversial, as many of Stanislavski's disciples had multiple variations on how to build and pass along his teachings.

There were two who towered above the others on how best to interpret Stanislavski's work. One was Stella Adler (who traveled to Russia to study with the master directly). The other was Lee Strasberg (who did not).

Over time Strasberg would become the most divisive interpreter of Stanislavski's teachings, dubbing his specific version of it "the Method." And when he died in 1982, Adler began one of her classes with a moment of silence for this "renowned acting teacher." Then she raised her head and announced, "It will take 50 years for the American actor to recover from the damage that man did." [18]

As an early member of the Actors Studio, Harris was one of a number of young actors studying at the altar of Lee Strasberg. Many were willing to subject themselves to his cruelties and "my way or the highway" approach to acting, but not Harris. "In the strict Stanislavskian sense of the word, I am not a 'method actress.' As much as I would like to, I can't respond to every moment on stage through the character alone. I often have to go outside the character and into my own life. This is *my* method." [19]

At the height of the Studio's influence, current stars of the stage (like Harris) mixed it up in classes with unknowns like Paul Newman, who wandered into the Studio one day to help a friend with her audition. She didn't get in and, naturally, it was Newman who was accepted (without having applied).

Of his time there, Newman remarked, "It was such a stunning thing just to be an observer there and to watch Geraldine [Page] and Kim Stanley and occasionally Marlon [Brando] and Julie Harris. So I kept my mouth shut and my ears opened and that was the way I seemed to learn." [20]

Newman, along with dozens of other Actors Studio progeny, lit up Broadway during the 1950s and dominated movie screens throughout the world. Their work was mostly misrepresented by the image of Marlon Brando in a torn T-shirt, allegedly mumbling his way through his lines. Not only did this do a disservice to his groundbreaking performance as Stanley Kowalski in *A Streetcar Named Desire*, but to many actors exploring new ways to find the truth in their work.

In a delightful interview from 1997 with the *New York Times* theatre critic Ben Brantley, Harris was joined by her frequent co-star, Christopher Plummer, where the two held forth on many subjects, including the Actors Studio. Though Plummer never studied there, on occasion he would be invited to watch and observe, giving him cause to mention the one thing which caught his eye: "It was never fun."

Julie Harris: "That's it. No, there weren't many laughs."

Christopher Plummer: "And isn't that the most important thing in the theatre? To have fun as well?" [21]

One of the greatest stage actors, Plummer adored Harris, as his comments spoken at her 2013 memorial service in New York attest:

> *I was to have the great joy of being her leading man in six different productions over the years. Poor thing—she didn't deserve that …*
>
> *A true, loyal and devoted friend with a husky voice and a shy little laugh, a woman with a mystery about her, but who owned her own light that could not be extinguished.*
>
> *In the mid-fifties, Broadway's last golden age, Julie stood alone high on her very own pedestal. Not just the first lady, but the first actress of the American theatre. A national treasure who for more than fifty years has continued to illumine and hold together the fragile fabric of our stage.*
>
> *For me, she will always be the Peter Pan of actresses: part-human, part-sprite. She could never hide the mischievous gleam in her eye and she never, never grew old. She took us by the hand and led us into the theatre and with one stroke of her talent she managed to disarm us of our cynicism and give us back our childhood.*
>
> *She will continue to live in my heart and in my imagination so long as there is something called eternity. And no matter what fate lies in store for the theatre, her curtain will never come down.*

Harris lived out the final years of her life at her home of more than thirty years in Chatham, Massachusetts. And though her stroke slowed her down and cost her much of her speech, there were still roles open to her in film and television which she enthusiastically embraced. Producers and directors (as well as her fellow actors) were always happy to be in her company.

Although her stage career was essentially over during those last years of imperfect health, she was instantly of a mind to return to her first love when an irresistible offer came through. Her friend and neighbor Alan Rust asked her if she would consider a part in something he was going to direct locally. The play was Paul Zindel's Pulitzer Prize-winning *The Effect of Gamma Rays on Man-in-the-Moon Marigolds,* and it was hardly a slam-dunk. Rust was fearful. "I didn't have the heart to ask her to play that old lady." [22]

The old lady to which Rust refers is the character of Nanny, who doesn't speak a word. But with theatre as her religion (and lifeline), how could Harris refuse one more shot at heaven?

When word got out that Chatham's local girl was returning to the stage, even if she had no lines, the five-day run immediately sold out. In one review, a critic wrote: "On opening night there were so many flowers from Harris's many friends and admirers from around the country that they had to be relocated to a separate room to let the cast move about backstage." [23]

Playing a woman in her nineties (a stretch—she was only eighty-three), Harris wrung every laugh out of the character. One report stated that a bit of business she discovered using her spoon as a comb was enough to justify the price of admission.

Such theatrical behavior brings to mind what playwright Donald Freed, for whom Harris performed in a one-person play called *The Countess,* said of her: "If she were not a great lady, she'd be a bag lady—prowling the centuries looking for bits of characters to pick up." [24]

There was also Harris's work ethic, upon which her old friend and colleague Fritz Weaver elaborated:

Once when I was in a long run and I was very weary, I called Julie up. And this was after her misfortune; her stroke. And there was that same, bright, cheery voice. And I said to her, "Please tell me, Julie, not to tire out in this long run. I'm thinking I can't take another day of this."

And she said, "Oh, but you must!" She then gave me fifteen

minutes of how you must find it new every night and how this
has to be your joy and your salvation as a person and as an
actor. And you must give a hundred per cent every time. Rainy
Thursdays and wet Mondays—you must give it your all.
　I needed to hear that. And it inspired me!

Even if she wasn't aware of it, Julie Harris held the power to inspire. Whether she spoke a few words, as she did outside the Morosco stage door with me when I was twelve, or decades later when no words were spoken at all.

On that particular evening, I had gone backstage after a show to visit my friend, Anita Gillette. Probably best known today to TV audiences as Tina Fey's mother on *30 Rock,* Anita is an actress with a long list of theatre credits.

I was with my whole family on this night. After the show visiting Anita in her dressing room, we were startled when a tiny woman with oversized glasses and blonde hair flecked with gray appeared as if out of the blue.

With her arms outstretched, she embraced Anita. It took me a moment to recognize her. But when she didn't speak, conveying her feelings for Anita's performance by holding her hand over her heart, I stood transfixed when I realized this was Julie Harris.

Time seemed to stand still. I was gobsmacked finding myself in front of her again for the first time since she had run her fingers through my shoulder-length hair.

Her aura was the real thing, for as soon as she left, my daughter Charlotte, then fifteen, turned to me and said, "Who was that lady?" And she asked not out of idle curiosity, but because she had experienced something special being in her presence.

"That was Julie Harris," I said. "One of the greatest actresses there has ever been."

I'm not sure I've ever said anything like that to anybody (about anybody) before or since. It wasn't hyperbole and Charlotte understood the honesty behind what I said. Nodding in assent, she knew this was no ordinary soul.

Ed Dixon related to me a similar experience:

> *I was in* The Persians *with Roberta Maxwell, a good friend of Julie's, so I met her after the show. I had this whole interaction with Ms. Harris and it was so joyful. She kept touching my arm and I was dazzled by her.*
>
> *It wasn't until after she walked away that I realized she had never said a word. Her friend had said things, and I had said things, and she touched me and interacted with me, but she had already had her stroke and she never said a word—and I didn't notice it.*
>
> *That was her power to communicate.*

For Harris, being a member of the audience gave her enormous pleasure. "My life wouldn't be as rewarding and exciting and richly endured if I didn't go to see theater." [25]

> *I took Charles Nelson Reilly, who doesn't like to go to the theatre, to* Nicholas Nickleby, *and when the [8 ½ hour] play was over he said, "Can we go again?"*
>
> *And I said, "We can go every day if you want."* *
>
> *At its very best, the theater is a balm for hurt minds. It unites us as human beings, gives us a home, brings us together. You say: That's what it means to be alive, to be human, to feel your heart beat. That's what it means. Theater does that.* [27]

In the latter part of her career, as a simple act of self-preservation, Harris did many solo pieces, which she sought out of her inordinate desire to perform:

> *I love to work in movies ... the bigger parts like Jessica Tandy would get, but I don't seem to get ...*
>
> *I have to think of things that I can do on my own, like these one-woman plays that I love doing, and love working on—that's something. That's an area when I am finding my own work.* [28]

---

* In fact, Harris liked *Nicholas Nickleby* so much she saw it seven times. She is quoted as saying about the show: "I would live in that theatre." [26]

There aren't many still around who shared a stage with Harris back in the day. Fortunately, I had a chance to speak with Maureen Anderman, who co-starred with her in *The Last of Mrs. Lincoln* (Harris's fourth Tony for Best Actress). She hit on the essence of what made Harris so unique:

> *I first met Julie at a party before rehearsals for* Mrs. Lincoln *began and she took my hand in hers and our eyes met and it was—well, we stayed friends for forty years. She was my mentor and my guide.*
>
> *And every night in performance, when I would walk onstage as her daughter-in-law, she would look into my eyes and take my hand as she had on that first day we met. And she used to tell people "I fell in love with Maureen every time she walked onstage." And it was that warmth and love that would emanate from her and cross into the other actor giving you confidence and your place onstage.*

Anderman also described how Harris prepared to play Mary Todd Lincoln:

> *The carpenters built a box for her backstage. It wasn't a changing room or anything. There was no door on it, but it allowed her a place to sit before a performance and collect her thoughts.*
>
> *I would always see her in that box, with her head down, concentrating and in preparation "getting" Mary.*
>
> *And it wasn't until the curtain came down and during the curtain call that she would remove Mary—and you would see Julie.*

Four years after *The Last of Mrs. Lincoln*'s disappointing short run, Harris returned to Broadway as Emily Dickinson in *The Belle of Amherst*. Finding the poetry deep within herself, Harris not only played the reclusive mid-nineteenth-century poet, but essayed a dozen other characters: the definition of a tour de force.

"Nothing thrills me more as an actress than to give recitations of Emily Dickinson's poetry," she said. "Her poetry has meant much to me personally, and I want to share this feeling with others. A simple line: 'the heart asks pleasure first, / And then, excuse from pain. /' It isn't enough to simply recite this line. I want to go into the audience and say the line to each person individually." [29]

This is perhaps the most insightful thing Harris offers by way of her methodology. It's not so much about her acting *per se*, but her approach to it: The need for the words she speaks to have meaning and to share that meaning with others.

Harris developed the Dickinson project herself with Charles Nelson Reilly, who directed her in eleven plays. Later, they enlisted playwright William Luce, who specialized in one-person shows, to craft it as a wholly integrated theatre piece.

For her performance, Harris received her fifth Tony for Leading Actress in a Play, although she wasn't in attendance. She was working on the road, touring with *The Belle of Amherst*.

Julie Harris as Emily Dickinson in *The Belle of Amherst* (1975)

Reilly was introduced to the world of Dickinson when he and Harris appeared in the musical *Skyscraper* together: "She did a benefit for an Episcopalian church on an off-night on a Monday," Reilly remembered. "She came out and read a letter of the young Emily. She leaned on a table like it was a desk and said two words: 'Dear Abiah,' and I knew from those first two words that it was a play. If anything belonged in a theater, it was these words. She truly breathed them and knew them." [30]

In conversation with Nathan Lane, while reminiscing about great performances that influenced him, *The Belle of Amherst* came up. With a matter-of-factness not open to dispute, he said, "Julie Harris was in a class by herself." Those feelings are completely understandable if you watch the 1976 PBS broadcast of *Belle*, readily available on YouTube.

With this performance, it deceptively appears as if Harris does not plan, let alone calculate. She knows where each laugh is, yet doesn't ask for a single one of them, as some actors are wont to do. She is confident they will come, so she speaks the lines honestly.

These sound like simple rules that, if followed, should make any actor equally good. But it doesn't work that way. Acting isn't a recipe—add two eggs, flour, sugar and mix. Otherwise, everyone would be a Julie Harris.

Watch how she handles difficult transitions, all alone onstage, without anyone to play off of. Pace and rhythm is everything. Not allowing for a proper beat or two rushes the moment and throws off the timing. If too many pauses are taken, then things become labored and the audience is lost.

In Harris's hands, it's a master class. A graceful, majestic performance that takes flight, yet is as grounded as anything you will ever see.

Harris embraced any part she played with every fiber of her being. Her discipline was enviable. In her book, her responsibility to a role is well-defined when she wrote: "Some actors will tell you not to even think about the play until you get to the theater that evening. I don't agree. Louis Armstrong once said that whenever he had an engagement in the evening, he would spend the whole day thinking about the first note." [31]

Lin-Manuel Miranda, the creator of *Hamilton*, is an old soul in tune with dedicated artists of the past. Highly disciplined, Miranda is in total agreement with Harris on the subject of preparation: "You plan your life around being at your peak at eight o'clock every night." [32]

As hard working and prolific as Harris was, Emily Dickinson fulfilled a need in her unlike other roles. It made her feel something which she would then pass on to the audience: unconditional love.

"I felt toward the end of the play as if it would never end, and I'd always be floating on this wonderful carpet, talking. And people were listening." [33]

Alec Baldwin was one who listened and learned from Julie Harris. In 1984, at the start of his career, a rare situation popped up when he had to decide which of two projects to take. One was a high profile mini-series; the other, a nighttime soap. According to Baldwin, his agent offered him the following scenarios:

"If you do the mini-series, it comes and goes. Or, you are a cast addition to a hit show, and your scenes are with the greatest living American actress." [34]

Baldwin took the soap, which is how he came to play Julie Harris's son for two years on the nighttime drama *Knot's Landing*. In the *Huffington Post*, a week after her death, Baldwin wrote: "Her voice was like rainfall. Her eyes connected directly to and channeled the depths of her powerful and tender heart. Her talent, a gift from God." [35]

"I found God in the theatre," Harris once proclaimed.

And in Julie Harris, audiences found a Goddess.

CHAPTER 5

The Obsession

1776 - March 15, 1969

I n March of 1969, the scenery for *1776*, a new Broadway musical, was being loaded on to the stage of the 46th Street Theatre. With only five preview performances scheduled before its opening on a Sunday night, it was slipping in under the wire as the final show eligible for that season's Tonys.

Awards were the last thing on the mind of its thirty-year-old director, Peter Hunt, who had wandered into the theatre in an uneasy state. The New Haven tryout had come close to disaster and without the blind luck of opening during the worst snowstorm in fifteen years (which kept the critics from attending) it might have closed then and there. Days before its Broadway opening, it had an advance sale of a paltry $60,000. Compared to the recent hit musical *Promises, Promises*, which came in with $1.3 million in ticket sales (more than twenty times greater), this was not promising.

Was it any wonder Hunt was worried? This would be his Broadway debut as a director. With the bulk of his youthful career having been as a lighting designer, hanging out in a theatre on this particular afternoon was a tonic. The lulling sounds of construction felt like home to him. His presence in familiar surroundings was enough to alleviate a few anxieties.

Then something happened that took him by surprise.

"I heard our master carpenter talking to the Local men," Hunt recalled to me in an interview forty-six years later. "And I heard him yell out, 'Hey guys! Don't use nails—use screws. This thing is going to be here a long time!'"

"I hung a U-turn, went to a bar across the street, and ordered myself a drink."

"Use screws." Could any words have sounded sweeter to a guy who began his career while still a student at Yale assisting the venerable lighting designer Abe Feder on the Toronto and Boston tryouts of *Camelot*? How did Hunt get the job in the first place? In his own words:

> *Stuart Ostrow couldn't get anyone to do it. Everyone turned the show down. So he was forced to go back and beg Jerome Robbins, who was the guy he asked in the first place. When Robbins refused (again), Stuart pleaded with him. "Don't you know some kid who's coming along that's really terrific and nobody knows about?"*
>
> *"No, I'm a dance guy," Jerry told him. "I don't know much about directors." So the lunch goes on and just before they're ready to get up Jerry says, "Wait a minute. There's this guy ... I don't know his name ... but he did this thing about Booth at Lincoln Center about eight months ago and he might be what you're looking for—if you can find him."*
>
> *They found me in Shubert Alley (on a break from lighting a show and having a cigarette), when a kid comes running up to me and says, "Who's your agent? Stuart Ostrow wants to offer you a Broadway musical."*
>
> *I didn't have an agent. The only person I could think of was Deborah Coleman, my friend Austin Pendleton's agent. I'd met her a couple of times but as a lighting designer I'd never had an agent.*
>
> *So I went to a pay phone by the stage door and called Deborah and asked her to be my agent.*
>
> *"Oh honey, I've got way too many clients as it is."*
>
> *"Dammit!" I said, "That's too bad, because Stuart Ostrow is going to call you offering me a Broadway musical."*
>
> *She said, "I'll get right back to you."*

So without even knowing his name, Jerome Robbins became the person responsible for Peter Hunt directing his first Broadway show (which also won him the Tony).

When I strolled into the 46th Street on March 15, 1969, to see the second-to-last preview of *1776*, it had been seventeen months between my first Broadway show and this one—my seventh—although it felt like light-years. I was certainly more mature (eleven days past my twelfth birthday) and was returning to the same theatre where I saw *I Do! I*

Do!—this time with no adult supervision and no longer anywhere near Row G in the orchestra.

This was also the first time I was seeing a show before the critics. From my seat in the last row I would have the luxury of deciding for myself if it was good or bad, with no pre-existing opinions to sway me one way or the other. What I was thinking was: Is it going to be old-fashioned? New-fashioned? Sincere? Irreverent?

I could never have guessed it would be all those things, beginning with the curtain flying up and twenty-one men congressman drowning out Boston's John Adams, singing in multiple harmonies "Sit Down, John!"

I was hooked. Bring it on. Then shortly thereafter, a book scene began ... and went on ... and on. Thirty minutes before the next song was sung.

And I was riveted. A revolution was taking place without a shot being fired. This play was about the brains, rather than the brawn, of what it takes to win a war.

A scene uninterrupted for thirty minutes had never been done in a musical (before or since). Such was the power and beauty of *1776*, whose concept sprang from the mind of its composer Sherman Edwards (1919-1981), a history major by education and a jazz pianist by profession. It was a passion project he labored over for more than a decade, initially attempting writing all of it: book, music and lyrics. After a series of "no's," Edwards finally got a "yes" from producer Stuart Ostrow, with the provision that a proper book writer be hired.

It fell to Peter Stone (1930-2003) to transform the confusing and unwieldy script into one of the most admired librettos of any musical. Stone wisely followed through on Edwards's original concept, which was to bring historical personalities such as Thomas Jefferson—with his head carved on Mount Rushmore and every nickel we take from our pockets—down to earth as men, not deities. Stone's finely tuned sense of construction, along with his dry and sensitive wit, took Edwards's well-researched script beyond mere paring and cutting.

With a cast of characters best known as visages in oil paintings, the members of the Continental Congress (as drawn by Stone and Edwards) sweat, bitch, moan and swat flies. They are humanized, though not demeaned—not an easy thing to accomplish.

There was one other outside (if not outsized) factor of why I was drawn to the show. It had to do with not being tall for my age. Looking to the future and what my career as an actor (if any) might have in store for me, being a leading man was doubtful. Yes, the unconventional (and fairly tiny) Dustin Hoffman had recently broken through in *The Graduate* a year and a half earlier. Three years later, *The Godfather* would bring stardom for Al Pacino (another short guy).

Though Hoffman and Pacino's leading man status came out of these film roles, the stage doesn't allow for below-the-camera tricks like standing on a box when one comes up short opposite a leading lady.

After seeing William Daniels as Adams, I vowed to play the part one day. He gave me hope that a somewhat small and slight person could be the star of a Broadway musical (without necessarily possessing the best singing voice in the world, either).

Brent Spiner, who led a Broadway revival of *1776* in 1997, had the same response as I did when experiencing the show:

> *I saw the touring company of* 1776 *in Houston when I was still in college. It was an extraordinary night because I was seated directly behind Lyndon Johnson, about a year into his retirement.* *
>
> *After, I went back to one of my teachers and said, "I want to do this show and play John Adams." My teacher said, "I'm sure you will."*

Asking Spiner about what pressure he felt playing a role so closely identified with the person who created it brought an interesting response:

> *I'm nothing like William Daniels so I did have to fight his voice in my head. I was a fan of the piece and had listened to the recording many times by then. It was a challenge.*
>
> *It's funny, but when I got the call the first thing I said was "There must be someone who's more right for this. I mean, I'm a Jew from Texas!"*

---

* Nice symmetry with the story of my sitting behind Lady Bird Johnson (see "Preface").

I had dreamed of playing it, but nearly twenty years later, and with reality staring me in the face, it was suddenly a different story.

William Daniels as John Adams, Howard Da Silva as
Benjamin Franklin and Ken Howard as Thomas Jefferson in 1776.

Author and theatre historian Peter Filichia claims that "having seen between 80% and 90% of the Broadway musicals produced in the last half-century, I still rank William Daniels's performance as the best I have ever seen a male lead give in a musical." [1]

Though I'm a long way from seeing anywhere near the number of plays and musicals Filichia has, I agree that the ferocity and commitment Daniels brought to the role was epic. His whole being was infused with that of the character; drawing you in so that you believed this was John Adams coming back to tell his version of these events. Barely offstage, his energy and drive propelled the show.

Daniels knew a thing or two about performing onstage. His career dates back to his Broadway debut in 1945 at age seventeen, when he joined the company of the long-running *Life With Father*. When I interviewed him in 2012, he elaborated for me:

> *I was a child actor, primarily performing on the radio with my sisters. We had an act and one day my mother told me to go to the producer Oscar Serlin's office. They were looking for new kids to go into year six of* Life With Father, *or something like that. Somehow I got the job without even reading. He liked me.*
>
> *And that's how I was hired to be in a play before I had ever seen one.*

I've often wondered why when William Daniels had captivated me so, did I instead ask to see Howard Da Silva when I went backstage? Why did I want to meet Ben Franklin rather than John Adams? Did Daniels scare me a little bit, whereas the warm and avuncular Da Silva offered the possibility of a friendlier face?

When I knocked on Da Silva's dressing room door, I was startled when I was greeted by his waving a green felt pen and declaring in his honeyed voice, "Where do I sign? Where do I sign?"

While Da Silva was autographing my *Playbill*, I looked into his dressing room and spotted William Daniels seated there, a look of total exhaustion on his face. I waved and he took one hand away from where he was cradling his head and meekly waved back at me. I simply didn't have the heart to ask this dog-tired man for his signature.

Many years later, when I told him this story, he looked at me with a surprised expression and said, "I was in Howard's dressing room?"

What was truly surprising was my discovery, long after my meeting him, that Da Silva was not a well man that afternoon.

The notoriously difficult Da Silva found ways to aggravate the whole *1776*

company. As Daniels told me, "Howard was a strange and difficult man."

Everything came crashing down four days before opening night when—during a tech rehearsal on the stage of the 46th Street Theatre— Da Silva had a heart attack.

Peter Hunt will never forget that Thursday afternoon:

> *Howard suddenly stopped and started grabbing at his clothes. The guys got a hold of him and they tore his shirt off and they took him outside and gave him CPR. The paramedics came and they got him to the hospital.*
>
> *They said "You need heart surgery."*
>
> *Howard said, "No, I'm opening the show. And then you can do with me what you wish."*
>
> RF: *So he came back and played Thursday, Friday, two on Saturday and opening night on Sunday?*
>
> PH: *All of them—with a doctor in the wings. And Sunday night he walked right out the stage door in costume and into a waiting ambulance. And he was off to the hospital.*

The story was spun in the press the next day that Da Silva had been hospitalized with pneumonia. The real story was the actor's own rigid stubbornness as well as the tired but true axiom, "The show must go on."

It's a wonder that Da Silva's iron-grip on the role of Franklin came about at all considering the rage he flew into after his big number was cut in New Haven. This led to a fly-on-the-wall conversation Peter Hunt wasn't supposed to overhear (but did):

> *I was having lunch at Casey's between the shows next to the theatre in New Haven, and Howard was in the next booth with Alfred Drake.* He had just seen the show and I could*

---

* Alfred Drake (1914-1992), one of Broadway's most enduring leading actors in musicals, starred in the original productions of *Oklahoma!, Kiss Me, Kate* and *Kismet*. A classicist, he also played Claudius to Richard Burton's Hamlet and Benedick opposite Katharine Hepburn's Beatrice in *Much Ado About Nothing*.

hear everything they were saying; Howard had an especially loud voice. Howard was going on and on about this terrible show, this terrible part, this awful director. "He's a high school kid. He's a lighting designer and what he's doing directing a Broadway show I'll never know!"

Finally, he ran out of steam. Then Alfred said, "Howard, when we did Oklahoma! *you were the dumbest fuck I ever knew. And you still are. This is the best show you've ever been in, it's the best part you've ever had and you're brilliant! And for you to drop out of this show would be the stupidest career move you could ever make."*

And Howard turned pale. "Oh, my God—Abe Newborn [Da Silva's agent] and the lawyers are going over it right now in Ostrow's hotel room."

And Alfred said, "If I were you I would get over there and stop it."

So Howard ran out to put the brakes on. Later I got a call from Stuart who (suspecting this would happen) told me Rex Everhart was available to take over the part. And I told him I thought what we needed to do was have Rex in the wings— and for Howard to be able to see him at all times. Then if he gets cute with us, we can replace him just like that!

As it turned out it was a godsend—because with Howard's heart attack we had Rex ready to go.

The night after its rave reviews, Da Silva was out and Everhart was in. Months later, and with the company enjoying sold-out crowds, Ostrow's office received a call for an unprecedented command performance at the White House. Only a handful of shows had ever been invited, and *1776* would be the first Broadway musical to be presented in its entirety from beginning to end.

Naturally there were a few hurdles to get over.

For one thing, a now heart-healthy Da Silva was back in the show. Getting a yes from him to play the White House would require diplomacy

As one who was forced to appear in 1951 before the House Un-American Activities Committee (responsible for launching the career of then-Congressman Richard Nixon), Da Silva took the Fifth Amendment.

Declared an unfriendly witness, he fell victim to the Hollywood blacklist, instantly ending his film and television career in the same way it was destroying those of his friends. A lot of bad blood there.

William Daniels was also a die-hard liberal and had no intention of entertaining Nixon either. He loathed the man as much as Da Silva did.

It was Stuart Ostrow who had to placate, cajole and shame this duo into agreeing to perform at the White House. First, William Daniels:

> *Stuart said, "You know, Bill, it'll be a salary for the rest of the cast. You can't deny these kids the extra money as well as this opportunity."*
>
> *So I relented.*
>
> *Only I never got any extra money. They all did!*
>
> *And the next Monday, we did it Sunday—Monday, I had no voice, so I missed the performance. One of only two times in the whole two years I did the show that I didn't go on.*
>
> *So I said to Stuart, "You know, I missed the performance on Monday night."*
>
> *He said, "Did you?"*
>
> *And I said, "Yeah, and I was docked for it."*
>
> *Stuart seemed surprised. "You were not."*
>
> *I repeated myself: "Stuart, I was docked for it!"*
>
> *He acted all miffed and said, "I'm gonna check that out."*
>
> *He called later and said, "I apologize, you were docked for it."*
>
> *And he still never paid me!*

As for Da Silva, his son Dan told me how his father handled the invitation:

> *Dad had two things happen when he went to D.C. He was with some old friends in a Jewish deli and someone at the next table said, "How can you perform for Nixon?"*
>
> *And his response was "It's at the White House. It's the office, not the man I'm respecting." But he also found himself feeling terribly guilty about it, what with his history with Nixon. So the next day he joined the protesters outside the White House. That helped ease his conscience.*

There were also fraught behind-the-scenes dealings in bringing *1776* to Washington, which threatened to derail it completely.

The White House was demanding that two controversial songs (perhaps the most effective ones in the show) be cut to appease the President: the antiwar ballad, "Momma Look Sharp" and "Cool, Cool Considerate Men," an ode to conservatism as relevant in 1970 as it would have been in 1776 (and just as relevant today).

Stuart Ostrow, another old-school liberal, stood his ground. The songs stayed, and when it was time for "Cool, Cool Considerate Men," Paul Hecht (who performed the lead vocals) delighted in informing me that he made sure to direct the whole thing pointedly at Nixon.

"Seeing that motherfucker *right there*—it was great," said Hecht. "I did it like I never did it at any other performance."

"Oh, it was agony," said Hunt. "I sat right next to Nixon and I had sweat pouring all over me. I'm thinking, 'Guys, give the man a break. He's the President!'"

* * * *

One of the reasons I became obsessed with *1776* was that during this period when I was seeing a Saturday matinee almost every week of the year, most of the time I would be out in the street after two hours.

Unlike today, where it is common for some shows to go on for three hours, *1776* was a rarity clocking in at two hours and forty-five minutes. This enabled me to sneak into the wings and watch the final scenes whenever I wanted.

I have no explanation of why the doorman allowed me to stop in with such regularity. I never took the time to learn the man's name. He was small and stooped with white hair and black-rimmed glasses and I would smile at him and he'd smile at me and that was all it took.

Maybe he thought I was related to someone. My hanging around never bothered anyone. The actors would come off after their curtain calls, pass right by me and wave, acknowledging my presence.

I got to know a number of them, especially Daniels's successor as Adams, John Cunningham. Though wonderful in the role, and possessing a similar drive as Daniels, Cunningham did not have the same intensity. Daniels's sense of danger made you fear he might burst a blood vessel.

The sheer power of his performance compelled you to believe no one else was capable of bringing as much to the role as he could.

A year into the run of *1776*, John Cullum took over the supporting role of Edward Rutledge. An established Broadway actor, having already played opposite Richard Burton in *Hamlet* and Barbara Harris in *On a Clear Day You Can See Forever*, he told me about initially turning down the chance to audition for *1776*:

> *When they were casting it originally I read the script, and thought, Hell, I want to play Adams. I mean, who wouldn't? It's the best part in the show. But I knew Billy. We'd done* Clear Day *together and he was perfect for it.*
>
> *So I passed. I wasn't interested in playing another southerner like Rutledge. I thought, stupidly, it was a part I could do in my sleep. I hadn't heard "Molasses to Rum" yet.*
>
> *So I held out for my Broadway lead and I didn't get one.*
>
> *About a year later I called my agent and told him that I would do any part in any show! I was going crazy. And he said, "Remember that part you turned down? It's available again."*
>
> *I said, "I'll take it!"*

Replacements were common throughout the three-year run of *1776*. Two actors recruited off its touring productions were Gary Beach and George Hearn. These future Tony-winners gave me even more reasons to see the show so many times.

Hearn shared his memories with me when we talked about it:

> *We opened at the Curran Theatre in San Francisco on the night of the Kent State shootings. People were boycotting and screaming and throwing things and I remember we all went out on the doorstep and tried to calm the crowd and said, "Wait! You don't understand. We're playing the good guys."*
>
> *Then we opened in Dallas the night the story broke about the My Lai Massacre, which is why I say it was an incredible year of change in America. And to be in that particular piece at that particular time was the gift of a lifetime.*

In addition to the countless viewings from the wings, I paid to see *1776* a dozen times from out front. I could afford this mainly due to coupons known as "twofers" (two for the price of one) that made it possible to attend Broadway shows in need of a boost for as low as $2.50. Before the invention of the TKTS booth in Times Square, these were lifesavers to theatregoers on a budget. With *1776*, I splurged each and every time, usually nabbing one of the best seats in the house—ninth row center—for $5.

Read it and weep.

There was one drawback to seeing *1776* so often. Something that caused a daydream to lodge in my head I couldn't shake. For whenever I took my seat in the theatre, my mind would go to the character of the Courier who comes in and out of Congress throughout delivering Washington's dispatches and, in a quiet moment, sings the ballad "Momma, Look Sharp."

I had a recurring fantasy that right before the show, someone would step out in front of the curtain, peer into the audience and ask: "Is the young man who's seen this so many times out here today? Our Courier has taken ill and we can't locate his understudy."

Then I would stand up and shout, "Here I am!" and rush backstage to change into the costume.

As another example of my fertile and creative imagination, I used to think that a talent agent might someday walk through the woods behind my house and discover me. Yes, hearing my singing along to a record in my bedroom, there would then be a knock at my front door and I would open it and find someone asking to represent me.

That the woods in my backyard edged a cliff and made a fantasy like this impractical on every level never entered my mind. But what do you want from someone who as a child used to imagine himself the host of his own talk show? Not too far-fetched, as I'm sure there were other kids who thought of themselves as the next Johnny Carson, but I'm pretty sure I was the only eight-year-old pretending to have their own talk show whenever they sat on the toilet. What can I say? It seemed a good use of the time.

* * * *

In 1968 when the original casting for *1776* began, the process went smoothly, until the creative team hit a snag with the casting of Jefferson:

> Ken Howard (Thomas Jefferson): *I had just opened in* Promises, Promises *where I basically had one scene as a Polish taxi driver who comes in near the end of the play and punches Jerry Orbach in the jaw.*
> *It wasn't very Jeffersonian, I know.*

> Peter Hunt: *I'd worked with Ken extensively up at Williamstown and directed him in many different kinds of things and knew he could handle the role beautifully. But I couldn't get Ostrow to see it.*

> Ken Howard: *Ostrow couldn't get the image of that Polish taxi driver out of his mind! Luckily no one else who came in was right for the part.*

Hunt remained a fan and friend of Howard's until his death in 2016. They had worked together on many projects over the years, and in the course of my talks with Hunt, a story he had long forgotten emerged from deep within his memory.

It had to do with Stephen Sondheim who, at the request of Stuart Ostrow, came down to Washington, D.C. to see *1776* during the try out. After the show, Ostrow was naturally eager to hear what Sondheim

had to say. Later, Ostrow sought out Hunt, who was taken aback by what
Ostrow had to report:

> *"I was right about Jefferson," Stuart shouted at me.*
> *"I told you he was all wrong for the part when we audi-*
> *tioned him!"*
> *I said, "What are you talking about?"*
> *"Steve told me, 'You should think about getting rid of*
> *the guy playing Jefferson.'"*
> *I couldn't believe what I was hearing as Stuart kept*
> *repeating what Sondheim told him. I asked what it was*
> *that he thought was so wrong and Stuart said, "He didn't*
> *articulate it very well, but he said he doesn't like him and*
> *doesn't believe him as Jefferson."*
> *I thought this was crazy. Because I really liked him.*
> *And it's a tough part to cast and, boy, did we find out how*
> *tough when Ken left the show. Nobody came close to Ken.*
> *Couldn't touch him.*
> *To this day, I don't understand what Sondheim didn't*
> *see or did see. But it was one of those things that makes*
> *you a little shaky. It's one of the reasons I was so nervous*
> *when we got to Broadway.*

Interviewing Stephen Sondheim for this book, I asked him about
1776, as I had never read anything regarding his thoughts or feelings on
the show:

> *Stuart Ostrow asked me to come down to Washington*
> *to see it. And I did. And I thought it was okay until the fi-*
> *nal moment. The final three or four moments, three or four*
> *minutes, when my hair stood on end and I started to cheer*
> *when the curtain came down.*
> *And that ending is all the arranger's ending. The dis-*
> *sonant music is what made it. And that was not Sherman*
> *[Edwards]. That was, I think, Eddie Sauter's ending.*
> *And what Eddie Sauter did is one of the greatest things*
> *I ever saw.*

As Sondheim rightly contends, the ending for anyone who saw it onstage makes for one of the most effective final curtains in American musicals.

And the chief theatre critic of the *New York Times* almost missed seeing it.

By 1969, some critics had begun the fashion of attending preview performances instead of opening nights. These happened mostly on a case-by-case basis at the invitation of certain producers. Wouldn't the critics want to write less hastily and take their time? After all, what was the point of rushing out of the theatre on a strict deadline to dash off something in forty-five minutes if they didn't have to?

Initially not all were on board with the new custom, though it eventually led to today's state of affairs where no first-string critics attend opening nights anymore. Lamenting its passing was the late theatre critic for the *New York Daily News* Douglas Watt, who said, "Having the time to mull it over, you could never display the same enthusiasm as fully." [2]

So when Clive Barnes of the *New York Times*, perhaps out of habit more than anything else, ran up the aisle before the curtain came down that afternoon on *1776*, he was in danger of not seeing the final tableau.

Recognizing Barnes (and what he was about to miss), Onna White, the show's choreographer, was not going to let him accomplish his getaway. Spying him heading up the aisle, she leaped out of her seat, grabbed Barnes by the shoulders, spun him around, and forced him to witness the smashing finish.

His review the next day would be an unqualified rave.

* * * *

Consider the opening of *Hollywood Reporter* critic Frank Scheck's 2015 review of *Hamilton*: "Forty-six years ago, a musical about the Founding Fathers entitled *1776* opened on Broadway at the 46th Street Theatre, going on to win the Tony for best musical and run for several years. History now repeats itself with another musical about the Founding Fathers, playing at the same theatre (now renamed the Richard Rodgers) and almost assuredly destined for perhaps even greater success." [3]

The comparisons between *Hamilton* and *1776*, each telling the story of the birth of our nation in different ways (even sharing the character of

Thomas Jefferson), are eerie in their similarities as musicals, but also in the eyes of theatre critics.

Take, for example, the following eight quotes:

> *"The most exciting and significant musical of the decade."* [4]
> *"One for the ages ... a one-of-a-kind theatrical experience."* [5]
> *"One of the most exhilarating experiences I've had in the theatre."* [6]
> *"A ground-breaking, one for the ages tale ... an amazingly thrillingly multi-layered musical."* [7]
> *"An American musical milestone."* [8]
> *"A musical with style, humanity, wit and passion."* [9]
> *"A brilliant and remarkably moving work of theatrical art."* [10]
> *"We now have an addition to the small roster of American musical classics such as* Porgy and Bess *and* Oklahoma! *It's a new kind of musical, new in every way, shape and form."* [11]

For the record: the first four were written for *Hamilton*; the last four for *1776*. Indeed, history repeats itself, albeit close to fifty years later. The comparisons continue with the cast of *Hamilton's* March 2016 visit to the White House, albeit in a truncated concert version without costumes or scenery, unlike *1776's* command performance.

Miranda possesses the heart of a theatre geek with a talent hot-wired to the history of composers and lyricists who came before him. As John Lahr has written, "Lin-Manuel Miranda actually understands the tradition of musical theater." [12]

One small example of this may be found in a not-too-subtle *Hamilton* homage to *1776*, which comes at a choice moment in Act II when the character of Hamilton yells to an offstage Adams, "Sit down, John!" In answer to the question of how this shout-out found its way into the text, Miranda said that "Adams, like Hamilton, can't shut up and knows he's right. So it came out of that exact same thing." [13]

Of Stone and Edwards's work, Miranda has said, "I think, [*1776*] is one of the best books—if not *the* best—ever written for musical theater ... that book is so smart, and so engaging ... I didn't know anything about this era of history until I started writing it [*Hamilton*]. And as I fell in love with the research, and these stories, I found that if you make the political personal, you can get away with putting in as much information as you want—as long as it *always* has a personal angle, and they remain flesh-and-blood creatures. Once everyone starts spouting, then you're dead in the water." [14]

This is exactly what *1776* gets right. When I saw it on a school trip for the second time, two years after my first experience, it solidified for me what an exceptional piece of theatre it was. Along with my fellow 8th graders, we took a bus into Manhattan for a Wednesday matinee. It does my heart good that this tradition of school groups continues, in spite of spiraling ticket prices. To help make it more affordable, *Hamilton*—the toughest ticket in many a season—has inaugurated a benevolent program that with any luck (and all-important underwriting) will spread among other producers interested in breeding a new generation of theatregoers. Through a $1.4-million-dollar subsidy from the Rockefeller Foundation, twenty-thousand 11th graders from low-income public New York City schools are getting to see *Hamilton* at the highly affordable cost of $10 a ticket. "The student matinees are the best part of our job without question," says Miranda. "They are our best audiences. And that's not on some idealistic 'I believe the children are our future' type thing. I mean, they are literally the best audiences. They don't know how to do anything but be honest, so they give us more energy than any other show. They give us more inspiration." [15]

It thrills me that kids like this, most of whom have probably never seen a Broadway show, are experiencing one for the first time—and that it's *Hamilton*. It must speak to them in much the way it did Harvey Fierstein when he talked about seeing himself onstage in *Fiddler on the Roof* as a child. Imagine what goes through these inner city kids' minds when confronted by an African-American Thomas Jefferson who looks like so many of them.

Writing of my fondness for *1776* has left me searching for some deeper meaning as to why it had such an effect on me. There had to be more than its just being good that made an impression on me in ways that have lasted a lifetime.

In so doing, something came up I had suppressed for a long time. I believe one of the reasons my younger self related to the role of John Adams was due to the character being described over and over as "obnoxious and disliked."

Regretfully, I must confess to relating to this, for as a teenager I *was* obnoxious. Not necessarily disliked as I had lots of friends, though that was mostly due to my being funny, which tends to draw people to you. I learned early on that funny can be a lifesaver. I know it's what bailed me out of being beaten up more than a few times.

And why was I in danger of being beaten up? Because I was obnoxious, that's why.

About six months after seeing *1776* this obnoxiousness caught up with me when my junior high school had auditions for a children's play called *The Stolen Prince*. I went up for it and landed the lead title character. I was the "star."

And I must have acted like one because after one week, the director, Ms. Fox, pulled me into her classroom and sat me down for a talk.

At first, I was happy to spend some time alone with Ms. Fox, who was young and pretty, with large blue eyes. But my bubble burst pretty quickly when she told me
she was going to have to let me go.

"You mean like fire me? Aren't I any good?"

"You're very good," she said. "but everyone thinks you're obnoxious. You're disrupting the process. I have to let you go."

Obnoxious. That word. Ouch.

And because of John Adams, and having listened to the *1776* cast album for the last six months, I knew *exactly* what she meant.

I left Ms. Fox's classroom and tears started flowing. Though humiliated, I knew that there was no injustice here, nor was I being unfairly treated. I took my lumps knowing this came of my own doing and there was no one else to blame but myself.

One of the cast members in that production of *The Stolen Prince* remains a friend of mine all these years later. And as strong as our friendship is today, he would corroborate that I was fired back then with cause.

I'm grateful to Ms. Fox for teaching me a lesson that nipped this behavior in the bud. And when given a second chance, I was on my best behavior as the first to be murdered in Agatha Christie's *Ten Little Indians*. I would describe my death by drinking poison onstage, except I think I've embarrassed myself enough for one chapter.

As for *1776*, it closed on February 13th, 1972 after its 1,217th performance — one-month shy of three years on Broadway. Aided by a twofer, I was there in the audience for my twelfth and final time to bid the show a fond farewell, paying $5.00 for my seat in G 107 of the orchestra.

Forty-four years later, *Encores!* at New York's City Center, announced they would be presenting *1776* in April 2016. This worthy series, offering great American musicals in concert, discovered there was a willing audience for this old warhorse when it proved to be the highest grossing one-week run in its twenty-three-year history.

Of course I made it my business to be in attendance. When I got to the theatre for its sole Saturday matinee, I headed for my seat, happy and excited. And in a moment of true serendipity, in a theatre of 2,570 people, who should I be seated next to? Wait for it! —William Daniels.

The author with William Daniels, 2016

This coincidence made me wonder whether I really chose to obsess all these years over *1776,* or if, in some odd way, it chose me.

And what of my long-deferred dream to play John Adams? With the ability to pass for forty-one onstage (no, really ... I can) I may still get my shot.

Till then.

CHAPTER 6

The Touchstone

Joseph Maher

"Joe's greatest gift, his great weapon, was his intelligence and the layer of authority he thus brought to his roles, particularly those of Orton. Joe's characters in Entertaining Mr. Sloane *and* Loot, *et al, weren't merely amoral or lascivious, looney or corrupt. They were dangerous and capable of anything, because Joe was so bright, verbally facile and cunning."*

This quote from Alec Baldwin, which he generously provided for this book, conveys all that was unique about the Irish actor Joseph Maher (1933-1998).

Intelligence, danger and cunning indeed were what forged his stage talents and contributed to his standing as the foremost interpreter of Joe Orton, the British anti-everything playwright.

I first took note of Maher when I was fourteen and saw him in a Georges Feydeau farce, *There's One in Every Marriage*, which came to Broadway by way of Canada's Stratford Theatre, where he played a number of roles over the course of his career.

Gerome in *Marriage* was one of the minor roles: an elderly retainer, who didn't make an entrance until the start of Act III, and is described in the text only as "old servant." In Maher's deft hands, a mixture of devotion and surliness was evident as soon as the lights came up on him, stooped and bent over, picking up clothing left on the floor in the wake of another of his master's sexual encounters. Shuffling and mumbling, his allegiance and indifference were somehow comically one and the same.

True farce, not to everyone's taste, is a favorite genre of mine and one in which Feydeau excelled (as did Joe Orton, though in a more sexually corrupt way). Classic farce, when expertly done, as it was in *Marriage*, can be breathtaking in its quick-wittedness and pace. Honoring all things essential to the form, *Marriage* had everything: slamming doors, mistaken identities, drunken and lecherous characters, and over-the-top acting grounded in reality. Maher, constantly poking his head through one entry or another, dropping an adroit comment here and there, brought the play to its climax while the world collapsed around him.

Gerome gets the last line, when he enters carrying a tray and says: "Aren't we going to eat? I bought some more potatoes."

You had to be there to see and hear how Maher could make a line like that positively sing. I can still hear his pronunciation of the word "potatoes."

And his personal notices for *Marriage* couldn't get much better than what Martin Gottfried wrote in *Women's Wear Daily*: "Joseph Maher— one of my most favorite actors—took the small but flawlessly written role of a valet and made perfect theatre of it." [1]

I also liked how Harold Clurman pointed out in his review in *The Nation* that "Joseph Maher is merrily 'Irish' as a senile French character." [2]

There are so many actors and actresses who thrilled me in the course of my theatre education that choosing a handful to write about was a challenge. It became important to me to include someone like Joe Maher, who managed never to stop working without becoming a "star."

Even as a kid, I thought about the kind of career I might have as an actor. In already naming Spencer Tracy and Paul Muni, it's important to note that they were anomalies: leading men who were also character actors. They became stars due to their abilities, not necessarily their looks. Each was striking, but not handsome by the arcane rules of Hollywood's old playbook. This led to dreaming in my adolescent years that one day I might get a chance to play leads, not just supporting character parts, once I began working as a professional.

But over time and study, an actor like Joe Maher became more of a touchstone for me than Tracy or Muni. Maher was the embodiment of an actor who rarely played the lead, but who led by example in everything in which he appeared, no matter how small the role. While speaking with many of those who worked with him, I discovered they all felt the same way: enormous admiration for his professionalism and versatility, and praise for how funny and generous a man he was.

Though an average theatregoer (perhaps even an above average one) might have difficulty matching the name to the face, the fact is that Maher appeared regularly on the New York stage for thirty years—a good long run considering he died relatively young of a brain tumor at sixty-four. And though he's been gone for twenty years, as long as reruns of old television shows bounce off satellites he'll still be with us. One example: his memorable episode of *Seinfeld* as an inebriated gentleman who, after becoming ill on an airplane, leaves his maniac of a dog (Farfel) in Jerry's care. Maher's scene stealing is grand theft, even if there are just two of them.

But onstage, what Maher could do with a "look" or a "take" is the stuff to which every comic actor aspires. The greatest performance I ever saw him give was as Inspector Truscott in a 1986 revival of Joe Orton's *Loot*. Though the play's initial 1968 New York production failed after three short weeks, re-evaluating it nearly twenty years later, critics were unanimous in their praise. An extension beyond its limited run at the Manhattan Theatre Club took the show and its cast to the Music Box Theatre, where Alec Baldwin made his Broadway debut as a replacement for Kevin Bacon, who was unable to make the transfer.

From very unlikely beginnings, the playwright Joe Orton rose to become the toast of the West End in mid-1960s London with ferociously funny comedies that have proven timely over the decades without losing their unseemliness. But Orton only enjoyed his fame for a criminally short span of time, as he was murdered by his lover, Kenneth Halliwell, who took jealousy to its limits and bashed Orton's head in with a hammer before killing himself with an overdose of sleeping pills.

Orton was thirty-four years old.

Both born in 1933, Maher discovered a kindred spirit in the playwright. His audacious stabs at *Entertaining Mr. Sloane*, *Loot* and *What the Butler Saw*—all with John Tillinger directing—redefined Orton's reputation in America.

To aid my memory of seeing *Loot* thirty years ago, I visited the Theatre on Film and Tape Archive at Lincoln Center's Library for the Performing Arts, taking along my son, Jeremy, who by this time had heard my raving over Maher's performance for years. And right from his entrance as Inspector Truscott of Scotland Yard, Maher had us both helpless with laughter. Every time Truscott declares he is not an inspector, but "from the Water Board," Jeremy and I went into fits of hysterics, since this violently lunatic-renegade detective is so *not* from the Water Board. With the term these many years later a widely known method for torture, the phrase had the newly added power to make the laughter stick in our throats—something that surely would have delighted Orton.

When the tapes had to be changed at *Loot's* intermission point, Jeremy took off his headphones and said, "I didn't think this would live up to your hype, but it's even funnier, if that's possible. Joe Maher is a genius."

Frank Rich, reviewing *Loot* in the *New York Times*, concurred: "It is surely the most unglued—and uproarious—performance of the actor's career. By the time the detective reaches an Act I gag in which he must identify (in part by licking) the corpse's gray glass eye, we certainly realize just why *Loot* was, in its author's own words, 'vulgar and offensive in the extreme to middle-class susceptibilities.' Those who are liberated rather than offended by Joe Orton's anarchic vision may be laughing so hard that they join Mr. Maher's victims on the floor in tears." [3]

Members who were part of that *Loot* company in New York—Željko Ivanek and Steven Weber (who understudied Ivanek, Baldwin and Bacon)—spoke with me of their fond memories working with Maher:

Željko Ivanek: *My favorite line from* Loot, *and it's one of Joe's, is "What has happened here must never go beyond these three walls."*

The reality with which he said that absurdity was proof how incredibly grounded he was in such completely absurd circumstances. And he never played that eccentricity. He was just so focused within that insanity. That's what was coming at you, the weird reality of it, as opposed to the quirkiness of it.

Joe set the tone for the whole production, but in the most casual way. He had the most incredible sense for the language of Orton.

Steven Weber: *I watched Joe do the eyeball moment every night from my perch in the balcony, where the understudies watched the show.*

Joseph Maher as Inspector Truscott in *Loot*.

And the act ending when the curtain dropped was taken off his cue, which was supposed to be a shocked gasp, only he'd make a noise that is impossible to imitate accurately. It was indeed a gasp—but it was also kind of a long, hilariously horrified hum, which took everyone by surprise, as they were expecting it to be something huge and splashy.

And he did it differently every time!

And then the behavior with the eyeball was insane. Sometimes he would lick it, sometimes he would just sniff it, caress it.

I could never get enough of it.

Nathan Lane, his reverence unmistakable, offered his personal assessment of the actor in something he wrote that was read at the New York memorial service for Maher:

I first saw Joe Maher as an actor in the play Loot. *From the moment he entered I was thoroughly captivated.*

His performance was outrageously funny yet grounded, impeccably acted yet dangerous, and full of surprises. But above all, funny; screamingly. From-the-gut funny.

When it was over I felt it had to be the definitive performance of that role. Joe certainly had a special chemistry with the works of Orton, but to me everything Joe did seemed definitive.

Echoing these sentiments was Maxwell Caulfield, Maher's co-star in Orton's *Entertaining Mr. Sloane*:

What Joe could do, which was such a lesson in comedy, was his ability to pull the rip cord on the laughing gas and shut it off on a dime. It was extraordinary. Particularly in Loot.

I was too wrapped up in the scenes from Mr. Sloane *with him, generally speaking, to be conscious of him beyond the fourth wall. But watching him from the audience in something like* Loot *was a very special experience.*

Maher appeared on Broadway a dozen times, as well as that many Off-Broadway. He also played leading roles for the most prestigious regional theatres in the country in addition to finding time for more than seventy TV shows and feature films.

A photo taken on the set of the 1989 Manhattan Theatre Club production of *What the Butler Saw* captures something about Maher in repose, nothing like what he was like in action. His Dr. Rance was another of Joe Orton's characters on which he put his distinctive stamp.

Joseph Maher as Dr. Rance in
What the Butler Saw (1989)

Though in costume, Maher's not in character. There is an ease and a relaxed quality that fits the man who people knew offstage. However, when onstage, in the blink of an eye, this master actor could produce total and believable madness with the mere pointing of two fingers—a device he invented for Inspector Truscott in *Loot*.

While swinging his arm around wildly, Maher would extend his thumb and hold two fingers together, keeping his hand positioned like an imaginary gun, a trick that "just somehow came" to the actor. "It seemed right for the character," as he described it to a newspaper reporter. [4]

That madness was something Peter Frechette, who played with Maher in the Los Angeles production of *Loot*, found particularly inspiring when we spoke about our mutual admiration for him:

> *Joe is a yardstick for me in terms of being true to your actual gifts. He was so technically proficient, but he also didn't sand down his weirdness. He used it. And over the years, I've tried to follow his example.*
>
> *It was a shimmering, moveable, but safe thing for the audience and for us to be on together. It was a ride—a magic carpet ride—and he provided this weird, mad, safe trip so the audience was blissed out with laughter.*
>
> *Since then only a few times have I ever heard such laughter from an audience, but I had never heard it before. Because it was real. He was always telling the story.*
>
> *The bad clowns forget to do that, but not Joe.*

* * * *

Joseph Sylvester Maher ("Sylvie" to those he grew up with) was born in Brackloon, Westport, County Mayo as one of seven children. His sister, Maureen Hogan, recalls how his future as an actor was assured when at four years old he was given the present of a baby donkey. "He was told that as a livestock owner, his first duty every morning would be to count his supply. So each morning he would go out, and having counted it, come in and holding up the index of his right hand he'd solemnly announce to all present, 'One Baby Donkey.'" [5]

Leaving County Mayo was essential for the bright and inquisitive young man, although notions of being an actor were far off in the distance. He claimed to have not seen a movie until he was ten or a play until he was a teenager.

His life was not easy in hardscrabble Ireland. "I went to Christian Brothers schools… they used to beat us with straps with pennies sewn into them. I've put a lot of that out of my mind." [6]

At age twenty-two, with preparations all set to go to Australia, a last-minute change of heart had him head for Toronto instead, where he arrived with $70 in his pocket in the middle of a snowstorm. He wound up staying with a Chinese family ("to this day I have problems with Chinese food"). [7]

Slowly, he began learning his trade while touring with the Canadian Players in classical fare like *Taming of the Shrew* and *The Cherry Orchard*. He further proved his versatility by being cast in a satirical revue co-starring John Cleese, prior to Cleese's international fame with Monty Python.

By the early 1960s, Maher had made his way to New York and Off-Broadway, landing in a British play by Henry Livings titled *Eh?*, which opened in 1966. The entire cast received great reviews, especially its lead actor, who had to take three days off during the run to fly to Los Angeles for a screen test (which is how Dustin Hoffman got *The Graduate*).

Additional Off-Broadway appearances found Maher opposite other young rising stars, among them Al Pacino in Heathcote Williams's *The Local Stigmatic*. This was such a special experience for the two actors that Pacino produced a film of it twenty years later with Maher repeating his performance.

It was also in this early time in Maher's career that he made his American television debut in a Hallmark Hall of Fame drama, James Costigan's *Little Moon of Alban*. Its star was someone who meant so much to him that he was prompted in an interview years later to claim, "My heart was beating to meet Julie Harris." [8]

His long-sought arrival on Broadway came at age thirty-four when in 1968 he appeared in Jay Presson Allen's adaptation of Muriel Spark's novel *The Prime of Miss Jean Brodie*. This high-profile hit, which won a Tony for its star Zoe Caldwell, earned Maher notices that soon brought steady work his way.

He wouldn't make a film until he was forty, and so it should come as no surprise that he was fifty-six by the time he stepped foot on the London stage, happily and triumphantly, in *What the Butler Saw*.

No matter that he was a late bloomer, the flowering was worth the wait. In 1976, he received the first of his three Tony nominations for Featured Actor in a Play for *Spokesong*, of which he was particularly proud. Maher played a dozen characters, sang five songs, and did most of it while riding a unicycle.

John Lithgow led the *Spokesong* company, and his remembrances of working with Maher made for a delightful conversation:

> *Joe was incredible in* Spokesong. *The way he would come confidently unicycling out of the wings always brought to my mind Samuel Johnson's quote that "It's not how well the dog dances, it's that he dances at all." It was completely amazing.*
>
> *If you'll remember, Joe appeared throughout the play as the Trick Cyclist, but then in the final scene he got off the bike and came out as an IRA gangster/extortionist. It's a dangerous scene and he is suddenly doing this turn as a threatening villain. He became very, very savage. And with his totally authentic Northern Ireland accent, he was absolutely chilling.*

His second Tony nomination came with Tom Stoppard's *Night and Day*, opposite Maggie Smith, who became a lifelong friend. He told a reporter in 1987, "I learned more from Maggie Smith than from anyone else. She's a genius. She's not an actress who does funny things. She just takes the material and makes it work. And that's rare." [9]

Maxwell Caulfield:

> *Joe learned from Maggie Smith how to emulate eccentricity based in reality. Between the two of them, I think they owned that sort of thing.*
>
> *The other thing I believe she taught him was stillness. Joe had that. His control over the audience, and how he could have them roaring and then just shut them down was absolutely masterful.*

Qualities such as these were of the utmost usefulness when the worlds of Joe Maher and Joe Orton came together, guided by the director John Tillinger, who I spoke with about what made his and Maher's connection to the playwright so special:

> *We started together as actors at Stratford. We were in the same play together. It was a wonderful experience because we found out quickly that we were kindred spirits ... Joe knew that I loved Orton and he did too. I don't know how he knew that, coming to think of it, but we talked about it for years.*
>
> *But I'll tell you what Joe understood: the plays are about hypocrisy. Joe understood that. I didn't have to explain it.*
>
> *He was born and raised in Ireland and he knew of the hypocrisy of religion and all the rest of it. Orton, though he was English, was of an Irish background. The tone of the plays is Irish, which people forget.*

How Irish was Joe Maher?

His heritage is best described in a tale told at the wake of his father, when a friend of his mother's asked what Mr. Maher had died of.

"Oh," said Mrs. Maher, "he died of a Tuesday."

The friend said, "No, I meant what did he die *of?*"

With no patience for stupid questions, the ever-pragmatic Delia Maher told the friend, "He died of *dying*. He was ninety-eight. He died of *death*."

His mother refused to leave the home Maher fled as a young man. She lived there until the end of her life, which came at the age of one hundred and three.

In an effort to make the desolate farmhouse a bit livelier, when Maher was earning decent money as an actor, he sent a television with instructions for his mother to watch him in something one particular evening.

When next he saw her, he asked what she thought of him on the television.

Lifting a crooked finger, she pointed at the screen and said, "You were right ... there!"

These last stories were told to me personally by Maher himself on an afternoon in Los Angeles in 1995 when I made it my business to meet him.

I was with my wife after seeing a mid-day movie at the Century City mall and there he was, standing in the food court, all alone. He was taking in his surroundings, dressed impeccably, probably doing some people-watching as actors are wont to do. Even though neither Margaret nor I knew him, there was no way I was going to let this moment pass without talking to him.

I had a dual purpose. I wanted to express my admiration for him, especially his work in the theatre. I also needed him to corroborate an anecdote about a *Julius Caesar* he was once in—a story I had heard from many actors, all told with the same authority as if they had witnessed it themselves. Personally, I shared it with friends for years as it's a foolproof tale with a classic punchline.

Now with Maher "right there" (as his mother would say), I would finally know if the story was true or not.

"Ohhhhh, it's true!" he said in a line reading worthy of that elusive Tony he never received.

He was also quick to point out that the only reason he would ever have dreamed of pulling the stunt he did was because "it was a very *bad* production of *Julius Caesar*. Absolutely the worst. I would never have done it if it had been any *good*."

What was the story? In his own words (as best I recall), here it is:

> *I was playing Casca in* Julius Caesar *at the American Shakespeare Festival in Stratford, Connecticut. This was in 1972 and as I say, a god-awful production. We all simply detested being in it.*
>
> *One night, the stage manager forgot to take the telephone backstage off its cradle. And at exactly the moment after we stabbed Caesar and were standing over his dead body—in that long silence just before Cinna shouts "Liberty! Freedom! Tyranny is dead!"—the telephone rang.*
>
> *And rang. And rang.*
>
> *Everyone froze. Finally, the stage manager had the presence*

of mind to pick it up and stop the ringing. But the silence in the theatre remained. No one knew what to do next.

It was then I looked out at the audience, stepped forward, and said: "What if it's for Caesar?"

As you can imagine, I got the largest laugh of my career. The actors left the stage in helpless laughter, abandoning me. How the play ever managed to right itself and continue I shall never know.

Then to conclude the story, he admonished himself by reiterating how he began it: "Mind you, this was a terrible production of *Julius Caesar*. I would never have done that had it been a *good* production of *Julius Caesar*."

For the perfect coda, when I began going over all the plays I saw in preparation for writing this book, I was stunned to discover I saw this Stratford *Julius Caesar* with Maher as Casca! I wasn't in the audience when this incident occurred … otherwise, I kind of think I'd remember it.

Damn! Why couldn't my school trip have been at this performance instead of the horrible Wednesday matinee I suffered through in the name of "education?" In my review I was particularly brutal, and wrote: "It repulses me to even think that this 'company' [quotation marks all my own)] actually had the gaul [sic] to try and pass this thing off as a professional production. … Director Michael Kahn has staged it with the grace and whimsy of a spastic."

So yes, Joe. If my review is any indication it was, to put it mildly, "a terrible production."

Margaret and I fell in love with the man right there. He asked us about ourselves and suggested we all get together and handed us his card. No actor I'd ever met had done that before. An actor with his own card? Printed at his own expense? Who ever heard of that?

It was white (or was it ecru?) and had his name and phone number in the lower-right-hand corner in an elegant font (what else?).

We called him a few days later and made a date to see *Shadowlands*, which starred Anthony Hopkins and Debra Winger. Meeting in front of a still-intact 1930s movie theatre in Beverly Hills we went directly inside—no stopping for popcorn—all business.

Back out on the street two hours later and chatting about the film, I had no inkling it would be the last I saw of him. A battle with a brain tumor began a short time later, although he kept on acting as long as possible.

Roberta Maxwell, with whom Maher first worked in Canada in the early years of his career, was his good friend until the end. She told me that when the initial surgery to remove the tumor had met with a promising diagnosis from his doctors, it wasn't enough to placate him.

"Joe knew his own mind, his own brain. He told me that even with the clean bill of health, he could tell there was still something wrong."

His lifelong agent, Joan Scott, was another devoted friend. "I adored Joe," she told me in 2013. "I loved a lot of my clients, but the one I loved most was Joe."

When it was close to the end, she brought another of her clients, Brendan Gleeson (a good friend of Maher's), to the hospital with her. As they stood over his hospital bed, to their complete astonishment, Maher recited—in full—Samuel Beckett's *Krapp's Last Tape*.

"Let me tell you," Scott informed me, "that was something."

The play, a solo performance by the actor portraying Krapp, requires the memorization of a nearly hour-long monologue. And here was Maher, slowly exiting this world, and reciting it from memory out of a brain being destroyed by cancer.

Upon hearing his death was imminent, Roberta Maxwell rushed to JFK airport to get to Los Angeles as quickly as possible.

I landed at LAX and was heading to see Joe to say good-bye when I got the call while in the car that he had passed. I missed him by twenty minutes.

When I arrived he was wearing a kerchief around his head, like in the old days when one was used to aid a toothache. It was to keep his mouth from hanging open. It was comical and kind of appropriate.

I sat with him. I just had to talk to him. So I did for a while. And one of the hospice workers said to me, "You know the hearing is the last thing to go."

And I believed that. His heart had stopped, but who knows what else was going on?

I asked Joan Scott, in all of the thirty years she knew him, if she was aware of any great loves in Maher's life. She thought about it for a moment and said, "I think Joe had a lover ... but I don't know where."

And one time, over a drink (or two) with Maher, Maxwell Caulfield was shocked when he heard something that completely took him aback.

"Joe told me he had had sex with one of the most storied linebackers in the history of the NFL. A San Francisco 49er. And I said to Joe, 'You're kidding?'"

And he said, "Would I lie to you?"

"Well, well ... I thought. And it was the only thing he ever told me about his sex life, too."

"He was always having affairs with doormen and people who were totally straight," Nathan Lane divulged to me. "He'd be having an affair with someone who had five children. Or some bruiser—whoever."

John Lithgow told a story that I had not heard from anyone else concerning a night when Maher had a close encounter with a mugger:

> *He was in the vestibule of an apartment building, about to turn the key, when someone came up from behind and pulled a knife on him.*
>
> *But what do you suppose Joe Maher did?*
>
> *He reached down as if to get his wallet and then—shockingly—he snapped up and knocked the guy's knife out of his hand. Somehow or other he was not robbed. And he is the only person I know that's gotten away with something like that. He took his life in his hands! We were all shocked he would do that. And I swear it's true. He defended himself in a physical way against a guy with a knife.*
>
> RF: *He came out of a hardscrabble life, to use his own words. This act of self-defense might have been simply imbedded in his DNA.*
>
> JL: *You may be absolutely right about that. But I still find it amazing.*

Maintaining something of an air of mystery about him, Maher could often be found at any number of Broadway haunts where liquor was served until late hours as George Hearn, who imbibed with Maher from time to time, recalled:

Ah dear Joe… we shared many wonderful nights at Barrymore's, let me tell you. It was my deep wish that he had played Georges in La Cage Aux Folles *with me. But he was so frightened of singing that at the audition he turned white and started shaking like a leaf. They almost thought they were going to have to take him to the hospital.*

But as an actor he would have been magnificent. He was simply the funniest man. When I first fantasized about us doing the show together he told me, "Oh, George, we shall play in this together, and we shall ride around in limousines and we shan't talk to anyone!"

He was a wonderful man.

Maher's delicious sense of humor was apparent in everything he did, so who best to supply one of his better moments than Nathan Lane?

Like all of us, Joe enjoyed a bit of gossip, and I can remember him discussing a certain well-known actress at the time.

Joe told me she was gay, and in an uncharacteristically naive moment I said: "But she's married, isn't she?"

And Joe said: "Oh, the husband's gay too."

And I said, "Really? Didn't they just have a child?"

And Joe said, "Oh, the baby's gay."

As a producer who had cast Maher in many of his films, Scott Rudin was quoted in the *New York Times* obituary for the actor: "He had incredible wit and style, and he could be subversive and affirmative at the same time. He could send up and embrace it at the same time. He was the kind of actor that doesn't exist so much anymore." [10]

Sad, but true.

Joe Maher was one of a kind.

CHAPTER 7

The Thriller

Child's Play - February 16, 1970

Not until my 50th play did I see one with my parents. Even after a year's worth of weekly theatre excursions and my witty and entertaining reviews around the dining room table, it never occurred to them that I might like being treated to a show. I was thirteen and still paying for it all on my own with the money from my paper route. I never received a nickel's allowance, nor did any of my five brothers and sisters, as it wasn't part of our family contract. If you wanted money to buy things, you went out and earned it, which I never looked at as a bad thing at all.

Sometimes they would hand me money to buy them tickets to see a show (based on my recommendation, naturally), but never for the three of us to go together and share the experience, much as I hoped they might come to the idea on their own.

Then one Sunday morning, I opened the Arts & Leisure section of the *New York Times*, and spied something that with a little cunning on my part could lead the way for the three of us to go to the theatre together.

Looking back, it had to have been odd for my parents to be saddled with a kid that lived and breathed show business every waking minute. And even though they liked going to the theatre, it was a luxury, so the cost of an extra ticket for me wouldn't have occurred to them. That—and being part of a big family with six children—meant that special treatment was considered ... well, a little too special.

Happily, they never did anything to prevent me from pursuing my passion. Case in point: when at the age of nine, I performed stand-up at my brother's bar mitzvah. "Why are there gates around a cemetery?... Because people are dying to get in!"

I wish that was blocked from my memory, but sadly it was one of the jokes I told.

Jerry Seinfeld, I was not.

Since no one in my family shared my interests, I was on my own in figuring out how to pursue this crazy passion, convinced for a long time I'd been born into the wrong household. When I used to watch something like the annual holiday episode of *The Dean Martin Show*, parading out his wife and their seven children, I yearned for that kind of a family of my own. I would often threaten my brothers and sisters that if they weren't nice to me, I wouldn't allow them on my Christmas special when I was famous. And *that* was no joke.

So with no direct connection to show business, I latched onto the sole *indirect* one my parents had among their friends—someone I never knew or met by the name of Dick Fallon. Always described in the most romantic terms, all I ever heard was how handsome and magnetic he was.

Rarely agreeing on much, Fallon's charisma and dashed potential was a subject that never failed to unite them.

By 1970, Fallon had already been dead two years, gone at the impossibly young age of forty-five. Probably for that reason, he was more a topic of conversation with my folks in death than in life.

They met Fallon in the days of the burgeoning Off-Broadway theatre movement of the mid-1950s, when he landed a job as an assistant stage manager of *End as a Man*, a new play by novelist Calder Willingham. They would meet up with Fallon afterward, along with cast members, staying out until three and four in the morning in Greenwich Village, joined by various spouses, boyfriends and girlfriends. It sure sounded wild and romantic to my ears whenever they talked of it, which was often.

The play made a star of Ben Gazzara, as well as other up-and-coming young actors also trained at the Actors Studio like Anthony Franciosa, Harry Guardino and Pat Hingle.

Ah, Pat Hingle. Whenever his name appeared at the start of an episode of *Dr. Kildare* or *Mission: Impossible*, my parents would take notice and cry out, "Pat's in this!" I couldn't believe they knew a real-life actor by his first name, but it was true. Times like these afforded me the chance to hear (yet again) about the most glamorous night of their lives, when they attended the opening of Tennessee Williams's *Cat on a Hot Tin Roof*—guests of Pat Hingle—who created the significant supporting role of Gooper, brother of Brick and son to Big Daddy.

Now let me set the stage here: When *Cat* opened at the Morosco Theatre in 1955, Williams had already written *The Glass Menagerie*, *A Streetcar Named Desire* and *The Rose Tattoo*, so there was extraordinary anticipation for the play, which would go on to earn him his second Pulitzer Prize.

The opening night was so star-studded that family legend has it my father nearly fell out of his seat in the front mezzanine while leaning over to get a better look at Marilyn Monroe when she came down the aisle to take her seat moments before the curtain rose.

I always pictured my parents walking the Red Carpet with flashbulbs popping, my accountant father decked out in a tuxedo, and my housewife mother in a glamorous gown.

In reality, my father wore one of the suits he put on every day for work, and my mother sported what in the late 1950s passed for chic: a mink stole.

All this brings me to that Sunday morning when I opened the *New York Times* (as was my ritual) and saw an ad that caught my attention. It was for a new Broadway show set to open soon entitled *Child's Play*, by Robert Marasco. And the top-billed star was Pat Hingle.

This ad was calling out to me with a portent of something wonderful to come. My parents, commoners though they may have been, might now provide a pathway to my genuinely connecting with a Broadway star.

But when I brought to them the proposition of seeing their old friend, I didn't get the enthusiastic reaction I expected. My first thought was that maybe I had gotten the story wrong.

"He was a friend of yours, right?"

"Well, *then,* yes," was their response. No question that those were amazing times and the most fun they ever had—memories conjured up nostalgically, endlessly, expressing how happy, young and free they were enjoying New York City's vast and fabulous nightlife of the 1950s. Only now, fifteen years later and settling into middle-age, they were more than a bit tentative about reacquainting themselves with someone who likely had forgotten them.

By 1970 Hingle was no longer a struggling actor earning Off-Broadway wages. He had gone on to substantial roles in film, theatre and television, among them leads on Broadway in such award-winning plays as William Inge's *The Dark at the Top of the Stairs* and Archibald MacLeish's *J.B.*

Although I had never seen Hingle onstage, I knew his work well from all the television I watched as a kid: *The Twilight Zone, The Fugitive, The Andy Griffith Show* … the list goes on.

Now with his return to Broadway, I would be that much closer to getting to know a true Broadway star. And after assuring them it would be no problem getting backstage (it was second-nature to me by then), I presented the *Child's Play* ad, making sure to highlight its low-priced previews.

My parents (however tangentially) knew—or once knew—the star of a Broadway show. There was no way I was going to take no for an answer and let this slip through my fingers. This was going to *happen!*

When the night came, I recognized the weirdness of the situation. I was a kid taking his parents to the theatre and not the other way around. I had bought the tickets, not them, and even if they paid for it I was in charge of all the details. I had even gotten them to splurge—a term that was pretty foreign to them in their tightly budgeted ways.

Hard to imagine with the high price of theatre tickets today, but it wasn't unheard of for producers to offer preview tickets at the bargain prices of $5 for orchestra, $4 for front mezzanine, and $3 for the rear.

Personally, I rarely spent the extra buck or two to move closer to the stage since I was happy to save the money and stay upstairs where I'd grown comfortable. Surprisingly, my folks approved the $4 front mezz seats.

Child's Play proved to be worth the extra buck per ticket and more than I could have wished for in celebration of my 50th show. To this day it is the most chilling drama I have ever seen in a theatre. In my review, I called it "tremendously horrifying."

Joseph Hardy's staging created an unsettling mood, and the performances he got from his cast brought him a well-deserved Tony. The tension was intensified by the set and lighting by the estimable Jo Mielziner, which won him his fourth and fifth Tonys.

Michael McGuire, Fritz Weaver, Robbie Reed, Ken Howard, Pat Hingle, Peter MacLean and David Rounds in Child's Play *(1970)*

Child's Play took place at a Catholic all-boys prep school. A former student, Paul Reese (Ken Howard), returns there as its new physical education teacher and is shortly confronted with an atmosphere of secrets and lies. The children begin turning on one another for no apparent reason, performing demonic acts beyond their comprehension—one boy has his eyes gouged out, and another is crucified.

The play ended with the students discovering it was Dobbs (Pat Hingle), their favorite teacher, who was responsible for driving his colleague, Malley (Fritz Weaver), to madness and death.

As the children menacingly converge on Dobbs, a terrified look in his eyes in realization they are moving in for the kill, shivers went up my spine as the curtain slowly fell—and is there anything better than a slow curtain for a great finish?

In speaking with Fritz Weaver about the effectiveness of this moment, I lamented how modern directors often eschew this device, thinking perhaps that there's something old fashioned about it. But there is nothing old fashioned about it at all.

"You are so right," Weaver said. "And may I add that you were at a highly impressionable age when you were going to the theatre all those years and your memories are acute and are a correct use of theatre. You were scared out of your mind by that moment and that's the great effect of the slow curtain. What you want, and what I would like, is that kind of theatre to come back again. But it's gone."

At its shocking conclusion, my parents and I were left speechless by *Child's Play.*

Afterward, we headed down the alley to get to the stage door—familiar territory for me. I had already gone down many such alleys, often invited into the dressing rooms of such warm and welcoming actors as Al Pacino, Shirley Booth, Bernadette Peters ... even the fearsome Nicol Williamson (more on that visit later).

I had more than a little confidence I could pull this off.

Being backstage was beginning to feel like a second home to me, but on this particular night it was special. Not only was I taking along my parents—they were acquainted with one of the stars of the show and it was something I was going to share with them. Evenings like this had been practically non-existent and would remain few and far between for years to come.

As I approached the stage doorman (they were all men in those days as they pretty much are today; no idea why that is), I proudly told him that Dick and Sylvia Fassler were there to see Mr. Hingle.

At this point I think my mom and dad were beginning to wonder if this was such a good idea. They were clearly nervous that Hingle would have no memory of them. But there was no backing down now. I was hell-bent on showing them I knew my way around and was fearless in the bargain, too. This visit with Hingle was different—the first time I would use the name "Fassler" to gain entry, and that meant something to me.

The doorman had us wait. The areas by most stage doors are tiny vestibules, cramped and uncomfortable, forcing visitors to make room as actors dart by to get home (or get a drink).

We didn't have to wait long before Hingle came out. Boldly, I stepped forward and introduced (re-introduced, really) my parents to him.

"I'm not sure you may remember, but this is Dick and Sylvia Fassler. They were friends of the late Dick Fallon."

And that's all that was necessary: the secret password.

Hingle's face lit up and that warm smile he would use for both good and evil in the roles he played over a fifty-five-year career let me know we were home free. He launched into his own personal reminiscences about Fallon and the times he had spent with him. Hingle knew he had passed recently and expressed his sadness that Fallon had died too young.

He asked if we liked the play in a way that indicated he was far from certain *Child's Play* would get a positive reception when it opened the next night. We were forthcoming in telling him we thought it was terrific and confident it would be a hit. Hingle seemed grateful, as our compliments were genuine.

We exited the alley with Hingle out onto 45th Street, his only visitors that night. No one was waiting in the street for him to sign a *Playbill* either. Nor was he recognized the whole time we talked out in front of the theatre under a giant photo of himself. After we bid him good night we watched as he walked away, probably heading for a bus or subway as most actors of his ilk (and his generation) were likely to do, as taxis were considered a luxury. In those days it was quite common to share a bus after a show with the star you just saw onstage.

This was a rewarding night out for my parents, who rarely treated themselves like this. They mostly led separate lives as their marriage increasingly turned into one of convenience. Things went beyond merely falling out of love; they really didn't like each other very much. With each unable to afford a single lifestyle, as well as provide for six children, they were never going to divorce.

When I was an adult, my mother confided in me that she had thought of leaving my father. She had even packed a bag, but had no idea where she would go. This confession went against my belief that she and my father stayed together out of at least some kind of commitment and duty to their children. That wasn't it. The truth is they stayed out of inertia, with little attention to how their constant fighting affected us all.

Would my parents have been better off had they divorced? What damage did my five siblings and I unnecessarily endure exposed to their mutual enmity?

Among ourselves we somehow were able to form a tight-knit unit over the years, bonded out of necessity to parent each other since neither our mom or dad had little interest in the job. They did clothe, feed and educate us and for that I am grateful. But anything more would have been gravy, and there's no doubt we led a pretty gravy-less existence.

I have no explanation why, long after all of us left the house, they remained together until my father's death in 2003 after fifty-two years of marriage. Very strange bedfellows.

I still consider myself lucky that they never impeded my love and interest in the theatre. If they had stood in my way, I'm not sure there was anything that could have been done to stop me, especially as my own hard-earned money funded it. With six kids constantly vying for their attention, my parents were often distracted, lending only half an ear to any of us. But they always seemed genuinely interested to hear what I had to say when I returned from the city every Saturday and reviewed for them what I had seen.

After *Child's Play* opened, the mostly positive notices included Clive Barnes in the *New York Times* calling it "a wonderfully powerful melodrama that will thrill audiences for a long time to come." [1]

All the critics hailed the work of its director, Joseph Hardy—an opinion shared by those cast members I spoke with:

Michael McGuire: *The story of* Child's Play *is Joe Hardy. Nothing else. He faced every problem that any director could possibly face, and solved them with such skill and grace it was just astonishing. That play was constantly being rewritten. We did an out-of-town run on our feet, in New York. That's the way it's done today, but back then it was a novelty.*

Ken Howard: *It was totally Joe Hardy's achievement. The work he did with Marasco created a much better play by means of improvisation and the utilization of his actors to the very best of their abilities.*

There were less than a dozen previews, but there was no sense to me that we were ever in any kind of trouble. And it was a great opening night and we all kind of knew it. It was like we may never quite get it there again—not that way.

Fritz brilliantly even went up a few times, which led to these awkward pauses— then I'd add something and he'd inter-rupt—it was like a great improvisation. And Pat Hingle, bless his heart, knocked over some coffee and had to clean up while he was talking. He loved that sort of shit! And it all added up to something wonderful.

Of course then Pat wanted to keep the coffee spill in as a bit of business he could do every night. But that wasn't going to hap-pen—not with Fritz. That sort of thing terrified him! It was so interesting as I was somewhat caught in the middle of them with that. Pat was very Actors Studio, and Fritz was very old school. In the way I work, I think I'm a little bit of both.

Fritz Weaver: *Joe Hardy was very clever. He deliberately set the schoolboys against me. They were instructed to annoy me in almost any way they could. They would stand in the wings with me before my entrance and bother me and disturb my concen-tration and pinch me and kick me a little bit and I would be in a rage sometimes and say, "Why don't they like me?" There were looks they would give me and I would say "What on earth have I done to these boys to deserve this?"*

And, of course, it paid off because I hated them! And they hated me!

Well, not really. They were just working little actors. But I

was annoyed by them. Distinctly annoyed by them. They were
malevolent little presences.
And that was all Joe.

After meeting and talking with his actors, I had the chance to sit
down with Joseph Hardy to get his set of memories, meeting at his Manhattan home, his Tony for *Child's Play* nearby on a bookcase:

> *After the first read-through, Pat said, "I don't know what this*
> *fucking play is about. What's going on here?"*
> *And I said, "We'll find out, Pat."*
> *So I got the cast together and said, "This is what we're going to*
> *do, because I know you're all capable of doing this: we're going to*
> *improvise in rehearsal, these scenes."*
> *So that's basically what I did. We would improvise everything,*
> *and then my assistant took it all down while Bobby Marasco was*
> *locked in a hotel-motel on 8th Avenue.*
> *He slept during the day. After rehearsal at night, I would*
> *go and put all these things under his door, and he would rewrite*
> *from those improvisations.*

> Michael McGuire: *Joe treated everybody differently*
> *and perfectly. What he did, because he could never really*
> *solve the play, was solve the performances. It was an infe-*
> *rior play with one great central character: Malley. And Joe*
> *tried to get a focused script, but he never actually got one,*
> *so he did everything else to create—when someone walked*
> *through one of those jagged shadows, it would stir you.*
> *It was a master class in directing.*

If McGuire felt it was an inferior play, he also knew it made for
powerful theatre. "But Pat helped it a lot, David Rounds … A lot of it
was performance."

A moment of praise for David Rounds, whose performance as Father Penny won him a coveted Theatre World Award, which is still given
annually to a dozen actors each season making their debut performances
either on or Off-Broadway. The award was a testament to his abilities,

considering his role was a very small one.

When I brought up Rounds with Fritz Weaver, he recalled him with great fondness.

> *David never had the career he was promised to have. He died of AIDS, a life extinguished far too young.*
>
> *I remember my favorite line in the play was his. He said, "You're telling your beads more than you're telling me."*
>
> *And he kind of did a little dance with it. He was very gifted.*
>
> *One night I went out with his parents, who loved him dearly. We went out and had an after-dinner celebration, and oh how much they loved him. Oh, my God ... they must have died when he died.*
>
> *I have a vivid memory of him. A sweet disposition. And funny, too.*

Ten years of solid theatre work for Rounds followed, the high point being a Tony for Featured Actor in a Play in a revival of Paul Osborn's *Mornings at Seven*.

He died three years later in 1983, one of the earliest AIDS casualties.

Child's Play's six Tony nominations were more than any other play in the 1969-70 season. Huddled in my parents' bedroom, we watched as it piled up its awards, heading for a clean sweep which would match that won by the original production of *Death of a Salesman* in 1949. Impressive company.

But when a short time later the envelope for Best Play was opened, an unexpected winner was announced: the Irish import *Borstal Boy*, written by Frank McMahon. This provoked gasps from the audience. *Borstal Boy* could now claim the distinction of being only the fourth play in the Tonys' short 23-year history to take home Best Play and not one other award.

And *Child's Play* would become the first play to win five Tonys without Best Play.

What the hell happened?

Enter the man responsible for bringing *Child Play* to Broadway: David Merrick.

The most prolific and infamous producer of his day, a genuine terror dubbed "The Abominable Showman," he was as feared as he was famous.

Anthony Newley worked with Merrick twice in the musicals *Stop the World, I Want to Get Off* and *The Roar of the Greasepaint—The Smell of the Crowd,* as both writer and star. His take on Merrick: "Hitler didn't die at the end of World War II. He went into show business." [2]

With his thick, dark mustache and coal-black eyes, he once formidably appeared on the cover of *Time Magazine.* Not many theatre producers before or since can claim that distinction. He also appeared with regularity on *The Tonight Show Starring Johnny Carson*, the most highly-rated late night broadcast of all time.

Merrick's list of credits dated back to 1944. By 1970, his *Hello, Dolly!* was in its sixth year and on its way to becoming the longest running Broadway musical. In addition, he had three hits held over from two prior seasons. But he was universally loathed, with a penchant for turning the creative teams on his shows against one another in the theory that a divisive atmosphere was conducive to good work.

Ken Howard relished telling me how after the ceremony, he sought out his producer at the Tonys ball for an answer to the question on everyone's minds.

"I went up to Merrick and asked him what he thought happened. How did we lose?"

"And Merrick, with a pained look on his face, shook his head and said, 'They hate me, Ken. They hate me.'"

"And you know," Ken said, "it was true."

When I repeated this to Fritz Weaver, his reaction was, "That sounds about right."

* * * *

After that night out with my parents, going to the theatre together didn't happen much. There was one time though when they were desperate for my help to get them seats for what was then the hottest ticket in town.

This was six years after our visit to *Child's Play* and I was now a college freshman. What they wanted to see was the current biggest hit on Broadway: the original production of *A Chorus Line.* Through a connection from my summer stock days now working for the Public Theatre (which produced it), I was able to secure three house seats at their face value—a whopping $15 apiece.

As on the night I went to *I Do! I Do!* the tickets weren't together. My dad took the single, volunteering to sit off to the side, and my mom and I took our places in the second row of the front mezzanine on the center aisle—amazingly good seats.

After the show my parents volunteered to drive me back to campus at Purchase College in Westchester before heading home to Long Island. It was nice of them, as they were literally going out of their way for me, and I was touched.

Was it so we could talk on the ride up about what we had just seen? About my dreams of being an actor, an issue that the show could have brought to their minds?

I know there was a silent bonding that occurred when we saw *A Chorus Line* that didn't happen with *Child's Play*, and it was for obvious reasons. The subject of parents and children was one of the resounding themes of the musical. Here I was, determined to have a life in the theatre with parents who didn't understand what that really meant, even after all the years they had to get used to the idea.

But nothing substantial was discussed on this car ride. It's possible I attempted a dialogue, only to have it sidelined with nonsense chatter, which is all my mother has ever been comfortable with.

My father, a man of few words, smoked his cigarettes.

After they dropped me off, I went to my dorm room and put on the *Chorus Line* album, which I'd owned for six months and had pretty much worn through already.

Sitting on the floor, my back up against my tiny single bed, I did something unusual: I wrote a letter to my parents.

I had never gone to sleep-away camp and, aside from a student-exchange trip to France at sixteen, this had to be one of the handful of times I was putting pen to paper to write them.

What I wrote was that I loved them. I was moved to do so because of the show and feelings it brought up in me about commitment and devotion and … what we do for love.

And I meant it.

They never commented on it.

CHAPTER 8

The Professional

Robert Ryan

Any actor taking on the role of James Tyrone in Eugene O'Neill's *Long Day's Journey into Night* must play moments of raw emotion, anger and despair. With most productions running more than three hours, depending on its pacing, it is a dramatic marathon packed with high-highs and low-lows for all four of its leading players.

But there is one quiet moment in the play that has always stood out for me. It belongs to Tyrone, the play's patriarch. It comes late in the evening and it has to do with a light bulb that is unscrewed, then later screwed back in.

A simple action for the actor taking on this role? Yes.

An interesting one? Certainly.

An intimidating one? Perhaps.

Sometimes the easiest bits of stage business can prove the hardest. I've seen many actors take a turn at that light bulb—from Jason Robards, Jack Lemmon, Brian Dennehy and Gabriel Byrne on stage, to Ralph Richardson, Laurence Olivier and William Hutt on film and tape. But it was Robert Ryan who screwed it best.

Robert Ryan (1909-1973) was responsible for first demonstrating to me how versatile an actor could be. I had the good fortune at a young age to see his final two New York stage appearances: as Tyrone in *Long Day's Journey,* one of the great American tragedies, and as Walter Burns in Ben Hecht and Charles MacArthur's *The Front Page*, one of the great American comedies. His performances in these two plays, encompassing different genres and sensibilities, have affected me to this day.

A leading player in some seventy films, Ryan was more often than not, the "heavy." He played anti-Semites, sadists, misogynists, homophobes and masochists—sometimes within the same character. If the role called for someone who could snarl really good, Robert Ryan was your man. But he was so much more than that. One film critic called him "perennially underestimated." [1] And no less a film authority than Martin Scorsese has written that Ryan was "one of the greatest actors in the history of American film." [2] I agree with Scorsese, and believe this was because all of Ryan's performances had a firm foothold in realism, never succumbing to caricature.

The dozens of lowlifes he portrayed were in stark contrast with the real Ryan, a crusading humanist who used his fame to publicly stand behind many unpopular causes of the day. He generously supported numerous charities and helped create what is still one of Los Angeles's leading progressive private institutions, the Oakwood School, which had its initial campus in his and his wife's backyard in North Hollywood. Ryan told people that the school was his most important accomplishment.

True as that might have been, it does nothing to diminish his work as an actor. A former boxer (he held the heavyweight title all four years he attended Dartmouth College), Ryan's formidable carriage made for a powerful film presence, upped a notch in brooding intensity when put forth on stage. In *The Front Page*, he used that imperiousness for comedic purposes, stalking his castmates from his height of 6' 4" like a tiger. Two years later, in *Long Day's Journey*, a role he mostly played seated in a straight-back chair, he made James Tyrone equally formidable. Ryan had a noble stature and a natural authority; so much so, that once he entered a play, he owned it.

The Front Page was only the fourth straight play I ever saw (sandwiched in between the original Broadway productions of *Hair* and *Man of La Mancha*). Upon entering the Ethel Barrymore Theatre on a warm May afternoon in 1969, I had no idea I was about to see an American classic. Almost as soon as I took my seat in the second-to-last-row, I was drawn in by the play's deft mixture of dark comedy and dramatic social issues. As young Chicago newsmen in the 1910s and the roaring twenties, authors Hecht and MacArthur weaved their true-life experiences into a colorful and authentic fictional story that was completely worthy of the stage.

Reviewing it from the perspective of a twelve-year-old (and with no shyness for hyperbole), I wrote: "This is one of the great shows of the twentieth century!"

I wasn't alone. Doug Watt's review in the *Daily News* was titled: "41 Years Later, *The Front Page* is Again the Best Show in Town." [3]

The role of Walter Burns has an entrance worthy of Molière's *Tartuffe*. In the same manner, a character's name is invoked with a mixture of fear, admiration and mistrust for a considerable length of the play, prior to his first appearance.

The printed text of *The Front Page* runs 141 pages. Burns isn't seen until page 98, and has such dominance that at any production's curtain call—among its 23-member cast—he always takes the final bow. When he does materialize in the middle of Act II (as if out of thin air during a wild commotion), the impact is sensational due to its perfect setup. And from the moment Robert Ryan appeared as Burns, it was impossible to take your eyes off him. He wore a bowler hat that I am almost positive he never took off. And with a stylized, pencil-thin mustache of the period, he created a brash and swaggering figure that was totally believable. Perhaps Ryan based the character on a boxing promoter who attempted to recruit him out of college during his fighter days. His ability to squeeze every last bit of juice from Hecht and MacArthur's crackling one-liners made for a vivid portrait of larcenous charm.

Robert Ryan as Walter Burns in
The Front Page *(1969)*

It was Ryan himself who made the production happen. He and Henry Fonda, along with their mutual friend, the actress Martha Scott, formed a group calling itself the Plumstead Playhouse. Finding some Long Island businessmen willing to invest in their idea at a theatre in the town of Mineola, the team opened with a production of Thornton Wilder's *Our Town*. It starred Fonda as the Stage Manager with Ryan in the supporting role of Mr. Webb. It was then followed by *The Front Page*, starring Ryan, with Fonda in the relatively minor role of one of the reporters.

A year later, reworked and recast from the Long Island versions, and with new directors hired, both productions transferred to Broadway. *The Front Page* cast included a wonderful group worthy of the old MGM contract players, filled with names that wouldn't mean much today but at the time of the show's run meant a lot to audiences of a certain age (even me at twelve—don't forget, I knew who Nigel Bruce was).

The task of putting together such a large company for the Broadway production wasn't easy, given its tight budget. So when director Harold J. Kennedy was attempting to cajole someone into doing the show, he would express how limited the resources were, which usually led to the question, "What is Robert Ryan getting?" Kennedy would then say, "$167.50." If the answer was, "Then it's okay with me," he knew he had the right actor. [4]

The Front Page boasts what is sometimes referred to as the most famous last line in the American theatre. Not knowing it was coming, I can attest to the enormous laugh it generated as the curtain fell. I may have laughed louder than anyone.

In the 2016 Broadway revival of *The Front Page*, Nathan Lane was entrusted with the role of Walter Burns. Is there anybody better at rendering comedic dialogue, be it a straight or a punch line? The answer is no, and Lane did not disappoint. I have no intention of giving away the play's famous last line, thereby spoiling *The Front Page* for anyone still unfamiliar with it after ninety years. I was thrilled (and so were its producers) that it was a sell-out in its limited run, proving once and for all its durability and timelessness.

I discussed *The Front Page* with Lane a few months prior to his beginning rehearsals, in which he made clear his level of excitement and appreciation for the play:

The Front Page *is just a beautiful piece of craftsmanship. Jack O'Brien [the director] and I spent two days comparing the Samuel French acting version and the original published version and they are very different. There are a lot of cuts and cleaning-up of language in the acting version, leaving things out that they must have thought were too risqué. But for the character descriptions alone that Hecht and MacArthur write, they are just gorgeous pieces of writing. And they tell you, the actor, so much about who it is you're playing.*

* * * *

At the point in his career when Ryan headed the company of *The Front Page* he had been a much in-demand actor during the twenty-five years after returning from World War II. Married with a wife and three children, he had served in the Marines, inducted late due to his advanced age—thirty-three upon being drafted. Common practice at the time had movie studios arranging deferments for their stars. Ryan was no exception, although it was done against his wishes. In this, the studios worked in concert with Washington in the belief that famous actors were in a better position to help the war effort by appearing in movies that promoted anti-German and anti-Japanese propaganda via the film studios' worldwide distribution arms, a useful tool during wartime.

Ryan spent most of the war neither home nor in battle, the sort of disappointment that plagued many men who served. It left him grateful to have survived, but guilt-ridden at not having had a chance to do what he considered his rightful part. Assigned as a drill instructor at Camp Pendleton in San Diego, it disturbed him to witness soldiers sent off and then to see them return damaged physically and mentally.

This led to a strong commitment on Ryan's part to make sure the country avoided another war in the immediate future. He was greatly influenced by his wife, Jessica Cadwalader, a Quaker and pacifist. With the arms race against the Soviets escalating almost daily, he began working with the National Committee for a Sane Nuclear Policy. In the fearful 1950s environment of "the Red Menace," such unpopular stands brought with them round-the-clock police protection when, on more than one occasion, the Ryans were directly threatened. One night, longtime family friend John Wayne (usually on the other side of most political issues from Ryan) stood sentry on their front porch all evening, his rifle at the ready.

One of Ryan's post-war films was *Crossfire,* a brutal examination of anti-Semitism in the armed services, in which he played a homicidal soldier. The role resulted in his single Academy Award nomination, though the horrific character he played effectively typecast him for much of the rest of his career.

His work grew exponentially with daring performances in *Act of Violence, Caught, On Dangerous Ground* and *The Set-Up.* But by the mid-fifties, Ryan sought new tests to his talents. This was when he began to explore stage work after being away from it for nearly two decades.

In 1953, the versatile John Houseman, co-founder of the Mercury Theatre with Orson Welles, made a tantalizing offer to Ryan: Shakespeare's *Coriolanus.* Hardly one of the more popular plays in the canon, it hadn't been done in New York since 1885. "I hedged a little by appearing in a play no one had ever seen and thus didn't suffer comparisons with famous actors," Ryan said. "I think every actor should want to do Shakespeare—an actor who hasn't played Shakespeare is like a lifeguard who's never been swimming." [5]

With Houseman directing as well as producing, together he and Ryan successfully solved a difficult play and were pleased with both the results and the reviews.

Eight years later, while in England, on the set of Peter Ustinov's film of the Herman Melville novel *Billy Budd,* John Neville came into Ryan's life. The British actor, who was also in the cast, headed a theatre in Nottingham, roughly two-and-a-half hours outside London. Ryan was intrigued to hear of the work being done there. A few years later, when Neville gave Ryan the chance to come to the hinterlands and take on Shakespeare's *Othello,* he agreed—but only after Neville promised to play opposite him as Iago.

It was the measure of the man that Ryan was paid $150 a week at Nottingham Rep and paid most of it to his dresser. His actions echoed the words of Tyrone in *Long Day's Journey,* who says of performing Shakespeare: "I would have acted in any of his plays for nothing, for the joy of being alive in his great poetry."

Speaking of Tyrone, the other reason Ryan headed to Nottingham was off Neville's suggestion to act in *Long Day's Journey* back-to-back with *Othello*. Ryan would be the first Irish-American to play Tyrone in England, an idea that appealed to him. His love for O'Neill as a playwright sprang from their similar Irish roots, as well as matched conflicts with regard to their Catholicism.

Unfortunately, Ryan was unhappy with the production, as he later told the *New York Times*:

> *It was an excellent company, but I was the only American and the others didn't really understand the Tyrones ... They say terrible things to one another, but it isn't meant the way others might take it. The English actors didn't understand that. They threw the anger away, understated everything, played with too much refinement, were incapable of busting loose.* [6]

A few years later, in the summer of 1970, Ryan discovered he had inoperable cancer. Given a fifty-fifty chance for survival, he was stalwart as he underwent chemotherapy. Keeping the situation under wraps, his main concern was preventing word from getting out, otherwise it would make him uninsurable for film and television work. And with the knowledge that his time was limited, Ryan was urged by his wife Jessica to return to his first love—the theatre—which led him to attempt one more crack at O'Neill's masterwork

As its title bears out, *Long Day's Journey into Night* takes place during the course of a single day at the Tyrone's modest seaside home in the late summer of 1912. Mary, the family matriarch, upsets the precarious balance, descending into her former drug addiction, when confronted with her youngest son's diagnosis of tuberculosis. The four leading characters (all based on O'Neill's real-life counterparts) play out scenes in monologues, duets, trios and quartets, sharing dark lies as well as harrowing truths.

In my conversations with Stacy Keach and James Naughton, who played the sons to Ryan's James Tyrone, both recalled the actor with fondness and intimacy:

Stacy Keach: *Bob was so warm and personable and he*

loved actors. He loved the theatre and was so much more than a "B" movie actor, which mistakenly some people believe he was. This kind of great, embittered persona he projected to a lot of people when he was in rehearsal or a businesslike mode, was by the book and serious. In truth, he had a great and positive attitude. And we were always hanging out together. We'd often have a drink at his apartment. He was very gracious to me and Jimmy [Naughton].

Bob nailed James Tyrone and he was a joy.

James Naughton: *Bob and I used to like to shoot pool. At that time, there was a pool hall upstairs on the corner of Broadway and 79th street. I think now it's like a rug place or something. But there was an old pool hall up there. And on breaks, or at lunch, or if we had some time when they were working the other scenes, he and I'd go up there and we'd shoot together.*

Bob also had a pool table in his apartment in the Dakota. He had taken out the dining room table and put a pool table in there. I had always shot pool and billiards, but he came kind of came late to it. He had the enthusiasm of someone who had discovered something in his adulthood.

Stacy Keach: *Bob was an extraordinary talent. Nothing would give me more pleasure than to sit around during rehearsals while someone else was working on stage and talk about Shakespeare with him.*

James Naughton: *Bob had a wonderful routine. Stacy and I were sharing a dressing room and, after a performance, once he was done changing, he'd open his door and say, "Okay, lads, come on in."*

And the two of us would walk into his dressing room and he had a bottle of bourbon, Old Sailor (I think), and three glasses. He poured and we all had a shot of whiskey together. Then off we'd go into the night. It was a nice ritual.

Robert Ryan as James Tyrone in *Long Day's Journey into Night.*

As this was my first exposure to *Long Day's Journey*, drama as good as this can have an intense effect on anyone, especially an impressionable fourteen-year-old passionately in love with the theatre. The play's story of familial love, hate and everything in between has the ability to force a connection for an audience, if they are open to the experience. One incident that occurred during the run, told to me by James Naughton, demonstrates why the play can have such a tremendous impact and therefore will always endure:

> *One night, I exited the theatre and nobody else was around, and I came instantly upon an older man and a young man who looked like dead ringers for each other. And they were holding each other, hugging. And I thought, "I've just come upon a father and son who've had a reconciliation because they watched this play."*
>
> *And I sort of stopped for a second because they were right in front of me, and they were crying and holding onto each other. And I went, "Holy ... " And I walked past them and I walked out into the street, onto Broadway and I sort of stood there for a minute and thought about it, like wow ...*
>
> *I mean, we were not getting paid a lot of money to do that show, but that was one of the most satisfying things I've ever seen.*

In this *Long Day's Journey*, all the actors were superb. But as I recall watching it, I felt that with Ryan there was something else going on. Speaking with the production's director Arvin Brown, some of the backstory he offered illuminated that:

> *Bob received his cancer diagnosis before we began working on the play, though he was in remission when we started rehearsals. He was sort of living under a dangling sword but none of us ever knew it. As far as we were concerned he was in remission.*
>
> *We were very careful with his schedule. I kept a sharp eye for when I thought he was getting tired. Bob only did the show six times a week, as opposed to the usual eight.*

Perhaps this is why I responded so passionately to the truth-telling in Ryan's acting. After all, it is what made him such a riveting and charismatic actor. Then why is his name not up there with others who once commuted between film and stage work regularly, such as his contemporaries did, like Henry Fonda and George C. Scott? The thought definitely crossed Ryan's mind, as his daughter Lisa once noted when discussing her father's career: "There were brooding monologues I would hear from time to time: 'Why does Gregory Peck get these parts and I don't?'" [8]

The fact that Ryan was too often consigned to playing the heavy on film undoubtedly contributed to this status. Though built for a leading man, the double-edged sword of playing evil thugs, even with such insightful depth, became his métier.

Thinking on all this led me to a memory of while in ninth grade, and still in the throes of my theatregoing addiction, I was cast in my junior high production of Agatha Christie's *The Mousetrap*. This was the spring of 1972, and a few years later, this intrepid mystery would become the longest running play in the world; still a record, having now past sixty-five years playing London's West End. Cast in the role of the murderer (I'll keep spoiler alerts to a minimum), my character is forced to reveal his true nature at the end of the play, intent on killing the woman who has discovered his wretched secret.

But how to find that dark spot in my soul where such feelings possibly lurked, especially at fifteen? Then it came to me: Robert Ryan! By this point, I had taken to his film repertoire in the study of his talents. That ability to seem sincere one moment, then turn on a dime the next, had the potential to serve as the perfect skill set from which to draw this characterization. The last thing I wanted was to appear like some villain in a melodrama.

Of course the play *is* a melodrama, and I'm sure I was about as subtle as a sledgehammer. With my small stature and high voice, I probably came off more Robert Morse than Robert Ryan.

Whatever the results, my fate (so far) has never to have been cast as a murderer again.

* * * *

After *Long Day's Journey*'s limited engagement ended, Ryan was happy. He had succeeded in a difficult role and was past his cancer scare. For the first time in a while, he was on an upswing. Then, nine months later, the good times ended irrevocably. Out of nowhere, his wife received her own cancer diagnosis. Ten days later, at the age of fifty-seven, Jessica was dead. In shock, Ryan was left a grief-stricken widower with nothing to console him but work. Desperate for anything that would take his mind off his pain, he agreed to high-paying roles in films mostly unworthy of his talents. Thinking not of himself, but of his children's inheritances, he filled his bank account while furthering his depression.

Nagging at Ryan was a feeling of wanting one last shot at something special, fearing his time on earth could be over in what seemed like a quick minute, as was the case with his late wife.

Arvin Brown offered me his perspective:

> Jessie's death was unbelievable. Just unbelievable. And one of the things I found so touching at the end was that she called every member of the family separately and talked to them about what her hopes and concerns were for Bob. She wasn't thinking of herself, but of him. I thought that was simply remarkable.
>
> And he told me afterward that when she talked to him about his future, she told him that she wanted him to go on working on the stage. That she hoped he would do more work with me. That he'd come to Long Wharf to work. That was one of her last wishes. Because I think she felt that he exhibited a joy in working on stage that she didn't often get to see.

After his wife's death, Ryan never returned to the stage.

Then one last chance at O'Neill came by way of the film director John Frankenheimer, who had worked with Ryan in the days of early live television. He invited the ailing actor to his home in Malibu to discuss a film version of *The Iceman Cometh*. He needed to convince Ryan (as well as himself) that the idea was even a credible one, given how ill Ryan was. After their meeting, Frankenheimer knew how much he wanted and needed the actor for the film: "He had a deep sadness inherent in most of these O'Neill characters. He was in touch with his inner self such as very few people are … he was a terribly honest actor. There was never any subterfuge in anything that Bob did."[7]

Putting together a cast with the likes of Ryan, Lee Marvin, Frederic March and Jeff Bridges meant the project was going to be a labor of love for everyone involved. Marvin's asking price for a picture at the time was $225,000 and he left $200,000 on the table so that he could play the demanding lead role of Theodore "Hickey" Hickman. I thought Marvin was outstanding, but his reviews were mixed. It was Ryan who received the lion's share of praise. Sadly, it came to him posthumously, since Ryan had been dead four months by the time the film premiered in theatres.

Paul D. Zimmerman in his *Newsweek* review wrote: "It is Robert Ryan, his face a wreck of smashed dreams, who provides the tragic dimension that makes this *Iceman* a moving, unforgettable experience. Ryan played this part in the shadow of his own death. He died this year, leaving behind a lifetime of roles too small for his talent, and this great performance as epitaph." [9]

When Ryan began shooting in January of 1973, he looked ravaged and far older than his sixty-three years. Lung cancer can do that to a person. His performance in the film is imbued with a sense of fatality, essential to getting under the skin of the character.

How good was Ryan as Larry Slade? Roger Ebert called it "possibly the finest performance of his career." [10] In a generally favorable review, Pauline Kael, whose strong opinions were often backed by her even stronger skills as a writer, praised Ryan as "[getting] right to the boozy, gnarled soul of the play … He becomes O'Neill for us, I think." [11]

In 2012, a thorough examination of Ryan and his work titled "The Actor Who Knew Too Much," was published in the *Dartmouth Alumni Magazine* (Ryan was class of '32). It was written by film critic Ty Burr (also a Dartmouth grad) who wrote of his *Iceman* performance: "Of all the rummies in Harry Hope's saloon, Larry is the one who takes the long view. He sees both the futility of dreaming and the need for it. Ryan grew his hair out into a lank, leonine mane, and the neurosis of his early roles seems burned away. All that's left is honesty." [12]

But allow me to bring things back to where I began this chapter: *Long Day's Journey*, James Tyrone, and the light bulbs. Throughout O'Neill's play, much is made of Tyrone being a "skinflint," going so far as to refuse to pay for his son Edmund's proper medical treatment. Late in the wee small hours of the morning, a drunken Edmund bangs his knee on the way into the house somewhere in the vicinity of 3:00 a.m. In pain and anger, he vilifies his father for being so cheap as to not leave a hall light on. Their argument escalates until Tyrone, to prove to his son that he's no miser, shakily climbs onto a table (in a dramatic fashion), and proceeds to screw in three light bulbs overhead in the hanging chandelier

There is so much underlying Tyrone's detailed movement here; the fear his son may soon die of the TB he's battling; the love he feels for him and can't say in words (but may be able to prove with this one gesture); the inner turmoil of knowing deep down he *is* a miser and can't bring himself to do the right thing.

It's *loaded*. And memorable—in the right hands.

It can't be overplayed and it can't quite be thrown away. It's a delicate balance.

Later in the scene, after Tyrone and Edmund's endless recriminations, hurling every insult in the book at each other, there's a quiet pause in the fighting and it is here O'Neill calls back the overhead lights. Tyrone (wily bastard that he is) looks up at the chandelier and softly says to Edmund: "The glare from those extra lights hurts my eyes. You don't mind if I turn them out, do you? We don't need them, and there's no use making the Electric Company rich." Then, climbing back up on the chair, he unscrews the three bulbs.

My memories of Ryan, aided by watching him play the scene in a blurry black-and- white video at the Library for the Performing Arts (one of the first ever taped for the collection), gives proof to the old adage "less is more." It's an effortless acting that isn't really acting at all—which is why it's so good.

Calling this chapter "The Professional" serves Ryan well, but in so doing it was my intention to bring to mind (for those familiar with it) the popular 1966 adventure film *The Professionals*. In this highly enjoyable Western, Ryan shines alongside Lee Marvin, Burt Lancaster and Woody Strode as hired mercenaries out to rescue the kidnapped wife of a wealthy industrialist, played nastily by Ralph Bellamy. It's a particular favorite of mine, and both its direction by Richard Brooks and cinematography by Conrad Hall were Oscar-nominated.

Once again, I rely on no less a scholar than Martin Scorsese, whose judgment of Ryan as a film actor is difficult to argue with: "In *Crossfire, Bad Day at Black Rock* and *Billy Budd*, he is consumed by hatred and envy—you can hear it in the cracks in his voice, you can see it in his smile. Ryan was a truly great actor." [13]

I only got to see Ryan twice on the stage, but twice was enough. His Walter Burns and James Tyrone taught me how certain subtleties allow for an actor to convey enormous reserves of strength. This quality alone set his work apart from so many others of his day (or any other).

The Tony Award trophy depicts the masks of comedy and tragedy. With *The Front Page* and *Long Day's Journey into Night*, Ryan perfectly embodied the goal to which every great actor aspires. He was worthy of such an award, even if awards eluded him in his lifetime.

I still marvel at his talent.

CHAPTER 9

The Near Miss

The Rothchilds - November 11, 1970

"If I do my job well, this show will not be a success." This is what Hal Linden told me his answer was when his agent asked him how the show he was rehearsing back in 1970 was coming along, right before he headed to Detroit for the tryout of a new Broadway musical, *The Rothschilds*.

Ironically, Linden turned out to be correct. He did do his job well; so well that it made his career—and *The Rothschilds* never became a hit.

Yet I believe *The Rothschilds* possessed 90% of the elements necessary to have ensured a much longer life on Broadway (and beyond) and thereby qualifies as the biggest "near miss" out of the 200 plays and musicals I saw during this period. Because of that it has stayed dear to my heart all these years. The one that got away.

In my review, written when I was thirteen, I wrote: "A spectacular musical ... Hal Linden is utterly fantastic. He sings the song 'Sons' so magnificently, you just want to hear him sing it over and over again ... the sets, lighting and costumes are all perfect. *The Rothschilds* is smashing."

So I liked it.

In 1962, Frederic Morton's *The Rothschilds* was published. This best-seller brought newfound attention to the famous family of Jews who rose out of the German ghetto in Frankfurt in the late 18th century to become the most powerful financial force in the world. A few years later, playwright Sherman Yellen was hired to adapt the eight-hundred-page book into a standard two-and-a-half-hour musical. A novice as a librettist, he was joined by the decidedly more experienced Jerry Bock and Sheldon Harnick to write the score.

Taking the assignment led to an unwelcome elephant in the room: that *other* Jewish musical Bock and Harnick had written so successfully. "We would not have undertaken it had we felt the similarities out-weighed the differences," Bock said. [1]

However, when the critics chose to unfavorably compare one show to the other in every review, it blindsided the team. Harnick explained to me that part of the negativity was based on what he believed was a per-ception that *"Fiddler* is about the underdog, so it works. *The Rothschilds* is about the Jew as conqueror, and people don't want to see that."

Though it is inarguable that *Fiddler* is the better show, when critics weigh in on such things, it sometimes forces talented and sincere men like Sheldon Harnick to feel as if they need to define themselves as either a winner or a loser. Even forty-five years later, Harnick remained stung by these lines of thinking, confessing how he was unsure whether he and his *Rothschilds* collaborators were shortsighted in their goal: "Whether just the idea of writing a show about wealth and the Rothschilds, who people associate with wealth, and whether that in itself put people off, I don't know."

Yellen also seemed to harbor a lingering unease about what the musi-cal represents to some of its audience: "I think it's the one reason it's not done as it really should be. I don't want to say it's because people don't like Jews, because that's not it. They sure like *Fiddler*. But I think the mixture of Jews and money is a little toxic."

Citing his primary goal then as wanting to make the story more contemporary to modern audiences and less about money, Yellen said, "You have to remember that I was contracted to write this in the '60s, and it didn't go on until 1970, the time of civil rights and the civil rights movement."

Coming of age in that time, issues such as the ones Yellen cites were a welcome subject in my home. Our talks around the dinner table were always infused with what was going on in the world: Martin Luther King, Vietnam and Richard Nixon were freely discussed—naturally at full volume.

And though loudness really has nothing to do with being Jewish, mysteriously it has everything to do with it.

Again, identifying myself as a Jew needs qualifying, as I grew up with little sense of any Jewish identity.

When my family moved to the Long Island town of Great Neck in 1964, it had a large and predominantly wealthy Jewish population (and still does). But the brand-new $28,000 home my parents bought was on the less affluent side of town, where there were almost no Jews. In fact, we were the first Jewish family on our block among Italian and Polish Catholics—the Ramazottis, Santinis, Pandolfis, Kovaleskis, Ravinskys and Kacpryzyks—all working-class, everyday folks.

Within a few years it was time to begin religious instruction in preparation for my bar mitzvah, just as my brother had done and many of my new Jewish friends were doing as well. Even at nine years old, I struggled with it. I found my studies at Hebrew school uninspiring, and at the weekly services, the pieties of the Rabbi's sermons did nothing to capture my imagination.

When it comes to religion, the problem dates back to the age of four and being brought to temple, made memorable due to the humiliation it caused me. As my parents gave me no instructions on the proper ways to behave, it seemed logical to me that when a song ended, I should applaud.

And so, I clapped for the cantor.

My two little hands smacking together, the only sound in the synagogue after the beauty of some hymn, had the congregation laughing uproariously. Sensing it was directed at me, I hid under the pew ashamed for the rest of the service.

Later, when Hebrew school started up for me, I was okay with it— at first. Though when Saturday theatregoing kicked in full-force, day-dreaming about what an upcoming matinee had in store for me made it impossible to concentrate on Moses and Abraham.

Things came to a head one day when my Hebrew teacher, whose name I've mercifully forgotten, got so mad at something I was doing that he kicked me out of the classroom (and not for the first time). Why? I'm sure I was disrupting things by cracking a joke—whatever happened to Jews having great senses of humor? —but this guy sure didn't think I was funny.

The by-now familiar routine involved my standing out in the hall, then going back in after class to apologize. Not this time. Once I exited the room, I walked up the flight of stairs, headed out of the school and never went back. That was it. I was done. A Hebrew school dropout.

When I walked into my house, my mother asked what I was doing home so early.

I told her what had happened and that I was finished with the whole thing. She said that if I didn't continue my studies I wouldn't be bar mitzvah'd. I responded by saying that was fine with me. My commitment had been lackadaisical at best. I had always been conflicted as to its point and purpose. Why did my essentially non-religious parents insist on my going through the motions with this?

When I told my friends of my decision they all said I was crazy. "Why would you give up all that money?"

"Is that why you're doing it?" I asked. "Shouldn't you be aspiring to the experience and meaning of it all instead of the cash?" (I know, it makes me sound like a better person than I am, but I really said it). I had seen my brother's bar mitzvah three years earlier for what it was: a pageant that left me with little desire to go through it myself.

And as for the money? There wasn't going to be any. My parents had used whatever my brother received to help pay for the beyond-their-means party four years earlier, so there was no reason to expect the drill wasn't going to be the same this time around.

I recall my father basically shrugging when he was told my news. I'm sure he was not-so-secretly relieved that by dropping out I had saved him a bundle. My sister, Joanne, only two years younger, quit Hebrew school soon thereafter, citing my example. Did this mean I was to blame for my parent's decision to stop paying dues and leave our temple? Or that by giving tacit permission to my younger siblings, I was the one responsible for all of them opting out of their religious training?

The bigger question: whether I intended to or not, did I turn a set of soon-to-be Jews into not-gonna-happen Jews?

The answer is no. Things fell into place as they were probably meant to, though there was one hoop left to jump through before I was free and clear. My parents forced me to honor the Rabbi's request to speak with me in one last do-or-die effort to keep me in the flock. So I went to see him at his home, which was located a bit too close for comfort. Yes, the Rabbi was a customer on my paper route. And not a very good tipper. So the guy already had one strike against him.

I remember sitting opposite him in his study. He wore thick black glasses and had a gap between his teeth, from which he noisily sipped tea. For about an hour, this kind gentleman pulled out nearly every stop in an exhaustive effort to connect with me.

"Did you know that the ancient Israelites put on plays?" was about all he had in his stash.

I was polite but firm. I told him my decision was final.

Poor Rabbi Spivak. I'm sure he prayed for me.

It was late November in the year I gave up on my bar mitzvah when I went to see *The Rothschilds*, eight months past the time I should have "become a man." I'm sure that wasn't what I was thinking when I took my seat at the way, way top of the Lunt-Fontanne Theatre. However, once the play began, the images of put-upon Jews, forced to bow to nasty children in the street ("Jew, do your duty!") stirred something inside me. The struggle of the main characters, Mayer Rothschild and his wife, Gutele, locked in at night behind wrought-iron gates and confined to a ghetto, had me deeply involved in their plight. It was 1970 and a story about fighting for human rights was relevant to me. I was relating to it unlike anything that had been taught in Hebrew school. Not that I had experienced anything close to what was happening onstage in my young life, but I was humbled by what the threat of it meant. The Rothschild family's rise out of dire poverty and religious persecution was potent to me.

It's not that I got religion on this afternoon. I got something else. Sometimes it takes a hit on the head to connect with the heart.

Nothing was more powerful to me than the end of Act I when Mayer, in response to the collapse of the German army by invading French forces, and under direct threat, scatters his sons across Europe. As he and Gutele bid them goodbye, the musical theme associated with each of their children from the song "Sons" (a different theme for each son) is brought back from when we were introduced to them as young boys. The haunting melodies underscore the drama with beauty and specificity.

When Mayer informs his middle son, Nathan, that his destination is England, he calls back one of the evening's earlier and most loaded lines.

With the orchestra rising to a crescendo, a father stares into his son's eyes and pronounces, "Jew, do your duty!" and the curtain falls. No longer will the Rothschild men bow and scrape to others. Their duties will be honest ones, forged in self-respect.

The original cast recording captures it all. Whenever I listen to it, that stage picture flashes in an instant, taking me back to that November afternoon. As with William Daniels's John Adams, I simply fell in love with Hal Linden's Mayer Rothschild. Though Adams was a part I dreamed of playing, the role of Mayer was more about Linden himself. I was fascinated by someone taking the stage so forcefully as if his life depended on it.

Hal Linden in his Tony-winning role

And in a way it did. After fourteen years in the business, this was Linden's first time entrusted with a Broadway musical to carry on his own (even if it was really for just one act). He was thrilled for the opportunity, although it almost didn't happen. It was slightly stunning when Sheldon Harnick informed me that the casting director for *The Rothschilds* had suggested he not use Linden. "She said, 'He's been around for a while, and if he was gonna make it he would've made it already.'"

The happy ending is that they hired Linden and fired the casting director.

Luckily, no such nonsense got in the way when Danny Arnold, the executive producer of a new ABC sitcom, *Barney Miller*, met with the network to discuss casting the title role. When handed a list they had put together, Arnold told them he already had the guy, as Hal Linden described it to me:

> *Danny Arnold was in New York having got a ticket to go along with his children to see* The Rothschilds.
>
> *Now he never told me anything, never sent me a note, didn't come backstage. I did not know the man existed until two-and-a-half-years later when I was in California doing a guest appearance on some TV show and I got a call.*
>
> *"Can you get on a later plane? You got a luncheon meeting with this guy Danny Arnold."*
>
> *And we met and he tried to convince me to play* Barney Miller. *I never auditioned, and no agent ever submitted me for it.*
>
> *Eventually I said to Danny, "What was it? Why me?"*
>
> *He said, "I wanted to imbue Barney with a sense of Talmudic justice."*

What Arnold wanted was someone who easily conveyed smarts as well as a healthy Jewishness. Linden had certainly revealed that to Arnold when he saw him play Mayer and, perhaps in a subtler form, that afternoon at lunch. What Arnold was tapping into was Linden's genuine nature—what he was born with—which resulted in the two best roles of his career. Both solely relied upon who he *is*, and that's something wrongheaded actors often try to erase about themselves.

For a man who had the unenviable reputation as Broadway's premier understudy, Linden was almost ready to pack it in right before *The Rothschilds* came along. He had only recently undergone his greatest triumph matched with his worst fear—and it happened with the same show:

> *I auditioned originally for Larry Blyden's parts in* The Apple Tree *but he got it, obviously. A year later, they contacted*

me. "Would I take over for Larry?" I was thrilled, of course, but they knew that when they replaced Larry with me the standby would quit. So the deal was take over for Larry, but also cover Alan Alda!

I was finally going to have my own part on Broadway and they still wanted me to be the goddamn understudy! Now I said, "I'll do it, but I want Larry's billing." The three of them [Alda, Blyden and Barbara Harris] all had alternating billing over the title. So as far as I know, at that time, I was the only understudy ever with star billing over the title.

I should be in the Guinness Book of World Records.

* * * *

During its tryout in Detroit, *The Rothschilds* was in real danger of not making it to the promised land of Broadway. While Linden may have been killing it in Act I, Act II was dying without him. Trouble in Motor City! Once Mayer scattered his sons across Europe to make their fortunes, the audience had a difficult time leaving Mayer behind, as they had grown to love him.

Act II's biggest problem was that it centered on a different central character as well as what happens when the Rothschilds are out of their poverty. "Poor people are always winners in theatre," Sherman Yellen said. "You have a harder time with rich people justifying their existence. That's why in later days I've asked the question why it would have worked better if the show just ended with Mayer sending his sons out in the world."

If the second act was, in a sense, superfluous, what was there to do? When on the road with a musical, if the patient is sick, a M*A*S*H unit is the only option. There's no time to strap the show to a gurney and take it to the hospital for major surgery. Though Act II had some excellent musical numbers, and the actors kept things interesting through their polished characterizations, changing protagonists was misguided.

Paul Hecht as Nathan, the son who becomes the main character in Act II, was well-aware of how it was playing out. "The problem was that it was two musicals. And as we all know a musical has got to be about one thing."

The shift in focus early in Act II (Nathan falling for the combative and liberated Hannah) introduced a modern love story in the hopes of sugarcoating the plot's primary attention to money. Even with Hannah played by the charming Jill Clayburgh (making her Broadway debut), the part was unnecessary. The storyline wound up with talented people painting themselves into a corner. Funnily enough, it was Jerry Bock's teenage son, with the wisdom of a critic beyond his years, who one day gave a piece of advice from the back of a taxicab to his father and Sheldon Harnick.

"You guys really blew it," the twelve-year-old pointed out. "The love story in the show isn't between Nathan and Hannah, it's between the father and his sons."

After Harnick told me this story nearly fifty years later, he indicated George Bock's critique, if implemented, might not have made any difference: "I thought that was a very insightful thing, and it might've helped a little, but otherwise, I don't think so."

Which brings things back to what Hal Linden figured out earlier than anyone: "If I do my job well, this show will not be a success."

There was no way around it. More of Hal Linden as Mayer was not only warranted, it was required. Sheldon Harnick:

> It wasn't that we needed to give Hal more to do—it was that our audiences were telling us they adored him. After we let him die when historically he would've died, the air went out of the second act, and you could just feel it! The audiences were not happy.

After seven Broadway musicals together, along with contributions to other entertainments that totaled hundreds of songs, *The Rothschilds* was the show that put an end to Bock and Harnick's twelve-year partnership. It also proved a harbinger for what was to follow: the death of the earnest, well-made musical they represented.

The breakup was precipitated by arguments over the man at the helm, director Derek Goldby. When he arrived from London three year's prior with Tom Stoppard's *Rosencrantz and Guildenstern Are Dead*, the play's rapturous reviews won acclaim for his work as well. But did the *Rothschilds* team really know what they were getting? The production's General Manager, Emanuel Azenberg, didn't think so:

Emanuel Azenberg: Goldby got a pass because he pur-
portedly did Rosencrantz, *which was brilliant. But it*
wasn't him, which I found out when I produced a Stop-
pard play and became friendly with him and he told me so.

I think every once in a while a director gets lucky
because he's in the right spot at the right time, and all the
other elements work.

And that's what happened, because notice what hap-
pened with Derek Goldby's career. He did Rosencrantz,
which should've made him, and then he did Rothschilds
and disappeared.

I was a bit apprehensive in telling Sheldon Harnick I was interested
in talking with him about *The Rothschilds* in that he might think my primary interest would be about the dissipation of his partnership with Jerry Bock. Common knowledge has always been that the tensions between
the two came to a boiling point with the firing of Goldby, though Bock
was quoted as saying that "the back of the camel had been weakened by
other straws along the way, so that *The Rothschilds* straw broke a vulnera-
ble back, not one broken by a sudden blow." [2]

As Bock was the only member of the production team who stood
up for Goldby, push came to shove, when over his objections, Yellen
and Harnick and the producers lobbied hard for Goldby's dismissal. For
Bock, not having the backing of his longtime partner must have felt like
a serious betrayal.

It didn't take long while speaking with Harnick, without any prompt-
ing from me, for the subject to come up on its own. It was clear Harnick
wanted to use our discussion to get a few things off his chest:

I think it was with The Apple Tree *when the problem with*
Jerry and me really started, because we were having terrible trouble
finding the score for The Diary of Adam and Eve [Apple Tree's Act
I] *and our producer said, "The problem may be that a one-act form*
may be too small to require a book writer and a lyricist."
This is when he said, "Sheldon, I'd like you to do book and lyrics."
I said, "Fine, and Jerry will help."
But as book writer, when we had Mike [Nichols] directing it,

there were times I had to meet with him privately, and I know Jerry was upset about that, because we'd always done everything together.

So that was the beginning of it.

Before Goldby's *Rothschilds* directorial assignment could commence, there was a long waiting period with numerous delays while the full financing was pulled together. This led the British-born director to take additional work to prolong his work visa to stay in the United States. So when asked to replace the director of a new musical, *Her First Roman*, that was floundering out of town in Philadelphia, he took the job and soon thereafter, Goldby summoned Bock and Harnick to help augment the score.

The show's composer, Ervin Drake, happened to be a friend of Harnick's, which was a cause for concern. But Goldby assured Harnick he'd discussed it with Drake, and that his and Bock's arrival would be welcomed. Not so much, as Harnick explained:

Poor Ervin Drake turned white when he saw Jerry and me show up in the theatre's lobby. He shouted, "Sheldon, what are you doing here?"

I said "Derek told me you were informed we were coming down."

He said, "No!"

I was mortified and said, "Uh-oh, we'll go back to New York."

But Ervin calmed down and said, "No, as long as you're here, I could use some help."

So we stayed. I had given up smoking by this time, but within a day I was smoking again. There was such a sense of intrigue in the company because Derek was going to this one and saying, "You're terrific, but how can we deal with that person?" Terrible.

Jerry and I wrote about three songs, and as far as I could see, we were not helping. And suddenly I'm smoking three packs a day and I was getting very anxious.

So I told Jerry after about a week and a half that I was going back to New York. And Jerry was furious because I'd abandoned ship.

I think that was the second place where the breakup be-
gan to happen.

When a song was needed while out of town to bolster Hal Linden's
presence in Act II, Bock and Harnick outdid themselves with the moving
ballad "In My Own Lifetime." However, the atmosphere of tension surrounding its composition brought Harnick back to a hurtful place when
describing what went on behind-the-scenes:

> *"In My Own Lifetime" has a very sad connection for*
> *me. Derek had been fired, and Jerry Bock was very, very*
> *close to Derek, and hated the fact that he was fired.*
>
> *Shortly after we wrote "In My Own Lifetime," I saw*
> *Lester Osterman [the show's co-producer]. He said, "I love*
> *the new song."*
>
> *I said, "Jerry played it for you?"*
>
> *He said, "Yeah" and I thought "Uh-oh," because we*
> *had always auditioned together—always. The fact that Jer-*
> *ry had auditioned the song by himself I thought was very*
> *significant in our relationship.*

Before our talk concluded, Harnick returned one last time to how
the relationship devolved, this time post-*Rothschilds*:

> *After the show opened, Margy and I invited Jerry and*
> *Patti to have dinner. And after about three or four times of*
> *"Let's go to the theatre, let's go to a movie," each time he ac-*
> *cepted, then the night before the day, he said, "Something*
> *has come up, I can't."*
>
> *So little by little, I got the message. And it was very*
> *painful.*

With no one else in the company experiencing anything as devastating as what Harnick went through, the communal reverie among the five
actors who played the Rothschild sons is as strong as ever. Not only are
they all still active and connected to the theatre in one way or another,

they also remain good friends with fond memories of this irreplaceable time in their lives together:

Allan Gruet (Kalman Rothschild): *The four of us shared a dressing room and they were like the brothers I wanted to have in my life. So walking from the dressing room to the stage was like a continuation, an extension of the script. It was so easy because there was an incredible love between us.*

Chris Sarandon (Jacob Rothschild): *We became a family on the road. After the show we always headed back to someone's room where we'd laugh and joke and have something to eat and goof off.*

Paul Hecht (Nathan Rothschild): *I was stuck because I was the lead and had to share a dressing room with Hal Linden. I missed out on all the fun going on upstairs with my brothers, and I used to sneak up there whenever I could.*

Allan Gruet: *Being together with that group of people was such a positive experience. Hal acted like dad and took on that role. We were all invited to his house for Seder, included in the family, included in everything. It was a totally unique experience. I was never a part of anything like it again.*

Paul Hecht: *It's very delicate what I'm about to say, but the memory of that show, as delightful as the memories in general are, is of pals. And how rare it is in the business to still be pals, forty-however-many years later. It's very rare.*

Timothy Jerome (Amshel Rothschild): *In 2010, at Jerry Bock's memorial service, I was the one who got us all back to sing "Rothschild and Sons" for the first time in over forty years.*

Paul Hecht: *I thought, "Oh, Christ, are we really going to crank up that thing?" And the audience went berserk!*

Allan Gruet: *I think they were excited because we were all still alive!*

Though accounts such as these consistently jibe, the stories of the firing of Derek Goldby do not. First hired as the show's choreographer, it was Michael Kidd who stepped in to replace Goldby. Kidd had a wealth of experience on Broadway with a dozen directing and choreography credits, including the dances for *Finian's Rainbow* and *Guys and Dolls*:

Sherman Yellen: *The problem was that Derek was nerdy, worrisome and hysterical. I can give you a whole list of negatives … He was also the guy that put it together.*

Chris Sarandon: *We all liked Derek. He was a very nice guy.*

Leila Martin (Gutele): *I hated Derek Goldby.*

Sheldon Harnick: *After Derek left, a lot of the cast came up to me privately and said, "We wondered how long this would take." The only one, I think, who was really upset was Paul Hecht because Derek had kept assuring him, "This show's gonna make you a star!"*

Chris Sarandon: *Paul had worked with Derek on* Rosencrantz and Guildenstern *so they had a relationship and, as I recall, Paul was very upset.*

Paul Hecht: *Derek told me, "I'm directing this musical about the Rothschilds," but I told him I wasn't interested because it wasn't the leading part. He assured me, "It's going to be the dad for the first half and you for the second. You'll get top billing," which I did, actually.*

Hal Linden: *Let me tell you something about that billing. It was because of my goddamn reputation for being a standby that they knew they could get away without giving*

Allan Gruet, Chris Sarandon, Timothy Jerome, Paul Hecht & David Garfield
at the recording session for *The Rothschilds* (1970)

Back row: Chris Sarandon & Timothy Jerome,
Front row: Allan Gruet, Paul Hecht & David Garfield (2013)

it to me and that I wouldn't turn it down!

It was my idea to be isolated. If I can't go first, I'll go last. So it read: "Also Starring Hal Linden as 'Mayer.'"

Paul Hecht: *We started rehearsal, lovely, lovely. Everything was good. I was good, and as we went out of town, gradually it was clear that the character the audience was responding to, and that Jerry and Sheldon felt they could write, was Mayer.*

Timothy Jerome: *Hal told the creators, "You can't cut the leading man out at the end of the first act and expect to have a second act."*

Hal Linden: *There's no way the audience was going to be able to cash in their emotional chips at the intermission and invest them in five new guys they never heard of. Well, not never heard of, but all of a sudden it's about somebody else!*

Allan Gruet: *After the Rothschild sons head off and make their way in the world, they didn't even have the good grace to fail. So who gives a shit?*

Emanuel Azenberg: *The second-act problems were already there before we left for Detroit.*

At the end of the rehearsal period in New York we did a run-through. After, there's a meeting in the basement. "Is there something missing in the second act?"

Yes! What was missing was Mayer Rothschild. You get the audience to like this old Jew and then he's gone. The story of the boys was less emotional.

So with something obviously missing, the decision they came to was, "We need a ballet."

Sherman Yellen: *Michael Kidd took over and he enhanced the movement, speeding it up, making it slicker, faster, but the show essentially remained Derek's.*

David Garfield (Solomon Rothschild): *I had no inkling Goldby would be let go. But I don't know if he was dying to do it in the first place. I think he was the one they could get.*

Hal Linden: *I was never privy to anything. It all happened behind closed doors.*

Paul Hecht: *We had no idea what was going on, we didn't see the fighting. Nor should we have. It was none of our business. Our business is to show up and bring something to it.*

Hal Linden: *I knew the show had this structural flaw. And I always thought, what are they going to do about it?*

Emanuel Azenberg: *A ballet! "The gold-smugglers ballet." Yes, that'll cure the problem.*
So I barred the door before they left, literally stood at the door and said, "Before we add this, can we at least wait until the opening in Detroit when we have an audience? This is going to solve the problem? Are you joking? It's an organic issue!"
Then we opened in Detroit and the ballet never came up again. We had bigger problems.

Leila Martin: *The damage was really done in Detroit, and there wasn't enough time to fix it. If they had been able to close down and work on it for another few weeks, it would have worked.*
It was almost wonderful.

Sherman Yellen: *Derek was beloved by the cast and by Jerry Bock, too. They all thought he was wonderful in what he did.*

　　Allan Gruet: *Goldby sent us telegrams for our open-ings in both Philadelphia and New York. He was a good guy.*

　　Leila Martin: *I only wish Jill Clayburgh was here to back me up because Goldby was just horrible to both of us. I have warm feelings for everyone in that show—ex-cept him.*

When it came time to replace Goldby, it is interesting that there is no evidence that Michael Kidd at any time lobbied for the job of direc-tor. When asked to take over, he even argued it wasn't necessary to let Goldby go, as Harnick explains:

　　We had a meeting with Michael Kidd, who was such a gen-tleman. He said, "We don't have to fire Derek. I will be Chair-man of the Board and determine what needs to be rewritten; what scenes and what dances. Derek will direct the new scenes, and I'll direct the new songs and dances. No one has to know that this has occurred."

　　So that's what we tried to do. And then, I don't know, about three or four days after that, Sherman had a new scene. And Hal Linden said, "I don't understand. Why do we need this scene?" And Derek didn't know either. So he took the scene and threw it at Michael and said, "Why don't you ask Michael Kidd?"

　　That was it. He killed himself by doing that. The next day he was gone.

　　I will never forget that. "Why don't you ask Michael Kidd?"

The Rothschilds opened October 19, 1970 to mixed reviews. In what is known as a qualified notice, the *New York Times*'s Clive Barnes was positive, but begrudging: "A good and solid start to the musical season." [3]

"Good." Not an adjective that sends audiences flocking to the the-atre, though John Schubeck of ABC-TV was more enthusiastic: "The first act may have been one of the finest I have ever seen." [4]

The Rothschilds hung around for a year, rarely playing to full houses. In the end, it only paid back twenty-five percent of its $850,000 investment. It took home two Tonys: one to Keene Curtis as Featured Actor in a Musical for playing four different roles, and one to Linden for Leading Actor in a Musical.

The other six competitive Tonys it lost were to Stephen Sondheim, George Furth, Hal Prince and Michael Bennett's *Company*, a game-changer if there ever was one. Perhaps time had just passed *The Rothschilds* by, as well as others shows of its ilk.

As *The Rothschilds* was the last Bock and Harnick musical, it brings up feelings of unhappiness for musical theatre fans. With Bock living a long and fruitful life until his death in 2010, and Harnick going strong into his nineties, they could have been writing shows for forty years beyond the end of their partnership. Would they have endured like John Kander and Fred Ebb, who wrote together that exact length of time until Ebb's death in 2004? If so, how many Bock and Harnick musicals were we denied?

As Harnick movingly said, "Every time I see one of our shows, I realize we had something special, and it saddens me." [5]

Though not wishing to end on a melancholy note, I will give the final word to Chris Sarandon, the last of the Rothschild brothers I interviewed. Near the end of our talk, I mentioned how amazed I was at the consistency with which he and his four "brothers" had the same memories.

Sarandon laughed. "That's because we were together the whole fucking time!"

CHAPTER 10

The Workhorse

Maureen Stapleton

I n going over the list of my first 200 shows, of all the actors who had their names above the title, the actress Maureen Stapleton was up there more than any other.

My earliest glimpse of her was in 1969 when she was starring in Neil Simon's smash hit *Plaza Suite,* a year and-a-half into its run. Directed by Mike Nichols, who had previously staged Simon's *Barefoot in the Park* and *The Odd Couple,* it won him his third Tony as Best Director (of his eventual seven wins in that category). *

When I saw *Plaza Suite,* Stapleton's original co-star, the brilliant and mercurial George C. Scott, had long since exited what was his first stage appearance in a contemporary comedy. It is Simon's contention that it was his dramatic skills that made him so good. "The best comedian I ever had in a play was George C. Scott," he said. "He was funnier than anybody in the third act of *Plaza Suite* because he was playing King Lear. He knew the essence of comedy is not to play 'funny.'" [2]

As talented as he was, Scott was also a tortured soul. An alcoholic, he would go on binges and disappear for days at a time, leaving entire casts and crews stranded. Stapleton battled a lifelong addiction to booze as well, but was the opposite of the unpredictable Scott. She was reliable and dependable: what many in the theatre affectionately refer to as "a workhorse." Not a thoroughbred, mind you. Stapleton would never have stood for such a fancy description. Workhorse would have suited her fine.

A few months before his death in 2014, I sat with Nichols for an hour-long talk about his life in the theatre and, in particular, about being in the orbit of Stapleton and Scott. He talked about their similar cravings for booze, as well as the drama that went with it.

*With a fifty-year directing career on Broadway, it was playwright James Kirkwood who once said, "A play always goes to Mike Nichols first: I think if an Eskimo wrote a play, he'd put it on an ice floe and push it towards Mike Nichols." [1]

"She was so terrified of him," Nichols explained. "She kept saying, 'Whatever the big pussycat wants.'"

Open and frank about Scott, Nichols told me stories that he asked I not repeat, and I will continue to respect those wishes. Having once truly loved the actor, Nichols was forced to end things with Scott when the abuse became too much to endure.

Maureen Stapleton was a much different story:

> *I miss her horribly. Oh my God …*
>
> *At some party we had, he [Scott] put her mink coat in the toilet.*
>
> *Maureen then came to rehearsal and said, "I took it to the furrier and he said, "My God, what happened to this coat?" and she said, "Well, it was in a toilet."*
>
> *And the furrier said, "Don't do that."*
>
> *She'd call me at three or four in the morning, and keep me on the phone for hours. Total gibberish.*
>
> *Where I fell in love with her was when we were in Boston. We were both staying at the Ritz and we went to dinner with our pals and the people in the show, had a great dinner and stayed out quite late. And we walked back, staggering a little bit, especially her, to the Ritz across that little park.*
>
> *When we got to the Ritz, she threw herself on the steps before the doors and said, "Fuck me or I'll start yelling 'rape!' It's a mercy fuck, you owe it to me!"*

Plaza Suite consisted of three one-acts all playing out in the same room at the Plaza Hotel with different characters "checking in." In the opener, Stapleton found both the humor and poignance in what was for Simon his first attempt at something other than flat-out comedy, a harbinger of many plays to come.

In a desperate attempt to reconnect with her distant and cheating husband, Karen Nash has booked the same room at the Plaza where they spent their wedding night. Hoping to reignite a flame long snuffed out by her husband's dalliances, the character's self-lacerating wit came easily to Stapleton, even if comedic timing like hers comes easily to but a handful of actors.

Though Stapleton was wonderful in all three plays, it was her work in Act I that was most special, as evidenced by her recreating the role in the 1971 film version. Funnily enough (or not so funnily as it turned out), it was someone's idea for Walter Matthau to be the sole male lead, with Stapleton, Barbara Harris and Lee Grant splitting the women's roles. As Stapleton remarked, "I was willing to settle for a solid single instead of a smashing triple." [3]

Making his Broadway debut in a small but critical role in the last act of *Plaza Suite*, was 23-year-old Bob Balaban. He was happy to reminisce about his experience working with such formidable personalities as Stapleton, Scott and Nichols:

> *My audition for Mike Nichols and* Plaza Suite *was one of the few I ever had when at the end of it a director said, "That's great. Come and be in the play."*
>
> *And I was young enough not to know that people don't do that. They usually have to talk it over with 3,000 people. But that's Mike.*
>
> *I actually had another offer when* Plaza Suite *came up. I had been auditioning for the musical* George M! *I had to choose and I thought, to have three lines in a play by Neil Simon with George C. Scott and Maureen Stapleton and be directed by Mike Nichols is, in the life of one's career, probably better than having a song in a Joel Grey musical.*
>
> *Mike did an incredible thing at the first rehearsal. He laid out the outline of a hotel suite at the Plaza on the floor and we had practically a full day of what it's like to check into a hotel room that you have never been in before. Do you look in the closet? Where do you put your coat? Do you open your bag first? How does it go?*
>
> *I quickly realized that he's a behaviorist. He knows how people behave, so the words come out of behavior. It's a very simple thing to say, but quite another matter to have no instinct about how to do that.*
>
> *So it was a great lesson watching him.*

After I saw *Plaza Suite*, I waited at stage door for Stapleton. Eighteen months into its run and she was, as always, giving her all, remarkable by current standards where a lead actor staying beyond a year in a show is rare. Stapleton was one of those special types who dedicated herself to her audience.

Meeting her, she seemed much smaller than she appeared onstage. She couldn't have been sweeter, if a little stunned anybody was waiting for her. You would think by this point in her career she might have gotten used to this, but no. Stapleton never seemed to grasp just how sincerely adored she was by her fans, as well as the theatre community as a whole. My single exposure to her as an actress prior to this had been as Dick Van Dyke's mother in the film of *Bye Bye Birdie*. Proof of how a character actor takes whatever work comes, she was thirty-eight when she filmed it—a mere five months older than Van Dyke.

I became better-acquainted with her a short time later, when I saw her in the all-star *Airport* in 1970, which earned her an Oscar nomination.* In what can only be described as a harrowing performance, two-time Tony-winner Cherry Jones is on record as stating: "I remember seeing her in *Airport* and recognizing for the first time that I was watching great acting. ... I'll never forget that performance as long as I live." [4]

For Stapleton, *Plaza Suite* marked a welcome stage success in a comedy. "I don't think tragedy and comedy are that far apart," she wrote in her autobiography, *A Hell of a Life*. "You start from the same place; it's just that comedy is so much more precise." [5]

For my money, that's as good an acting lesson as can be expressed in one sentence.

Plaza Suite would be the beginning for me of seeing Maureen Stapleton on Broadway—and it would be far from the last over a remarkably short time:

> *Plaza Suite* - July 1969
> *Norman, Is That You?* - February 1970
> *The Gingerbread Lady* - December 1970
> *The Country Girl* - March 1972
> *The Secret Affairs of Mildred Wild*, November 1972

---

* In 1958, Stapleton became the first actress to be nominated for the big three in the same year: The Tony (*The Cold Wind and the Warm*), an Emmy (*All the King's Men*) and the Oscar (*Miss Lonelyhearts*). She lost all three.

Maureen Stapleton as Karen Nash and
George C. Scott as Sam Nash in *Plaza Suite*.

Five Broadway shows in three-and-a-half years—and none was a limited engagement. Yet in spite of being popular and beloved, there were personal demons Stapleton fought her entire life, many of which she sought refuge from with alcohol. Her need to seek solace in drink was well-known and not altogether different from many of her acting contemporaries, though the extent of her phobias were highly uncommon.

She wouldn't fly (once up in the air was enough) or cross bridges by car. Later in life, going up a flight of stairs held a certain terror. The worst and most improbable fear was that she lived in abject terror of being shot while performing live.

She explained her two most essential vices succinctly: "Smoking was a part of my life from early on [eleven or twelve years of age]; but drinking was an acquired skill." [6] And it's probably no accident that two of her finest stage performances were as alcoholics: Evy Meara in Neil Simon's *The Gingerbread Lady* in 1970, and Birdie in a 1981 revival of Lillian Hellman's *The Little Foxes*, opposite Elizabeth Taylor.

One would think Simon wrote Evy with Stapleton in mind, especially with the caustic wit and drinking that were the overriding aspects of the character. Not so. When Simon sent the play to Mike Nichols for a first read, Nichols (although unable to direct it because of pending film projects) told Simon in no uncertain terms: "There is only one actress. You must send it to Maureen." [7]

Simon was conflicted. He adored Stapleton and thought her perfect for the role, but was concerned she might somehow feel he'd ripped off her life in constructing the character. Those fears were both confirmed and allayed when, after reading it, Stapleton phoned him and said, "You bastard! ... You no-good dirty bastard! ... When do we go into rehearsals?" [8]

In what was Simon's first attempt at serious drama, Stapleton delivered on Evy's deep reserves of sorrow as well as uncovering every ounce of comedy. She also managed to warble a few songs with more than enough respectability to make for a convincingly successful, if albeit washed-up, chanteuse.

A review in *The Nation* by Harold Clurman praised her as "one of the four or five outstanding actresses of the day. She is effortlessly humorous; it is virtually impossible for her to strike a false note. ... She is open to all the slings and arrows of outrageous fortune without seeming to beg for them." [9]

Maureen Stapleton, on the street where she lived (45th), her name in lights.

In my write-up of the show, I called her "illustrious." Illustrious of *what* I have no idea. Then again, I was no Harold Clurman.

* * * *

Stapleton, the product of a childhood mired by an alcoholic and absent father and an unhappy and unstable mother, found her only source of freedom was to go to the movies for hours on end, often sneaking out of classes and playing hooky to do so.

Once high school was over and having already told her single mother she was saving up to move to New York City to be an actress, she worked hard until she reached her magic number—$100. No one, not a soul, had encouraged her in this goal. Her ambitions were all her own, preparing for this day since the age of twelve.

"The first time I informed my mother that I was going to be an actress, she said, 'Okay, okay, be an actress.' She didn't get that I wasn't asking her permission." [10]

As a child I *did* ask permission to audition professionally, and I'm grateful my parents always said no. I think there was a fair chance I might have made a go of it, but at what price? What would success have brought me? Had I gone on to even the tiniest degree of fleeting fame or fortune, I might easily have wound up on an *E! True Hollywood Story* with a title like *1960s TV Stars: Where Are They Now and Who Cares?*

If my parents weren't on board, I still had Aunt Helen looking out for me. One time she called to say she had heard on the radio that a new version of *The Little Rascals* was holding open singing auditions in Manhattan. She had written down all the information and told me, "Go!"

I have no idea how I got into the city that day. Who took me? I was all of ten years old. It was an open call, something I knew nothing about. I had no idea how to prepare. The information I got from Aunt Helen was that I should bring a song. That meant I should bring sheet music, but I didn't know that. I brought a song—the one in my head. I also had no résumé and no headshot, so I arrived completely empty-handed. I was batting a thousand.

I signed in and waited. That part I do remember, the waiting.

When my name was eventually called I went up on the stage. The auditions were held at the Bert Wheeler Theatre, located off the lobby of what was then the Hotel Dixie on West 43rd Street, a disreputable hovel back in 1968. Known today as the Hotel Carter it is *still* a disreputable hovel. A recent review from a tourist on the Internet travel guide Trip Advisor bears repeating: "This place service sucks security sucks front desk is sucks." (verbatim.)

The carpet was threadbare and the place reeked. And believe it or not, the musical that was running on the stage at the time was an actual hit that, when it opened, featured in a supporting role a young unknown—Bernadette Peters.

It was a spoof of Shirley Temple movies called *Curley McDimple*. Peters had already left the show by then. I'm sure either her mother, her agent, or her sense of smell got her out as soon as possible.

When I stepped onto the stage I was directed to the pianist who dryly asked for my sheet music.

I didn't have any.

He sighed, then asked what I would be singing.

I told him "Someone Needs Me."

He sighed again. He'd never heard of it.

As it was from *I Do! I Do!*, he dropped a level in my book right there. Now we were even. If he was going to judge me, I was going to judge him. Of course, "Someone Needs Me" is a song sung by a middle-aged person about time having passed them by—totally inappropriate and all but killing any chance at my becoming a Little Rascal. Only that wasn't my biggest problem.

"Don't worry," he said. "I'll follow you."

I didn't quite know what that meant, but let me tell you how it went: I sang the entire song *a cappella* and when I hit the last phrase "for someone needs meeeeeeeeee" he came in with a "da da da dummmmmm" on his piano.

That was it—that was "following me."

Basically, a final chord.

The song stank, I stunk, and I went home.

Not the last time that happened, though it was the first time on a somewhat professional stage.

And they never made that particular *Little Rascals* film either. I always liked to think they didn't have the right eye for talent.

* * * *

When Stapleton came to New York City to pursue her professional career, she worked a series of odd jobs, among them artists' model and hotel clerk. "I was 17 years old, I weighed 180 pounds and I had a hundred bucks in my pocket. ... I was invincible." [11]

Her looks were atypical, not fitting any pre-cut pattern. An unattributed remark, which I love, showed up in her obit in the U.K. newspaper *The Guardian*. It praised Stapleton as having "big showgirl eyes, a small mouth, the skill of a Japanese tumbler, the radiance, and a voice that combines harridan and chamber music with layers of cello and violin." [12]

It wasn't until 1951, as a still-fledgling twenty-five-year-old of Irish decent, that Stapleton transformed herself into a Sicilian widow with a sixteen-year-old daughter in Tennessee Williams's *The Rose Tattoo*—the breakthrough of which she had always dreamed.

It was the playwright himself who fought for her to play it. In his autobiography, *Memoirs*, Williams wrote of Stapleton: "She was a very young girl at the time but nevertheless I thought she was so brilliant in characterization that the obstacle of her youth could be overcome. So I kept insisting that she read and read again. Finally, I assisted her in 'making up' for a reading: I had her dishevel her hair and wear a sloppy robe, and I think even streak her face to look like dirt stains. And that reading she gave made all agree that she was the one." [13]

If the role of Serafina at first seemed a stretch for Stapleton, then Birdie in Lillian Hellman's *The Little Foxes* some thirty years later was no natural fit either.

Friends with the tempestuous Hellman since 1959 when they collaborated on the Broadway production of *Toys in the Attic*, Stapleton was surprised when in 1981 she was in consideration for a revival of *The Little Foxes* that was to star Elizabeth Taylor. Having lost out on the part once already when she auditioned for Mike Nichols's 1967 *Foxes*, Stapleton told Hellman, "I can't play Birdie. I'm too fat. And besides, she's an aristocrat; I'm a peasant."

In response, Hellman snapped, "Maureen, stop it, this is acting we're talking about." [14]

At this stage in the game, Stapleton was fifty-five and overweight (a struggle she dealt with her entire adult life). Austin Pendleton, the director of this *Foxes* revival, shared with me his surprise when Hellman suggested Stapleton for Birdie:

> I told Lillian that I thought Maureen was a great artist, but I didn't think she was right for it.
>
> Then one day I'm in Lillian's apartment, which was always an adventure, and suddenly she said, "Rita!" to her assistant, "Get Maureen on the phone!"
>
> And she made her way to the phone and said, "Maureen, I'm sitting here with Mr. Pendleton"... and then I'm sure Maureen said some obscene thing and Lillian cackled and sex was described ... and then she said, "We could talk like this forever, but Maureen, Mr. Pendleton doesn't think you're appropriate for the role."
>
> I'm waving my arms and gesticulating wildly, then I heard Maureen through the phone: "Tell him I'll audition for him."

I'm still waving no! Lillian then hangs up and says, "She's going to audition for you, Austin."

This was just before Christmas and I went over the day after and it was like ten in the morning. She was hung over and in her robe and we pulled down the play from an anthology and we read the big scene in the third act. And it was breathtaking.

I saw this *Little Foxes* and Stapleton was indeed a standout. Regardless of her bulk, she made Birdie appear waif-like. Her talent was such that she could make you believe anything.

In 2012, six years after her death, Stapleton's hometown of Troy, New York, held a celebration of their favorite daughter. Jane Scovell, who co-authored Stapleton's autobiography, spoke at the ceremony and described a scene in *The Little Foxes* where Elizabeth Taylor was center stage, her glistening violet eyes burning a hole through Stapleton as the mistreated Birdie. "But all eyes were on Stapleton," according to Scovell. "She was doing more acting with her back than dear Elizabeth was doing full frontal. Her back was deflated. You knew exactly how her character was feeling." [15]

I spoke with Scovell and asked her how *A Hell of a Life* was arrived at for a title:

I came up with it and the publisher liked it, but Maureen objected. She suggested we call it A Heck of a Life. *That was particularly funny having come to know her so well. It wasn't that she was objecting to a curse word. It was more along the lines of "Who am I to say I had a hell of a life?" Maureen was afraid it would come off boastful. That's how modest she was.*

Also modest and extremely forthcoming was Austin Pendleton, telling stories of what it was like directing Stapleton in *The Little Foxes* (for which he received a Tony nomination for his direction):

She staged the big scene herself. She said to me, "Look Austin, they always stage this as pure bullshit. She sits there and has this long emotional scene. But when you're an al-

coholic, and you confess to people that you're a drunk, you move around."

RF: *Out of nervousness?*

AP: *And shame. So we started playing with it and she said, "Let me just do it." So she staged it.*

And Walter Kerr tore it apart. He wrote: "Maureen Stapleton somehow manages to survive the inept staging of Austin Pendleton."

And I thought I can be objective about the staging because I didn't do it! It's brilliant staging. I could never have come up with that. It's so intuitive. It's the way people are.

RF: *Did it vary?*

AP: *No. In fact, I tried to make little changes in it and she said, "No!" But she was wonderful.*

The Little Foxes would be Stapleton's final stage appearance. Not long after, she packed up her New York apartment and moved to the Berkshires to be closer to her daughter and grandchildren. She took on the occasional role in film or TV, but for all intents and purposes she went to Lenox to retire.

Still, she remained on many a filmmaker's wish list. In 1996, writer-director Albert Brooks tried to coax her back to the big screen for *Mother* (a role that went to Debbie Reynolds). Brooks described for me his phone conversation with Stapleton:

She told me she was flattered, that she loved the script, but had no intention of ever stepping foot on the West Coast again. It wasn't an L.A. thing either, since we were going to film a lot of it in Sausalito. She said she would do it if we could film it where she lived—in the Berkshires.

I explained to her that it wasn't feasible; that I had just gone to great pains and expense to secure the rights to Simon and Garfunkel's "Mrs. Robinson" for a sequence where I drive over the Golden Gate Bridge, like Dustin Hoffman did in The Graduate. *The film absolutely needed to take place outside San Francisco.*

Her response? "Can't you build it here?"

Another reason for Stapleton's retreat from New York was due to the sudden death of her beloved friend and agent, Milton Goldman.

Goldman was that rare breed—the gentleman agent—whose consistent good taste and advice garnered him lifetime clients. Once signed to Goldman, few ever left. John Gielgud, Laurence Olivier, Helen Hayes, Mary Martin, Christopher Plummer, Vanessa Redgrave, Albert Finney and Stapleton were but a few who came under his care.

Stapleton's feelings for Goldman are best articulated (in the way only she could) by a story in her autobiography:

> *One time we were at a theater party and I'd gotten rather tight. ...   I wanted to leave and needed my escort to take me home. I found him standing with a bunch of people.*
>
> *"Boy, am I glad to see you!" I cried, throwing my arms around him. "I love you, Milton. I wanna go home."*
>
> *Milton smiled, politely extricated himself from the group, and started steering me toward the door. I was overcome with affection for him, and as we left the room I gave him what I considered my biggest compliment:*
>
> *"Milton, you're a doll. I really love you, and if you ever decide to fuck a woman, I'm your man."* [16]

Stapleton possessed the ability to raise that kind of salty language to the level of high art, with full knowledge that her saltiness had the power to get her into a lot of trouble. While appearing opposite Melvyn Douglas in Arthur Laurents's *The Bird Cage*, her cursing, along with that of several other ladies in the cast, caused the actor to report to the show's director, "I've been in the army and I've been in show business all my life, and I've never heard such language." [17]

Laurents, who himself had a well-known propensity for bitchiness, concurred: "Their conversation and the language transporting it could curl a steel beam." [18]

Foul mouth aside, among her contemporaries, Maureen Stapleton was beloved. Not only for her talent, but for the depth of her friendships with everyone from Marlon Brando to Noël Coward. A mother-hen, she collected friends the way people collect books. Nights spent in her apartment until all hours of the morning were mandatory and legendary. Secrets were shared, advice was dispensed, much alcohol was consumed.

James Naughton recalled a time for me when he was working with Stapleton on the television film *Tennessee Williams' South*:

> We shot the thing in a hotel in New York. And I was living in New Haven and I missed my train. And somebody said, "If you need a place to stay, you can stay—" and Maureen shouted, "He's staying with me!"
>
> And she took me home, Maureen did, and put me up that night. And we sat up and drank champagne, because that was her drink. All night. I mean until dawn—light was coming up outside. And she had a rehearsal in the morning—I didn't.
>
> But we had a wonderful time, and she told me stories ... If I could remember them, I'd write a book.

Piper Laurie, in her autobiography, *Learning to Live Out Loud*, describes the time she played Laura in *The Glass Menagerie*, opposite Stapleton's Amanda:

> Maureen was the only one of the cast who had actually seen the legendary performance with Laurette Taylor twenty years earlier. Poor Maureen—she was haunted by it and couldn't shake her inhibitions until the very last night with us many months later. Her performance that night was one of those recorded in heaven. I was touched by something miraculous with her on stage that night.
>
> She was the most gifted actress I had ever worked with. [19]

William Youmans, a wonderful actor with whom I went to college, appeared with Stapleton in *The Little Foxes*. "Here's what I remember about Maureen," he told me. "Every night before going on she would always say, 'Cut the fuckin' pauses and let's get outta here!'"

When they first met on *Plaza Suite*, Bob Balaban had a sort of secret life that Stapleton wasn't aware of. Later, it caused a brief moment's tension between them in what otherwise was an idyllic and longtime friendship, as he explained to me:

> *I was twenty-one and she was naturally maternal. I looked like a lost soul with my schleppy clothes and not knowing what to do with myself. She would take me out to lunch and ask if she could help me in any way.*
>
> *Then after I'd left the show, I was shooting a movie in Mexico, and she called me at what must have been 3:00 a.m. East Coast time. "You fucker, you're rich!" she shouted at me.*
>
> *Yes, my family was well-to-do and she suddenly found out about it and accused me of pulling the wool over her eyes—"I've been taking care of you!"*
>
> *So I apologized and told her that when I got back to New York I would take her to a fabulous restaurant. And she said, "You better." And I did.*
>
> *Maureen Stapleton was the gutsiest, nicest, coolest lady I ever met, not to mention the best actress on the planet. I loved her.*

A deeply sensitive person, Stapleton's willingness to share her inner life and vulnerability with an audience was what made her the actress she was. Outsized when a role called for it (and sometimes hilariously so), every part she played spoke to her heart.

However, the price for that kind of access to one's emotions can sometimes make the cost incalculable. An actor with the power of empathy such as Stapleton's brings to mind the relatively short life of Philip Seymour Hoffman, who took his commitment to playing the depths of despair as Willy Loman in the 2012 Broadway revival of *Death of a Salesman* to its ultimate limit. During the run of the play, he returned to addictions that twenty years earlier had almost killed him.

Hoffman's death from a drug overdose came up in my conversation with Mike Nichols, who directed *Salesman*. Meeting three months after that tragedy, the rawness of it all was still difficult for him to talk about:

> Salesman *was the most personal play I ever worked on and we all fell in love. And the Phil thing was so...*

unbearable. You felt like, "Of course," and we all felt,
individually, we could have helped him. And why didn't
we? But that's an illusion, although it doesn't go away.

Whether an artist who digs into such unadulterated feelings can ever be repaid for such a sacrifice is an important question. Bob Balaban expanded on this notion when discussing Stapleton's gifts as an actress:

I have a feeling that some people, Maureen in particular,
were born with too much sensitivity to everything. A kind of
overload of sensitivity, which is maybe why she could act those
emotions so well. Or was so phenomenally empathetic. Or was
simply too sensitive to not be drunk whenever she could be, to
anesthetize herself to the pain of all that sensory overload.

The penetrating soul of Maureen Stapleton was so delicate that, as Balaban notes, it had to have been a hard thing to live with. As she once admitted: "In the Tennessee Williams roles I've played, the emotional problems were so great I was living under terrible tension and pressure. That's when you have to call on all that interior jazz." [20]

Examining all the shows I saw Stapleton do on Broadway, it wasn't until adding them up that I realized I hadn't missed a single one from the time I first saw her in 1969 until her retirement in 1981. Eight shows in twelve years—and she shined in all of them. She could take a lemon, like the three-week failure *The Secret Affairs of Mildred Wild*, and make a lemon-drop martini. Her good friend Doris Roberts, who co-starred in that show, reminisced about Stapleton when we met in 2013:

Long after Mildred Wild *closed I remember going to*
her house and there were a whole bunch of English theatre
people there and it was kind of dull. So Maureen went up-
stairs and put on the dress she wore in in the show that was
her Scarlett O'Hara outfit with an enormous hoop skirt—
and she came out and took a huge fall and couldn't get up.
She had us all in stitches.

RF: *Did* Mildred Wild *play out of town before com-
ing to N.Y?*
DR: *Boston, yeah.*
RF: *Was it rocky?*
DR: *Rocky, but funny.*
RF: *So you had a lot of fun doing it?*
DR: *No.*

At her memorial service, the story of an exchange between Stapleton and a reporter was told. It summed up the qualities that gave her the reputation of having been a truth-telling, no-bullshit, profanely funny individual like no other.

"How does it feel to be recognized as one of the greatest actresses in the world?"

"Not nearly as exciting as it would be if I were acknowledged as one of the greatest lays in the world."

How do you not love someone like that?

CHAPTER 11

The Bomb

Dude - September 30, 1972

The self-named Joe Allen restaurant has held the same spot on West 46th Street in the theatre district for more than fifty years. A chief reason for this, besides doing a good business, is that Mr. Allen need never fear eviction: he owns the property and is his own landlord.

It is also his home—he lives right above his long-successful establishment.

Allen bought the brownstone that houses his restaurant in 1965 (from Fred Trump, as it happened) at a time when the street between 8th and 9th Avenues was "red-lined."

When Allen mentioned that term to me in an interview I conducted with him in 2014 I had to ask what it meant. He explained that the street was so undesirable that no bank would loan money towards the purchase of any property there. It was considered worthless.

With help from some friends as investors, Allen was able to buy two of the buildings—one for $75,000 and the other for $80,000—before adding a third a short time later. This trio of townhouses now has a market value roughly in the neighborhood of at least $15,000,000 (a very nice neighborhood).

The street, designated "Restaurant Row" in 1973 by the City of New York, offers more than thirty eateries—three of which (Joe Allen, Orso, and Bar Centrale) are Allen's.

And it all began with one man and a vision.

Allen's initial goal was to attract working-class members of the theatre community, as opposed to its stars, to a safe haven that was cheap and comfortable. This meant young (and sometimes not so young) struggling actors, chorus people, stagehands and everyone else "trying to scratch out a pleasant simple tune without breaking their necks." It wasn't easy.

As Allen tells it: "Nobody had any money. In an effort to seduce chorus people, I said, 'Go ahead and sign for it.' Everybody paid—they could be slow, but they all paid, because they had to be able to come in here to see their friends." [1]

This proved a smart template. Eventually Allen would cater to the biggest stars on Broadway, mindful of keeping things low-key enough to also make a humble, starving artist feel welcome.

To this day, prior to a matinee or evening show, tourists enjoy its juicy burgers or its famous banana cream pie. Later, after 10:00 p.m., when the theatre district sidewalks fill with folks getting out of shows, Joe's is home to more than the tourists. It is a communal place to unwind after a performance until the food and drink stop being served and the waiters gently urge customers to go to their real homes. Whenever I came to New York during the thirty years I lived in Los Angeles, I would visit Joe Allen and always find a familiar face there (besides Mr. Allen's).

So why is a chapter about a show called *Dude* and titled "The Bomb" devoting its opening paragraphs to a restaurateur? Even if Joe Allen could easily pull off the moniker of "the Dude" (he's very cool) and his establishment may, in modern parlance, be "the bomb," there's another reason.

Upon entering the restaurant, one of the first things likely to be noticed along the walls are framed posters, or window cards, as they are referred to in the trade. These provide a "who's who" and "what's what" of the worst flops ever produced on Broadway.

They also reflect an insider's sense of humor that makes the place feel like somewhere it would be wise not to take yourself too seriously. Have a drink, relax and enjoy the fact you may be in a hit (for now) because tomorrow the poster of your latest failure could be on the Wall of Shame for all the world to see. I can say with pride, if that's the correct term, that I had the misfortune of seeing a good number of the more than three dozen posters adorning the walls—but thankfully was never in one of them.

Although if unwanted notoriety, foul reviews and short runs are the requirements, then by Mr. Allen's standards, there was a show I was involved with that qualifies: Howard Schuman's *Censored Scenes from King Kong* certainly had the goods. Or, in this particular case, the bads.

This was my first hire under a Broadway contract (I turned twenty-three two days before opening night) and, as with *Slab Boys*, I was understudy to some worthy actors of note: Stephen Collins, Peter Riegert and Chris Sarandon. The cast also included another twenty-three-year-old, Carrie Fisher, a freshly-minted box office draw due to *Star Wars*.

The title of the *New York Daily News* review for *Kong* was "Drop It Off the Empire
State Building." And in the *New York Post*, Clive Barnes wrote: "Obviously even in a
theatrical season as bad as the present something had to be the worst. … This season still has a fair distance to run. However, I doubt whether anything is going to outmatch in horror a little number called *Censored Scenes from King Kong*."

You don't ever forget reviews like that. In fact, I memorized them.

Burned as they must have been, the *Kong* producers didn't rush over to Joe Allen and ask that their poster go up. Allen has said that he would mostly hear from a producer only by way of their pleading, "'Please don't put up that poster,' and I'd say OK … then, three months later, 'Could you put the poster up?' They suddenly realized that the poster is all that will be remembered." [2]

There is one flop on Allen's wall that stands out among the rest. If not the biggest turkey, it's unquestionably the biggest poster. With every show represented by a window card of a standard 14" x 22", there is one five feet high on the back wall of the restaurant. And that show is *Dude* (though at full measure it also includes a subtitle). *Dude: The Highway Life* can best be summarized by borrowing a line from Mel Brooks' *The Producers* as "a show so bad it'll close on page four."

The interior of Joe Allen, flops on the wall to the left, *Dude* straight ahead.

In the view of theatre historian Ethan Mordden, "*Dude* was apparently more hallucinated than written." [3] The crackerjack team involved with the show truly hoped to have another *Hair* on their hands—not so much of a misguided notion as two-thirds of *Dude*'s creators were responsible for that revolutionary musical.

Dude was the brainchild of Gerome Ragni, the co-author of *Hair's* book and lyrics. With James Rado, and composer Galt MacDermot, the trio became millionaires after their "American Tribal Love Rock Musical" rocked Broadway. A huge hit, its notoriety was secured for all-time when at its Act I curtain, some cast members took their clothes off while singing "Where Do I Go." What had been the domain of Off-Broadway was suddenly front and center and in your face on Broadway—full-frontal nudity.

When I attended *Hair* a year into its run, I was twelve, and naked people were something to which I was most definitely looking forward. So imagine my disappointment when, at the moment of truth, the lighting was so dim I could barely make anything out from up in the cheap seats. I was titillated, naturally, and somewhat immaturely wrote in my review: "You might think buying the album would be the same as seeing the show … but see it anyway … because there's plenty to see."

If *Dude* had aspirations to be another *Hair*, it needed more than a great production and an exciting score. Spiking the proceedings with nudity wasn't going to cut it, since by 1972 it was no longer shocking. Also, without James Rado, Ragni's co-lyricist, librettist and partner, he was flying solo with *Dude* on a wing and a prayer. Ragni shopped around a draft that weighed in at over 2,000 pages—ten times the length of an average musical script. I'm sure this original doesn't exist anymore, and from all I've read, something tells me it may not have been typed in the format of a play. Or for that matter, even typed.

Ragni's vision was to set *Dude* in a circus-style environment with the audience on all four sides. Though some shows had been produced in this manner Off-Broadway on smaller scales, utilizing a Broadway house for this purpose was a new concept. Such an undertaking had to include not only the expense of its construction, but that of its deconstruction, as the theatre would have to be returned to its original configuration once it closed. The projected cost for that was $100,000 which, in today's dollars, would be four to five times that amount.

So who would take on this dubious enterprise? What producer in his or her right mind would get involved with something so out of control before it even started? Surely it would have to be someone with an enormous desire to get a foot in the door and their name as producer above the title ... someone with ambition and perhaps a touch of deviousness ... someone maybe a bit pathological, slightly delusional and with an assured ability (at least in their own mind) to get things done, no matter what the cost.

Make way for Adela Holzer.

A self-made woman with a suspicious background, Adela Lafora arrived in New York in her early twenties (that point is debatable) from Spain (okay, that much is true) and barely speaking English (or so she said). Relatively quickly, she married a wealthy shipping tycoon, Peter Holzer, becoming his business partner and sharing the high life in a well-appointed townhouse. She refashioned herself into a glamorous woman of means, edging her way into society. With a desire to make a name for herself, she began investing in the theatre.

Luckily for her, the first check she wrote was for *Hair.* Telling anyone who would listen, Holzer never varied from her claims that her $50,000 investment yielded $2 million in return, which wasn't true. But telling a lie came as easily to Holzer as telling the time. Her autobiography, *If at First ...*, is as close to reality as anything in *Game of Thrones.* Its cover features an attractive photo of Holzer and the tag line: "The Cinderella story of a young Spanish woman who became an American tycoon." It was published the same year she was arrested on charges of grand larceny for looting her investors of $9 million.

Bernie Madoff-style, Holzer semi-mastered the art of the Ponzi scheme, proposing tantalizing opportunities too good to be true. Staving off clients who demanded to see results, she would con them by finding new victims and distributing their investments, disguised as incoming profits. These illegal activities sent her to prison in 1983. After serving two years, she was released, no longer with a husband (Peter Holzer divorced her), a place to live, or any money.

With the ferocity of the "wrongfully convicted" and working every possible angle, within a few years Holzer painstakingly secured enough up-front cash to reestablish her reputation—where else?—in the theatre.

Her new project was one with the potential to make *Dude* look dull and tranquil by comparison: a show about the red-baiting 1950s zealot, Joseph McCarthy. It should go a long way towards describing what a freak show *Senator Joe* was in that it featured an actor playing an enzyme in McCarthy's diseased liver—and it was a musical!

After a couple of meagerly attended previews, the show gave up the ghost in the course of two days in early January. By the end of February, Holzer was arrested again, and soon sentenced to another term in prison.

The dual shambles of *Dude* and *Senator Joe* were staged (in the broadest sense of the term) by Tom O'Horgan, a director who was able to secure a good deal of work on Broadway based solely on his two biggest credits, *Hair* and *Jesus Christ Superstar*.

It was no coincidence when one critic wrote of *Dude* that "it combines the worst of *Hair* and the worst of *Jesus Christ Superstar*—a void-plumbing feat."[4]

As for *Dude's* subtitle, "The Highway Life," no one ever knew what it meant. As one critic wrote "There's no suggestion of anyone actually going anywhere in any way." Among *Dude's* cast of survivors is Dale Soules (currently killing it as Frieda, the convicted murderess on Netflix's *Orange is the New Black*), who recalled *Dude* for me with a tender fondness:

> *I believe Gerry Ragni started out with the intention of telling a kind of parable about the journey of a young man making his way along the "Highway Life" … life in the theatre universe. But we were confused from the beginning and continued to be so. Despite the many problems, the reward was meeting wonderful and talented people, including Billy Redfield, Rae Allen, Michael Dunn, Louis Falco's dance company … many of whom are still friends, including the gentleman on the poster. ***
>
> *There is nothing quite like a difficult experience, gone through collectively, to bond a group of people.*

The initial ad in the *New York Times* gave the first clue that something out of the ordinary was going on with *Dude;* for instead of seats in the orchestra, front and rear mezzanine, it designated these sections as

---

* Kevin Geer, a friend of Ragni's, began rehearsals as the star of *Dude*, until it was discovered that he couldn't sing. Quickly let go, Geer's posterior remained on the poster for posterity.

Foothills, Valley, Mountains, Trees and Tree Tops. In what amounted to a massive overhaul of the Broadway Theatre, all its seats were removed on the floor to create a stage in the round at the center of what was formerly the orchestra. A raised row of seats was constructed on the actual stage, now mirroring the still-existing balcony, which is where I sat: up in the "treetops," for $3.

As it turned out, this construction escalated with misfortunes. Eventually it became a toss-up as to which was worse: problems with the show's story or its gargantuan physical production—neither of which made any sense.

For starters, there was actual dirt distributed onto the stage floor, part of Ragni's demand for "realism." This served mainly to soil the expensively distressed costumes and cause dust storms whenever the actors trampled on and off, to the accompaniment of coughing fits from the audience.

The first remedy for correction was to hose it all down, turning everything literally to mud. The second fix involved scraps of brown felt laid down to fake the
look of things which, after failing, gave way to plastic—the opposite of dirt.

Besides the uncomfortable physical environment, the actors were in revolt of the script, filled with so much gibberish as to make them not only confused, but angry. To combat the chaos, Actors' Equity was called in to investigate what union rules, if any, were being violated. One such transgression involved Ragni's sister, who had been recording all the rehearsals. This might not have been so terrible, except that the actors discovered things said of a personal nature offstage finding their way into rewrites, and then having to speak them onstage.

Ragni also allowed his brother, a priest, in on the process. His main contribution was demanding the show take on more religious overtones. In time, both Ragni's brother and sister were barred from the theatre.

Within this turmoil it fell to two veterans with impressive résumés in the theatre to rise above the fray, William Redfield and Rae Allen. Unfortunately, their roles, which may or may not have represented Adam and Eve (they were never sure), prevented them from doing their jobs properly.

Redfield, who died in 1976, was quoted in an article for the *New*

York Times as saying, "The show was never completely blocked. And we didn't dare discuss the script. How could we? There was none."[5] In the spirit of self-survival, Redfield admitted he and Rae Allen made up their own dialogue. "We had to. It was either write it or stand mute in the confusion."[6]

Redfield's widow, Lynda, spoke with me about this anomaly in her husband's rich and diversified career, which dated back to his Broadway debut at age eleven in the original cast of *Our Town*.

> *Poor Bill. He signed on with such hopes that this would be a bold new experiment and it was quickly apparent that everyone was in over their heads. And the physical exertion was so awful with all that mud and dirt. I had to go to Hammacher-Schlemmer and buy a portable Jacuzzi so he could soak it all off!*
>
> *I was there at the last performance. They played it to an empty house in that cavernous theatre. It was all so sad.*

When I entered the Broadway Theatre that September afternoon for *Dude*, my mind went straight to it being my first time back since a few months earlier when I attended the 1972 Tonys.

That's right. At fifteen I somehow managed a ticket to the Tonys. Though I've since forgotten how I got there I do remember what I paid—$10—as I had never spent that much on a night at the theatre before. Even more expensive was the cost of renting a tuxedo. By this point I was supplementing my income from the paper route by babysitting, as well as sidelining as a ticket broker for some of my *Newsday* customers. Being handed a few bucks for my troubles was great, especially as it was hardly any trouble.

This made it possible to come up with the cash for the Tonys, the tux and my tickets to the Tonys ball, which I think cost an extra $25. The entire evening was a mind-blower, but the absolute highlight was during the awards when Ethel Merman was given a special Tony for Lifetime Achievement. As the story goes, when "the Merm" was informed that an all-star cast would perform her most famous numbers, she told them, "No way! No one's doing my songs but me!" Which was how everyone got to enjoy Ethel Merman—starring in a salute to herself.

And I got to see the whole show from the last row of the Broadway Theatre about as far away from the action as possible (the Broadway is enormous). I didn't care. After all, there was never any problem hearing Ethel Merman.

But now what to make of the Broadway Theatre and all that *Dude* wrought five months later? What I saw was a circus, center ring and all. Ropes dangled overhead and the orchestra was split on various levels (good luck to *that* conductor). It all made for a very confusing jumble that caused one critic to state: "It's the first time I ever felt sorry for a theater." [7]

My ticket for the Treetops was exactly that—way up at the highest point. I took my seat, found the view fantastic, and was kind of exhilarated.

Then the show started.

By the time I had gotten to it, *Dude* was in one of its countless previews, with no announced opening date in sight. O'Horgan had replaced the first director after three performances. Although I'm sure he tried to bring order to the confusion, in characteristic fashion he contributed nothing more than his patented (and predictable) sense of weirdness.

What little chance he had to get at the core of what ailed the production was blocked by Ragni, who was incapable of seeing the forest for the trees (or treetops, as it were). Since he believed everything he wrote was gold he couldn't bring himself to engage in the necessary rewrites. Ill-equipped to handle the intense pressure cooker of an out-of-town tryout *in* town, his nerves were shot and he was often spotted by the company walking around in a daze, which is not uncommon for writers at the epicenter of a troubled musical.

In my review, I didn't mince words, and wrote: "*Dude* is horrible."

I wasn't alone.

"Spectacularly bad." – Leonard Probst, WNBC-TV

"A bulging trash basket of a musical." – T. E. Kalem, *Time Magazine*

"Extremely pretentious and juvenile." – Doug Watt, *New York Daily News*

"Incoherent, childish and boring." – Martin Gottfried, *Women's Wear Daily*

"Tom O'Horgan stage manages this debacle like a mass epileptic convulsion."

 – Walter Kerr, *New York Times*

And for sheer melancholy, nothing topped Richard Watts, whose last line in his review from the *New York Post* read: "After the first half hour it made me unhappy."

The day after its opening, *Dude's* box office take came to $500.

Continuing to heap abuse on this poor excuse for a show is akin to shooting fish in a barrel. The truth is that I've chosen *Dude* to represent all the bombs I saw in this period. Were there worse shows? You bet.

Earl of Ruston quickly comes to mind. A country-western musical for Broadway, it featured songs with titles like the enchanting "Mama, Earl Done Ate the Toothpaste Again"; the wistful "I've Been Sent Back to the First Grade" and, let us not forget, the tender and charming "Insane Poontang."

What I will always remember about this unmemorable show was that it featured the composer's grandmother in her rocking chair seated stage right the entire evening, occasionally commenting on the action.

You read that right—his grandmother.

The *Playbill* bio for the resistible Leecy R. Woods Moore, featured the folksy line, she "is making what theatre folk here call her acting debut on the Broadway stages."

My one-word review of *Earl of Ruston*, dated May 1, 1971: "Ugh!"

Such distinctions of horror need not extend solely to the musicals I saw.

Case in point: a play from 1969 titled *Angela*, by Sumner Arthur Long, a poor excuse for a comedy in which a bored housewife kidnaps a TV repairman, ties him to her bed and holds him hostage in his underwear—all to make her philandering husband jealous.

An "intolerably bad play," said one critic. [8]

This show holds a special place in my heart (I mean, that plot *alone*!), due to having seen it with my sister Joanne.

It fell to Joanne, two years younger than I, to attend shows with me that I couldn't get anyone else to see. In good times, my paper route earnings made it possible for me to buy two tickets in advance, though this meant I would often be searching for someone at the last minute (usually in vain) to accompany me. I recall long Friday nights, with the next day's matinee looming, calling everyone I knew to find a taker for my extra ticket. To make matters worse, I had to sell a lot of shows that had opened that week to pitiless reviews. Talk about working on my acting skills!

My fellow teenagers had no idea what I was talking about. Mostly I was pitching them on the excitement of seeing a Broadway show for $3 bucks, rather than try to explain titles like *The Chinese and Dr. Fish.*

There should have been one more line on my "Play Evaluation Sheet" that indicated who I saw each play with. There are some people I can remember dragging along with me (I mean accompanying me), though most I cannot. In an effort to complete the list, I recently contacted someone I hadn't seen since our high school graduation. When we spoke, the first thing he said with regard to what we saw together was, "I have no idea what it was called, but I remember Sandy Duncan in her underpants."

Without batting an eye, I said, "*Love Is a Time of Day.*"

Its author, John Patrick, had achieved far greater success with *The Teahouse of the August Moon,* which won the Tony for Best Play and the Pulitzer Prize for Drama, running for close to two-and-a-half years.

Love Is a Time of Day ran from Monday to Saturday.

And in the small world department, this two-character play co-starred the same actor who played the TV repairman in *Angela*—Tom Ligon!

Not only did he have the distinction of starring in these two awful comedies, Ligon had to play a number of scenes nearly naked in both of them. In my review of *Love Is a Time of Day,* I wrote: "Tom Ligon still has on the same pair of underwear."

These two shows opened two months apart—and at the same theatre. I imagined Ligon must have felt royally cursed, but that wasn't the case when I put the question to him:

> *Cursed? No, not at all. Please! Who was I at that stage in my career to turn work down? Back-to-back Broadway shows in leading roles? And, in the case of* Angela, *the chance to work with Geraldine Page? Come on!*
>
> *But those were not the two worst shows I did at the Music Box. I had previously done another one at that theatre*

in December 1963 called Have I Got a Girl for You. *It
opened one week after the Kennedy assassination. Not exactly
the right moment to open a comedy.*

*And to make matters worse, Dick Van Patten played a
character named Ruby! Talk about bad timing—and, unfortunately, bad luck.*

But back to *Angela*. My sister has remembered this play all these
years since it holds the added pleasure of our going backstage and meeting Geraldine Page, one of the most accomplished actresses of her time. I
remember the night almost twenty years later when Page won the Academy Award (on her eighth nomination), and Joanne called me and said,
"She was so nice after we saw her in that funny show."

Yes, my sister was a pushover. Whenever I left the theatre with her
after some stinker, I would always apologize. I could then count on my
sweet sister to usually say, "I liked it."

On this Saturday afternoon I took her backstage, as I once did my
older brother Allen, to meet the star of the show. My recollection is that
of startling a rather depressed woman dressed in a frumpy bathrobe who
stared at us wide-eyed.

Why wouldn't she? Besides the sight of a twelve-year-old and a ten-
year-old at a sex farce (unaccompanied by their parents), the matinee
played to an audience of about fifty people, as *Angela* posted its closing
notice the morning after its catastrophic reviews. It was to ring down its
final curtain that evening.

Angela marked the first time (and not my last) that I handed my ticket to an usher and was stopped from heading to my usual seat upstairs.
"Honey, don't bother," she croaked in a world-weary sigh, waving at the
empty orchestra. "Sit wherever you want."

Ms. Page was spared the critics' venom, but make no mistake, venom
was spat. In an almost existential comment, Clive Barnes in the *New York
Times* wrote: "For some unaccountable reason, *Angela* opened last night
at the Music Box Theatre." [9]

Sometimes critics take on a larger target than just a show when they
feel threatened. For the last word on *Dude,* Jack Kroll in *Newsweek* went
a different route from his colleagues. Published nine days *after* the show
closed, Kroll's review would have been unnecessary, except that he had

a considerable ax to grind. Coming out swinging, he called the show "a stupid mess," then went out of his way to attack its producers personally. This was due to a statement in the *New York Times* from the usually silent half of the producing partnership, Peter Holzer, Adela's shipping magnate husband. Angry over *Dude's* universal pans, he called out its critics as "a bunch of stone-faced old men that should not have the right to make up the public's mind." [10]

Kroll lashed back angrily, stating, "Such people are the brazen imperialists of the theater, which can well do without their piratical illiteracy. Only in America can a million dollars be thrown into the garbage disposal that is the cultural machine operated by the Holzers and their ilk." [11]

Leaving it to others to roll around in the mud, director O'Horgan, either an eternal optimist or certifiably insane, was quoted in the aftermath as saying that *Dude* was "still better than *Follies* or *Hello, Dolly!*"

So *there!*

Post-*Dude*, Gerome Ragni lived in near obscurity another twenty years, dying of cancer at age forty-eight. His one other show for the theatre was produced Off-Off Broadway in 1977, reunited with his partner James Rado once again. It was called *Jack Sound and His Dog Star Blowing His Final Trumpet on the Day of Doom*.

No comment. Let sleeping dogs lie.

As for Adela Holzer, if only she could have learned her lesson. But in 2002, she was sentenced to her third (and hopefully) last stint in jail. It was her longest incarceration—nine years—and her most serious criminal offense. She was found guilty of extorting 91 immigrants (it was thought to be as many as 700) with fake promises of facilitating their citizenships.

Oh Adela, you saucy minx!

Released from prison in 2012 at the supposed age of eighty-two, she is today, for all we know, searching for investors to fund a 50th anniversary revival of *Dude* in 2022.

Leave it to Joe Allen and a lifetime spent in the restaurant business, to sum it all up:

"Life is a cruel joke. But less cruel and more of a joke when you're in a good bar." [12]

CHAPTER 12

The Natural

John McMartin

O f the four actors I chose to profile for this book, the first
one I knew I would write about was John McMartin.
I call him "the natural," as he never took an acting lesson.
As good as he was on screen and on television, if you never
got a chance to see him on the stage then you never got a chance to *really*
see him. I am one of the lucky ones. For if there was anyone else I saw in
more shows with more pleasure than John McMartin, I can't name them.

The gift of being invited to his home by this gentle and gentlemanly
actor to speak with him about his life in the theatre was an afternoon I
will treasure forever. But between the three years of our meeting and the
time it took to complete this book, McMartin died from cancer on July
6, 2016, a month shy of his 87th birthday.

He influenced me when I was in my teens, dreaming of becoming
an actor, keeping up the promise of a contract between us (one he never
knew existed) by teaching me through his consistency in everything he
did and to which I paid close attention.

My connection with him goes back to the beginning of when I started going to the theatre and runs deep. I saw him in many different plays
and musicals and it was sometimes hard to find an actor "acting." He
just *was*. Add to that his high level of professionalism (performing with
a broken arm as recently as 2014 in *All the Way*) and you had in John
McMartin a worthy hero of the stage.

Much like Robert Preston, McMartin excelled at everything: drama, high and low comedy, farce, classical theatre and musicals. Since his
Off-Broadway debut in the operetta spoof *Little Mary Sunshine* (a big hit
in its day at over 1,100 performances), McMartin rarely stopped working. He appeared in twenty-four Broadway plays and musicals and, when
added to his Off-Broadway and regional theatre work, they encompass

close to a hundred and fifty productions in fifty-seven years.

That is a life in the theatre.

With five Tony nominations in three different categories, does it really matter if McMartin never took one home? This versatile actor was always a winner.

Some additional McMartin stats: He was directed in four shows by Harold Prince and in three by Bob Fosse. Authors and composers who featured prominently on his résumé included Tom Stoppard, John Guare, Neil Simon, Luigi Pirandello, Georges Feydeau, Eugene O'Neill, Cole Porter, Jerome Kern and Oscar Hammerstein II, Cy Coleman and Dorothy Fields, Irwin Shaw, Molière, Mark Twain and two by Stephen Sondheim—all of them on Broadway.

Modestly, he told me: "I've been luckier than most actors. I have no complaints." It is we who were lucky to have had him onstage for nearly six decades.

His roots were humble. Born August 21, 1929 in Indiana, raised in Minnesota, then Illinois, McMartin lived the rest of his life in New York City since he first arrived in 1958 ("my cold-water flat days"). Reluctant to discuss anything about his childhood when we met, all he would confess was that he lived in small towns where there were only movies:

> *My life didn't begin until I got into the theatre, so we'll start there.*
>
> *I was in the paratroops, 82nd airborne, and they came through the barracks once and asked, "Does anyone want to do a soldier show?"*
>
> *I raised my hand. I was carrying a fifty-seven recoilless rifle which weighed like fifty pounds. And we did a show called* Room Service *and I had a grand time of it.*
>
> *I thought this is interesting stuff. I always wanted to be an actor, I just didn't know how you'd go about it. I didn't know anything about theatre.*
>
> *I was in a play before I ever saw one. So there was that.*

After the army, McMartin kicked around for a time, finally settling in at the Allenberry Playhouse, located in south-central Pennsylvania. A year-round theatre since 1948 when it offered a top ticket price of $1.50, McMartin appeared there in thirty-five shows from 1954 through 1959.

Heading to New York after that, he landed *Little Mary Sunshine* directly off an Allenberry connection. His friend Eileen Brennan, cast in the title role, recommended McMartin when another actor was not working out in rehearsals. As it turned out, both she and McMartin received Theatre World Awards for their New York debuts. *

McMartin's Broadway debut was in 1961's *The Conquering Hero*, not quite up to the usual standard of its director and choreographer, Bob Fosse. Based on Preston Sturges's 1944 antiwar comedy *Hail, the Conquering Hero*, after a war-torn out-of-town tryout, it limped into New York severely wounded. Having fired Fosse, it was that rare commodity: a show with no director listed in its opening night program. It ran one week.

This would prove to be an all-too-common occurrence for the young McMartin, as his next three Broadway shows over a period of two-and-a-half years came to a combined total of about three months' worth of performances.

"I always liked to say I managed to use the same box of Kleenex."

McMartin's connection to Fosse would eventually yield his first Broadway success—Cy Coleman, Dorothy Fields and Neil Simon's *Sweet Charity*. Cast as Oscar, opposite the Charity of Gwen Verdon, McMartin said: "She was magnificent … a true wonder. I would just stand in the wings and watch her when I wasn't on." [1] He would enjoy doing so for eighteen months of the show's run.

Hal Prince cast the actor as often as he could. When I told him it was my intention to write a chapter on McMartin for this book, he said, "You should. He's one of *the* great actors. His performance in *Love for Love* was the funniest thing I ever saw in my whole life. He can do anything. I'm glad you have good taste."

If that's the case, it's a taste I share with many to whom I spoke. John Glover had a long association with McMartin, as he worked with him in the early part of his career in a Broadway revival of Eugene O'Neill's 1926 drama *The Great God Brown* (directed by Hal Prince).

---

* 1959 was an auspicious year for the Theatre World Awards. McMartin and Brennan were joined by such fellow future success stories as Warren Beatty, Carol Burnett, Patty Duke, Jane Fonda, Anita Gillette and Dick Van Dyke: a group that has collectively received four Oscars, fourteen Emmys and a Tony—to date. Not too shabby.

When Hal cast me in The Great God Brown, *it was right before summer in 1972, so it would start in September and this was maybe May or June.*

And he said, "Listen, in the play you take John's personality and become him. He's in a play now. Howard Haines is the house manager. I'll tell him you're coming. Knock on the door and Howard will let you in any time you want to come."

So I saw Follies *about 35 times, down in the orchestra, because people weren't coming.*

I sighed so loud it made Glover laugh.

Follies was a major achievement for McMartin, doubly-so when taking into account his being a last-minute replacement for an actor who backed out a few weeks before rehearsals began. He also had the added disadvantage of being the sole lead for

whom the audience held no nostalgic association, something the rest of the casting hinged upon. The company was a who's who of "who's that?"—former stars of the stage and screen, many of whom had been out of the spotlight for years.

I saw *Follies* at its second-to-last preview the day before it opened. It should be no surprise to report that the physical production was more sumptuous and overwhelming in size and beauty than its photographs convey. Most of what transpired that afternoon confused and slightly bored the fourteen-year-old in me. I tuned out much of the mid-life crises of its four lead characters and instead concentrated on the extremely tall and beautiful chorus women, slinking about like ghosts in the background.

Below are two sentences from the review I wrote for *Follies* when I returned home late that Saturday afternoon. It is included here with some reluctance, as I know it's good for a laugh:

> The book is the weak spot, but its a pagent more than a story. Stephen Sondheim has written some good numbers, but his dramatic ones are bland and dull.

Yes, I spelled "pageant" wrong. Hardly my worst transgression as "<u>some</u> good numbers" takes the cake. And if "Losing My Mind" and "In Buddy's Eyes" were bland and dull to this teenager, I apologize. I have now come to understand their greatness and then some. Thankfully, the closing line of the review states "*Follies* is a very good show," so there's that.

The most memorable moment for me came courtesy of McMartin as Benjamin Stone, a wealthy philanderer, cold to his wife and trapped in his own head for much of the evening. At the show's end, the 'Follies' portion of *Follies*, its leading characters fantasize their emotional travails through a prism, performing their inner angst in musical numbers (*that* I got). In this sequence, Stone is the star of his own Fred Astaire-style song, "Live, Laugh, Love." McMartin, dressed in a white suit, complete with top hat and tails, danced and sang with aplomb. Enthralled by this number, my heart went into my mouth when McMartin staggered for a moment and appeared to go up on his lines. No doubt about it. He was stumbling. The orchestra had to vamp a bit and he couldn't find his way back into the song.

This was my 101st play and I had never seen anything like this. I turned to my companion that day with an expression of "Is this really happening?" And suddenly it all came clear: this was part of the show. This wasn't McMartin's breakdown, it was *Stone's*! When Ben screams his wife's name, "Phyllis!" I had been hoodwinked with everybody else in the theatre. The *Follies* cast album had yet to be recorded so there was no way anyone knew this was coming. It was shocking and heartbreaking. And McMartin played it to perfection.

"Someone came up to me after the show when we were trying out in Boston and thought I'd been in genuine trouble with the song," McMar-

tin confided in me. "I said to Hal, 'People think that I'm up for real.' And
he said, 'Yeah,' with a gleam in his eye. And so we kept it in."

For a glimpse of the effortless style McMartin brought to *Follies*,
there is the televised 80th birthday concert for Stephen Sondheim from
2010, where McMartin sings another of Ben Stone's solos, "The Road
You Didn't Take." Some forty years after its original production, the performance by a more mature McMartin (eighty-one at the time) is proof
of how an actor can convey in song a complexity of ideas worthy of a
Shakespeare soliloquy. If you doubt it, check out the DVD and see what
true art looks like, provided by both McMartin and Sondheim.

In his book *Finishing the Hat*, Sondheim describes McMartin in *Follies* as "thrilling." When I spoke with him, he told me, "I think my favorite three performances in musicals were, off-hand, Alfred Drake in *Kismet*, Alan Alda in *The Apple Tree*, and John McMartin in *Follies*." When
I asked him to elaborate on that, he refused. "No, I can't elaborate," he
stammered. "I can't … you can't describe those …" and his voice trailed
off.

I understood what he was getting at. For someone like Sondheim,
an artist for whom words have the ability to cut deeply into his soul,
performances can be evaluated but they cannot be quantified when they
touch or move you like that.

A favorite quote of mine comes from the actress Charlotte Rae.
When asked to discuss her favorite performances over a lifetime of going
to the theatre, she said, "It's hard to analyze the great performances. They
just are." Exactly so. If Sondheim says McMartin was "thrilling," that
should suffice.

I have my own difficulty putting into words my feelings about
McMartin's performance in Molière's 1662 tragi-comic *Don Juan*, a
turning point for me as both audience member and fledgling actor. I sat
transfixed by the comedic (as well as the dramatic) complexity of what
McMartin was doing.

At the time I saw this performance, I was in rehearsals for a school
production of Mary Chase's *Harvey*, a play that ever since its Broadway
premiere in 1944 has been one of the most produced plays in America, particularly with school groups. The plot concerns Elwood P. Dowd,
a genial drunk who befriends (much to his family's consternation), a
mythological Pooka, a six-foot-one-and-a-half-inch rabbit that no one

John McMartin as Benjamin Stone in *Follies*.

else but Elwood can see.

I was resolved to give my all to the role of Judge Omar Gaffney, the family retainer of Elwood and his sister, Veta. In the hope of bringing as much as possible to my characterization (and all I had learned at the Ruth S. Klinger Theatre Workshop), I decided that the Judge was in his sixties, which is how I became intimate with a can of "Streaks N Tips." That, along with crepe hair and latex, created an accompanying droopy mustache for the full picture.

I cut my hair shorter for the part (if that can be believed)
and costumed myself in my brother Allen's five-year-old
bar mitzvah suit, which no longer fit him.

Judge Gaffney is a small role, but I was resolved to find a moment to shine, even though the character doesn't get much stage time. His main purpose is to move the plot along without anything really juicy to say or do. However, with a few years of seeing some pretty great comedic actors on the Broadway stage (like McMartin), I was fast learning how to appreciate and discover where the "funny" was.

I had also observed how a clever actor, if given the right line, could garner some exit applause. I was determined to get mine, even if it would require a bit of business to get there and something more than the words and a firm door slam to achieve it.

The situation, minutes before the play's conclusion, is that a doctor at the local sanitarium is about to inject Elwood with a serum that will banish Harvey from his mind forever. My character has come to Veta's aid in her quest to rid her brother of his delusion. When Veta, in a last-second change of heart, can't go through with it, the Judge's frustration is set loose.

Here I must confess to going a little "over the top" (translation: overacting).

"Have it your own way," I shouted, crossing the stage for my overcoat.

Then, while thrusting my arms in its sleeves and smashing my hat to my head, I opened the door and stood my ground: "I'm not giving up my game at the club again, no matter *how* big the animal is."

Requisite door SLAM and exit applause!

A triumph.

It has taken me a *lifetime* to rid myself of such bad habits.

* * * *

I don't consider myself a singer. I did a musical, The Boy Friend, *and I wasn't supposed to be in it. But they fired the guy. I didn't think that's where I was going to go—in musicals. But you go where it takes you.*

When McMartin told me this, it struck me as a bit odd, as the musical-comedy form fit his talents perfectly. His exuberance, showmanship, and sheer joy in performance was never displayed better than in the lavish 1992 Broadway revival of *Showboat*, directed by Hal Prince. As Captain Andy, McMartin balanced his duties as master of ceremonies, caring father and harried husband, all while projecting a kindly stage presence, not an easy feat without appearing cloying. And late in the musical when he traded in his sailor's cap for a top hat, it quickly brought to mind his Ben Stone in *Follies*. I thought, "Hand John McMartin a top hat and all is right with the world."

Then there's his physicality. Fair, thin and tall, he always found a way to use his wonderful set of hands with great efficiency. When he played someone distracted (or drunk), his hands seemed detached from his body. They would flounce about as if devoid of connection to any brain signals being sent.

His voice was unlike that of any other actor. Capable of high highs and low lows, sometimes reaching falsetto, McMartin could then drop it suddenly to a distinctive growl to unique comic effect. This brings to mind his virtuoso turn as Uncle Willie in the 1998 musical *High Society*. A friend of mine once described this performance by saying, "McMartin slipped the show in his side pocket and walked away with it."

Months later, when this same friend saw McMartin in a restaurant in New York, he said to him, "I really thought you were going to win the Tony for that." McMartin replied, sighing, "So did my wife."

To whom McMartin referred was his partner Charlotte Moore, the actress and artistic director of the Irish Repertory Theatre in New York City; its founder and guiding force since it opened its doors in 1988. They met in 1972 during the time they were performing on Broadway in rep in *The Great God Brown* and *Don Juan,* and they were together forty-four years.

In November 2015, I asked Charlotte what her thoughts were on what made McMartin's acting so special:

> *What kind of actor do I think Jack is? He's a natural. He never had a lesson. The first time he appeared onstage he had never seen a play. He didn't know what a play was and he was up there doing one.*
>
> *And he's been at it ever since.*
>
> *When I'm cueing him, which is often, it never fails that I'm unsure if he's just talking or whether I'm cueing him. I find that*

extraordinary, because I don't know of anybody else who fools me like that.

Even when we were in a play together and he would talk to me onstage, he would say something and I would be like, "Wait a minute? Is that a line?"

No, Jack tells the truth.

The deep sensitivity McMartin brought to his acting also permeated his personal life. George Hearn told me that he once inquired of Charlotte, "How's Jack doing?" and her response was, "Oh, he got some bad reviews for something and now I can't get him out from under the dining room table."

That notwithstanding, the good will and respect McMartin earned from critics, as well as from his peers, was substantial. It was a pleasure to speak with a small sample of the hundreds who have worked with him, and for them to share a few memories of their experiences:

Ed Dixon: *I was with John in the 2011* Anything Goes *revival just before it closed. He had this one bit of physical humor at the end of the show where he would do this great take. It had about five parts to it. He'd lose his balance, stamp his foot down, and run across the stage.*

At the very last performance he added something else to it that made it better than it had ever been and the whole company could barely keep a straight face. It was so funny.

Afterwards, I asked him, "How did you come up with that?"

He shrugged and all he could say was, "You have to keep trying."

After doing the show a year ... and on closing night! How about that?

When it comes to comedy, John is like a brain surgeon.

Randy Graff: *I was so thrilled when I got the opportunity to work with John in* High Society *as we were going to have a lot of scenes together. And in order to be at my very best, I not only memorized my lines, but his as well. I was going to be a full partner and be on top of everything in every way I could.*

*So one night, we're singing "I'm Getting Ready for You,"
and I went up! I had no idea where I was. I stared at John
and it felt like three minutes, even though it was probably
thirty seconds, but still a long time to do nothing onstage.
And this was in the middle of the song!*

*The orchestra was vamping and it was all on me be-
cause John was now as lost as I was. We stared at each other
like two deer in the headlights. Finally, John made a gesture
with his hands, pretending they were paws, and purred like
a kitten. I did it back to him, pawing and purring, and the
audience loved it, but it still didn't help us find the lyrics, so
we went into a little soft-shoe.*

*To this day I don't know how we found our way back
into the song. Resourceful as always, John saved the day.*

John Glover: *One of my favorite stories is from the time he
was auditioning for something and they asked him, "How tall are
you."*

John shot back "I'm 6'2."

They said, "Ugh, we need somebody shorter!"

"Oh," John said. "Did I say 6'2? I meant 2'6!"

That's John McMartin.

Viewable on YouTube is a *David Frost Show* from 1972, when leading cast members of *Follies,* as well as Sondheim and Prince, sat for interviews and performed on the broadcast to promote the show. Grinning
with a nervous, tight smile, McMartin goes through the paces of answering questions, visibly squirming as if he'd rather be anyplace else. Yet he
is funny and endearing. At one point, Frost asks "I've heard you are very
ill at ease on talk shows. What happened?" McMartin half-smiles and
replies, "This isn't me talking."

That shyness was perhaps why McMartin made so few other appearances like this on television. Such thoughts were on my mind when
I discussed with Hal Prince how I needed to speak with McMartin for
this chapter.

"You should," he said.

"He's so shy though. To get him to talk about himself would be—"

"He's shy, but he'll talk. You call Charlotte and say 'Hal said—' and then Jack will talk to you. I don't know how *much* he'll talk. You'll see."

And thanks to Charlotte, that's how I wound up in 2013 in the study of their home on West End Avenue in New York City.

Some highlights:

The absolute first Broadway show I ever saw was My Three Angels. *And I did it the very next season in summer stock.*

Then the second show I saw was The King and I *and that just blew me away. Jesus, it was eye-opening and light-bulb time for me. Simply beyond magnificent.*

Once when I was in A Little Night Music *regionally, I was having a terrible time with one lyric in the first song, "Now, as the sweet imbecilities tumble so lavishly onto her lap."*

So I called Len Cariou, who had created the role, and I launched into the problem over this one damn lyric and Len interrupted immediately.

"Now, as the sweet imbecilities tumble so lavishly onto her lap, right?"

I said, "How did you know?"

He said, "Jack, everyone has trouble with that!"

I resent when people try and put me into one category or another. You do plays or you do musicals. It really kind of pisses me off.

One day I was coming out of Follies *at the Winter Garden and somebody said, "I brought up your name the other day with a teacher of mine, and she said 'Well, we don't know what he can do, he does musicals. We don't know if he can act.'"*

I certainly had no training in the classics, but once I got to them they were a gift from God. It's all there in the text.

All the stuff I was getting to do in Allenberry, that was still off the press—a lot of it was comedy—and I got to test it in front of paying audiences. Oh, the audience can teach you so many things.

To his core, McMartin was a true creature of the theatre, doubly so on the subject of the ritual of what happens after the curtain comes down. For many years, he could be found after a performance in some theatre-district haunt enjoying a libation. The names Christopher Plummer and Jason Robards were some of the high-profile types (and celebrated drinkers) with whom McMartin would, in his own words, "hoist a few."

Many of those post-show marathons were at Sardi's, the 44th Street bar and restaurant that has been a fixture in the theatre district for ninety years. When you first enter, there is a cozy side bar to the left where an oversized black-and-white photo is on display. How it got there is best told by McMartin himself:

> *Vincent Sardi was a lovely friend and when I was doing that play, I would come in every night because we were just up the street from Sardi's. And Vincent said he would love to have that photo of me from outside in front of the theatre after we closed. "Could you get me that picture?" he asked.*
>
> *I said, "Yeah, I think so …" and this was when Sardi's had the bar where the cloakroom is today. And after I got permission and gave it to Vincent, the next thing I know it's the centerpiece of this new bar and it's just towering over everyone that walks in there! It's so embarrassing—you come in and "Ahhhh!" At first I thought he wanted it for his wallet or something. Now when I look at it I figure that no one knows who it is anymore.*

I do. And so would any number of people who saw this performance or others in his series of unforgettable portrayals.

John Glover appeared in *Don Juan* with McMartin. When I quoted the last lines of the play to him, "My wages, my wages," and told him how I would never forget the way McMartin cried and the look in his eyes, he smiled.

"That's because you feel he loves you," he said.

And he was right as that feeling of love was also a source of inspiration. For when it came time to audition for college acting programs, my path to acceptance was to outright steal McMartin's Sganarelle characterization. I would open with George from John Steinbeck's *Of Mice and*

John McMartin as Sganarelle in Don Juan *(1972)*

Men to highlight my dramatic skills, and then follow with my knock-'em-dead Molière.

Upon finishing both pieces at my Purchase audition, my first-choice school, I was surprised when the auditioner, Joseph Anthony, said to me, "I'm interested in George."

I'll never forget his saying that. What he was proposing was that I had more of myself to offer. We took the time to discuss who George was, who I was, and look for attributes that lined up. He then asked me to do it again, where I made some improvement. How much, I had no idea.

I was uplifted being directed by a man of Anthony's experience and reputation. He had only recently retired from a first-rate career as a director on Broadway. I left the room elated, even though I had no way of knowing if I had given him what he wanted. For years, the way I measured an audition was by whether they liked me or not—totally the wrong way of thinking. What's important is whether *you* like what you did. If you leave satisfied, you have been successful. The mistake is measuring success based on getting the job. Hiring may often have nothing to do with the quality of your audition. It's more often to do with how short or tall you are, or if you look enough like the actor cast as the father to play his son.

Happily, I did well enough to be one of the twenty-five students chosen for Purchase's fourth year of admittance. The education I received there helped shape me as an actor, but more significantly, as a person.

* * * *

On July 8, 2016, two days after his passing, I attended a gathering held for friends and family of John McMartin, where there was sadness and joy in equal measure. I found myself among a small group discussing his final role, a guest appearance in 2015 on the Netflix comedy series *The Unbreakable Kimmy Schmidt.* McMartin played a well-to-do though addled senior citizen who goes out on a blind date with Kimmy (Ellie Kemper) and mistakes her for a Nazi. Chasing her out in the street he hurls a pine cone at her shouting, "Grenade!" Carol Kane, one of its series regulars and a longtime friend of McMartin's, told us that at the table read, "Jack was so funny we couldn't go on. We all had our heads down on the table, pounding it with our fists." McMartin's performance as Grant Belden proved a heck of a send-off, exiting with a bang, not a whimper.

Three months prior to his death, I received a prized email from "Jack," after I had sent him this chapter for his approval:

> *Dear Ron,*
> *I was blown away by your kindness in your forthcoming book.*
> *The best review I ever received! Or any actor could hope for.*
> *Charlotte and I enjoyed your company so much, it never occurred to us we would be treated with such care in print.*
> *Congratulations on all your hard work. May you be praised as high as you did me.*

All the best,
Charlotte and Jack

At the conclusion of our one-and-only time together, after talking for two hours, he said to me, "This wasn't an interview. It was a conversation."

Kind soul that he was, I wish there had been more of them. Rest in peace.

CHAPTER 13

The Critic

The reviews I wrote as a teenager are more than just a chronicle of the shows I saw. They demonstrate a yearning to be taken seriously in my opinions.

I read a host of critics back then. Their writings on productions old and new emboldened me to think that perhaps I could do the same thing. This is what inspired me every evening after returning home from a matinee to file my own review. Since I was already an inveterate list maker who enjoyed nothing more than a good ritual, this was an easy thing for me. I did it with drive and discipline.

I knew that my writing could never measure up to the professionals, what with my awkward mix of youthful enthusiasm and ambitious over-reach. I looked to cultured critics like Brendan Gill of the *New Yorker*, who, in one brief sentence, had the ability to combine in equal measures both humor and truth. For example, of the only time Katharine Hepburn ever sang in a musical, Gill wrote: "*Coco* is a terrible show and well worth going to see."

Re-reading all 200 of the reviews I wrote makes it clear that I was creating a writing style all my own; taking opinions I wasn't shy about offering in conversation and preserving them for what I guess I hoped would be posterity. The takeaway, however, is less about posterity and more about how unintentionally funny they are—never more so than when a play or musical made me angry.

The Year Boston Won the Pennant, by John Ford Noonan, prompted a cruel review—so it's as good a place to start as any. A strange and dark comedy, I brought up *Pennant* with John Lahr. It was produced by the Repertory Theatre at Lincoln Center, when he was the literary advisor there.

"You know," he said, "that's not really a bad play."

I admire the hell out of John Lahr so my immediate thought was I should take another look at it—except the play has been out of print for decades. When I did find a copy at the library, it was available solely for reference and I wasn't allowed to leave the room with it. As I sat down with the play, I felt as trapped as when I took my seat in the Forum Theatre (now the Mitzi Newhouse) all those years ago.

Not really. I enjoyed reading it. With its absurdity, it's clear now that Noonan was writing a metaphor for Vietnam. Did this realization make me want to read everything I ever panned and reassess them all? No way. But this was instructive nonetheless.

Here's my review, which fairly or unfairly is possibly more entertaining than the play. It was my 16th show and the 6th straight play I saw. The "Play Evaluation Sheet!" (you gotta love the exclamation point!) tells the rest of the tale:

PLAY # 16

<u>PLAY EVALUATION SHEET!</u>

PLAY _The Year Boston Won the Pennant_ (LIMITED-RUN)
STARS _Roy R. Scheider and Marcia Jean Kurtz_
DIRECTOR _Tim Ward_
AUTHOR(S) _John Ford Noonan_
MUSIC _____
LYRICS _____
SEAT _A 30_
PRICE _$300_
DAY I SAW IT _June 1, 1969_ (SUN, MAT)
THEATRE _Forum_

PLOT — _A baseball player who has lost his arm tries to make a comeback._

(REVIEW)

This show is probably supposed to be in some way symbolic, but I faid to see it. The play shows the rise and fall of Marcus Sykowski's rise and fall as a pitcher for the Boston Red Sox. The fall due to his losing his pitching arm (how, we don't know) It shows him desperate for money, a man after his life, his wife faking their baby being kidnapped for publicity, his being beaten up and losing fingers on his only hand, his going to someone's funeral because it was said the boy killed himself because of Marcus, the wife kidnaps the people after Marcus, Marcus gets a fake arm, pitches at a stadium, and is killed. It was so bad I would have slit my wrists.

Ted Chapin, president of the Rodgers and Hammerstein Organization, is fond of asking theatregoers who began at a young age (as we both did), what was the first experience that made you realize: "Wait, they're all not going to be so terrific?"

Going through my reviews it appears that it happened for me at play #9:

PLAY # __9__

PLAY EVALUATION SHEET!

PLAY George M!
STARS Joel Grey and Jerry Dodge
DIRECTOR Joe Layton
AUTHOR(S) Michael Stewart and John and Fran Pascall
MUSIC George M. Cohan
LYRICS George M. Cohan
SEAT C 2 (Box)
PRICE $4.00
DAY I SAW IT April 13, 1969 (Sun. Mat.)
THEATRE Palace

PLOT - The life of George M! Cohan, as portrayed by Joel Grey.
(REVIEW)
Tsk, tsk, tsk! That's all I can say. My hopes were up high, and they fell faster than a bird with no wings. George M! was awful. Joel Grey was not up to par, and the supporting players were all 2nd rate. The music, by George M. Cohan, is a little outdated, but there are a few good tunes, and a few good numbers. But it never gets off the ground. The second after you walk out you don't remember what you've seen. It ain't no "Hello, Dolly!"

"My hopes were up high, and they fell faster than a bird with no wings." Clunky, yes. But at least at twelve I was experimenting with metaphors.

My disappointment in *George M!* reminds me of what James Wolcott once said about his friend and fellow critic, Pauline Kael. Before a film would begin, Kael would take Wolcott's hand and say, "Let us pray."

Whatever god Kael was appealing to was in the hope of a transcendent experience, which is the reason any of us go to a play, film or concert in the first place, isn't it?

When it came to playwrights like Harold Pinter, who wrote in a less linear and more indirect style than his contemporaries (to say the least), I have to admit my younger self was at sea. I had no frame of reference for his work, and I couldn't grasp the point of his plays. Over time, through maturity as well as study, I gained enormous respect for Pinter. Now I revere the man and rarely miss an opportunity to see his plays when they are revived.

It would appear from my review of *Old Times* that I walked out on it, something of which I have no memory. Considering it is about memory and what we choose and don't choose to remember, this feels like a Pinter-style mystery in the making:

PLAY # 137

PLAY EVALUATION SHEET:

PLAY Old Times

STARS Robert Shaw, Rosemary Harris and Mary Ure

DIRECTOR Peter Hall

AUTHOR(S) Harold Pinter

MUSIC

LYRICS

SEAT D 111

PRICE $3.50

DAY I SAW IT Dec. 4, 1971 (SAT. MAT)

THEATRE Billy Rose

PLOT -- Who cares and who knows!

(REVIEW)

I remember them taking about "Odd
Man Out" James Mason, Robert Newton,
and a ~~casserole~~ casserole. Barf! I
never in all my years ever thought
I'd walk out on a show, but this was
it! I never would walk out on something because you know something's
got to happen. But with Pinter you
know nothing ever happens. So
why stay? (So why go?)

The Philanthropist* was a comedy that failed to entertain me on any level. I found it an incomprehensible piece of theatre for my "fragile little mind," as Eric Cartman of *South Park* fame is wont to say:

Naturally it received over-the-top reviews. What did I know? Since it ran only 64 performances, it is possible there were more folks who agreed with me than with the critics.

PLAY # __101__

PLAY EVALUATION SHEET:

PLAY __The Philanthropist__
STARS __Alec McCowen and Jane Asher__
DIRECTOR __Robert Kidd__
AUTHOR(S) __Christopher Hampton__
MUSIC ____
LYRICS ____
SEAT __D 107__
PRICE __$3.00__ (REG $3.00)
DAY I SAW IT __Mar. 13, 1971 (SAT. EVE, PREVIEW)__
THEATRE __Ethel Barrymore__

PLOT --- __A teacher of words, knows nothing.__
__(REVIEW)__
__During the first act, a man sneezed__
__in the balcony. It was the high-__
__light of the show.__

* * * *

The story of my review of the first Shakespeare I ever saw should be told in tandem with the story of my visit backstage after the show.

It was a 1969 production of *Hamlet* with an all-British cast that was headed by Nicol Williamson, an *enfant terrible* renowned for behavior of the worst kind, much of it onstage in front of paying audiences.

En route to New York during its Boston engagement, Howard Panter, the production stage manager told of how "the first night was going very badly. The audience was restless … and the performance was deteriorating." [1] Williamson, angry with himself, threw down a goblet during the first scene and walked off the stage. As stage manager, it was Panter's call and he brought down the curtain. "Everyone was so shaken. … I didn't think it was a stunt at all. He was deeply depressed." [2]

Years later, on two separate occasions, Williamson's unprofessional antics again made the papers. In 1976, while appearing as King Henry VIII in the musical *Rex*, Williamson slapped a chorus member across the face at the curtain call when he thought he heard something negative said behind his back.

In 1991, things got even more contentious when during an onstage duel in Paul Rudnick's *I Hate Hamlet*, Williamson struck his co-star, Evan Handler, in a way that Handler instantly knew was no accident. Dropping his sword, Handler walked off the stage, out the stage door, onto the street, and never returned to the production. It played another seven-and-a-half weeks with Handler's understudy—and without further incident—but the die was cast. Williamson returned to the New York stage only one more time before his death in 2011—in a 1996 solo show, taking no chance interacting with other cast members.

With little knowledge of who he was at the time (let alone his reputation), I had no idea what was potentially in store for me going backstage to meet Williamson. I was so fired up and excited by what had just transpired that as soon as the curtain came down, I ran from my box seat and raced to the stage door. Arriving breathless, I was met by a brusque doorman who blew me off. "Wait outside," he said.

This was a first. What happened? Was my kid charm wearing off? Maybe I wasn't as irresistible as I thought.

After a long wait, during which time about two dozen people had gathered on the sidewalk surrounding me, the doorman popped his head out, looked straight at me and in the same gruff manner said, "You!"

I looked back at the others as if to say, "So long, suckers."

Once inside, my new friend pointed upstairs. "First door on the right."

I went up, knocked, and a deep voice ordered me to enter. And there was Nicol Williamson, an imposing sight at 6' 3". He barely looked up while attending to buttoning his cuffs, a cigarette dangling from his bottom lip.

"Hello." Then, looking past me, he asked, "Where are your parents?"

I said, "At home."

A look of surprise crossed his face. "You came by yourself?"

"Yeah," I said. "I couldn't get anyone to go with me."

Williamson laughed. I didn't realize I'd said anything funny. It was the truth. No one I asked was interested.

"Did you enjoy the show?"

"Oh yes. Very much."

"Did you understand it?"

"I think so. I do have one question. When you saw the ghost, did you really see him or was that in your mind?"

Williamson stared me down. For a moment, I believe he considered having a real conversation with me. But after a brief deliberation, he smiled, went back to his cuff-buttoning and said, "I think I'll leave you to consider that."

He then signed my program with a flourish and I was on my way.

Here's my review. Take note of the price ($2.75) and the plot summary (I *think* I was trying to be funny):

PLAY # 17

PLAY EVALUATION SHEET!

PLAY   Hamlet (REVIVAL; LIMITED RUN)

STARS   Nical Williamson and Franchesca Annis

DIRECTOR   Tony Richardson

AUTHOR(S)   William Shakespeare

MUSIC

LYRICS

SEAT   AA 7 (BOX)

PRICE $ 2.75 (TU-FER)

DAY I SAW IT   June 7, 1969 (SAT. MAT)

THEATRE   Lunt-Fontaine

PLOT -   Hamlet, Prince of Denmark is the going to avenge his
father's death by murdering the man who killed him,
his uncle, who's married his mother, so his uncle
is now his stepfather and King of Denmark. In
the process 8 people are killed.

(REVIEW)

A great production of "Hamlet" Shakespeare's immortal
classic has opened here with a multi-talented actor,
Nical Williamson in the title role. First of all it's
one of Shakespeares or any other author's greatest.
Williamson does Hamlet so the audience can understand it. Instead talking in his mind, he talks right
out to the audience, you became involved. He
plays Hamlet, in my mind, better than Olivier
in his Oscar winning movie. Williamson is accompanied by other fine players such as Mark
Dignam as Polonius.

"Instead [of] talking in his mind, he talks right out to the audience;
you become involved."

I imagine that was due to this being my first time seeing a soliloquy.

* * * *

Before exiting this fun home of one young boy and his strong opinions, allow me to provide a few more stand-alone comments for additional amusement:

- In reviewing Peter Luke's 1969 drama *Hadrian VII*, the story of an Englishman who imagines himself made Pope, my reaction signals my ignorance about religion: "This play is for someone Catholic like *Light, Lively and Yiddish* is for someone Jewish."
- The actor Robert Shaw wrote a mesmerizing play, *The Man in the Glass Booth*, that was directed in its 1968 Broadway production by Harold Pinter. I really liked it and closed out my review by saying, "There are many questions this show asks, and when you discover the answers, they will make you think."
- My misspelling here gives this bit of praise for the 1968 revival of Noel Coward's *Private Lives* a whole new meaning: "Brian Bedford and Tammy Grimes are too fine character actors."
- In that same vein, here is my negative comment of Martin Gabel's performance in 1970's *Sheep on the Runway*, by Art Buchwald: "Martin Gabel is stiff as a bored."
- Of the two Broadway shows Joan Rivers wrote, the one I saw was a pretty poor excuse for a comedy called *Fun City*. It closed in a week in January 1972. The last line of my review was an homage to TV critics of that time who always signed off with something pithy. I wrote: "*Fun City* tries to be topical, but it is only typical and predictable."
- Shamefully, at my young age, there were times when the more innovative the show, the less I seemed to grasp the nature of the ground it was breaking. I had severe reservations about Sondheim and Furth's *Company*. In the spirit of full disclosure, I wrote: "This play needs a doctor. In other words, with a little patching up this *could* be a very bright musical comedy." Of course, no one involved with *Company* was shooting for that.

CHAPTER 14

The Finale

Why did I suddenly stop my weekly theatregoing at 200 shows? Why after that did I never fill out another "Play Evaluation Sheet" again?

The red letter date was January 13, 1973. As usual, I attended a Saturday matinee. Only this was no ordinary day: it was the occasion of my 200th show.

To commemorate my 100th, nearly two years earlier, I had taken my mother's 8mm Revere silent movie camera into the city with me. In quick cuts, I filmed the marquees of all the shows running at the time, as well as the exteriors and interiors of my Times Square haunts. Something of a time capsule, it's a fun keepsake of a not-so-fun day.

The play that landed by sheer chance in the 100th slot was *Father's Day*, the second Broadway production in the infamous career of playwright Oliver Hailey. Once called "the most produced, least successful playwright in the New York theatre," [1] his Broadway debut was in 1966 with a play entitled *First One Asleep, Whistle*. It closed in one night.

His last, produced fifteen years later, *I Won't Dance*, also closed in one performance.

Father's Day, which I saw at a preview, was Hailey's middle shot at fame and fortune that—you guessed it—opened and closed on its opening night. What are the odds? Not without a sense of humor, Hailey joked about his three bombs saying that "they ran all evening." [2]

This is to point out that the musical *Tricks*, my 200th show (much like my 100th), was a flop. Not a milestone, but a millstone, to paraphrase a Stephen Sondheim lyric. All I wanted was to see something fun to mark the event. Was that too much to ask? Why keep track so diligently if the numbers had no intrinsic meaning? Where were the perks along the journey?

Tricks, loosely based on Molière's *Scapin*, was about a scoundrel and his wily ways. Coarse when it should have been witty, it didn't have a single song worth singing (I'm sparing the names of all concerned).

I had already read the half-hearted reviews earlier in the week, so I knew heading in this wasn't going to be remotely what I had in mind as a way to celebrate.

Still, *Tricks* shouldn't bear all the blame for my disenchantment. Broadway had been brought to its knees in these rough early years in the 1970s and I had been seeing an increasing decline in quality for some time. In going over the final eight months of this period, here is a partial list of titles of some shows I saw, followed by the number of performances each one managed to squeeze out:

May 20, 1972 - January 13, 1973:

- #173: *Heathen* (1) One night was all it deserved.
- #178: *Dude* (16) See Chapter 10.
- #179: *Hurry, Harry* (2) Opened on a Thursday, closed on a Friday, not even a weekend's run—which if not a record, is certainly an ignominious achievement.
- #181: *Mother Earth* (12) A rock musical about the environment, produced by Roger Ailes before his Fox News days. I wrote: "We know we shouldn't litter or use colored toilet paper already and that's about as far as this thing goes.
- #182: *The Lincoln Mask* (8) As in Abe. As in dead on arrival.
- #184: *Lysistrata* (8) Greek actress Melina Mercouri in a musicalized Aristophanes fun fest.
- #185: *Ambassador* (9) A Henry James musical—what we were all waiting for.
- #186: *The Creation of the World and Other Business* (20) Arthur Miller's first attempt at comedy. And what's a comedy without Cain killing Abel?
- #187: *Via Galactica* (7) Contrary to *Alien*, in space they *can* hear you scream.
- #188: *The Secret Affairs of Mildred Wild* (23) Even Maureen Stapleton tap dancing as Shirley Temple couldn't save this one from Pulitzer Prize-winning playwright Paul Zindel.
- #200: *Tricks* (8) I called it "tremendously vulgar and pushy." As the

last original musical from Herman Levin, a man whose name was once listed above the title as the sole producer of *My Fair Lady,* I felt sorrier for him than for myself.

These 11 plays averaged a total of roughly 10 performances each, which goes a long way toward explaining why I burned out. Going to the theatre had become a debilitating experience as well as something of a chore. In retrospect, the burning need to see every show that came in each season had grown from a genuine desire into an obligation (and dare I say compulsion). In truth, I was becoming more critical with every review I wrote; less a kid with a hobby and more a young adult with considered opinions and expectations, matured out of experience.

After the final matinee of *Tricks,* and feeling miserable, I suffered additional insult to injury as this rotten spectacle had cost me $4.50. It sounds trivial, but my budget was a strict one. And with the next show on my to-do list, a new musical called *Shelter* that was asking $5 for the last row—outrageous!—I decided then and there it was time to get out (*Shelter* ran a month, by the way).

And just like that, I quit. I needed money for other things—like dating. I was sixteen, and the nice Great Neck girls I was interested in going out with had little enthusiasm for traveling into Manhattan by train to see obscure plays and musicals.

I'll never forget the look I got from the girl I took to *Elizabeth I*, a play with music which featured the 3' 10" Hervé Villechaize (soon to become well-known from the ABC series *Fantasy Island*). In what had to be the show's low point, he got a fart in the face from the Virgin Queen. Talk about diminishing returns.

I didn't stop cold turkey. There were a few things I saw over the next couple of months, including Stephen Sondheim and Hugh Wheeler's *A Little Night Music* in 1974, which was something special. It was also the last musical produced by Harold Prince where he offered the last row of the theatre for $2.

I brought up the subject of that $2 ticket when I interviewed Prince, glad to finally have the chance to thank him for making his shows so affordable back in the day. To my surprise, he told me, "Not many people took advantage of those seats, whether you think they did or didn't. They went begging night after night after night."

In the two remaining years I lived in Great Neck before I left for college, my weekly theatregoing was essentially over. My biggest disappointment over a show I didn't see, was one that proved once and for all I was no longer the same obsessive kid anymore. It was *Mack & Mabel*, by Jerry Herman and Michael Stewart, starring Robert Preston in what would be his last Broadway musical. What further proof is there of my apathy than not mustering the enthusiasm to see my favorite actor in his first musical to come to Broadway since *I Do! I Do!*? My indifference may have had something to do with reading about the show's bumpy road in the four cities where it tried out before New York. By the time it opened on Broadway, the reviews were generally dismissive and did nothing to encourage me to buy a ticket.

Perhaps the real reason I didn't see it is that I couldn't face another disappointment. When I caught the announcement in the *New York Post* that *Mack & Mabel* was closing after an ill-fated eight-week run, I considered for a moment catching its final Saturday night performance. But it conflicted with having promised my girlfriend that I would take her to the opening weekend of Bob Fosse's film adaptation of *Lenny*, a play I had seen twice during its year-long Broadway run.

It was around this time that I was getting to know my girlfriend's family. Invited to dinners at their home, I was connecting with her parents and two brothers in a far more civilized environment than the one I was used to. I was introduced to grown-up ways of behavior by example of another family's respect for communication and real listening. This was a revelation when, after all, seeking out a family is what led to my desire to become a part of the world of the theatre in the first place. Chasing after my childhood idol in a Broadway musical felt somewhat frivolous, so passing up seeing *Mack & Mabel* was a sign of maturity as well as a rite of passage. I was putting my girlfriend's wants and needs above my own. I chose to see a movie I could have seen any day of the week and missed out on a once-in-a-lifetime event. On that night I sat through *Lenny* without once thinking, "I wonder what's going on at the Majestic Theatre right now."

A year later when I arrived to start my freshman year at Purchase, something immediately opened up inside me. For the first time in two years a desire to pick up going to the theatre—if not exactly where I left off, then close enough by—took over. The school's proximity to New

York City made it ideal to organize field trips for my classmates. In no time at all, I was heading expeditions into Manhattan. Going back to Broadway was as much about rekindling my passion as it was about sharing it. It also helped forge long-lasting unions with many of my classmates.

While at Purchase I put myself on so many mailing lists I wouldn't be surprised if Box 137 in the mail room continues to get discounts addressed to me forty years later. Among the shows I arranged to see were Andrei Serban's celebrated production of Chekhov's *The Cherry Orchard*, James Earl Jones's superb performance in Phillip Hayes Dean's one person-play *Paul Robeson*, and most memorable of all, the Sirs, Gielgud and Richardson, in Harold Pinter's *No Man's Land*.

And who did I often buy a ticket for and invite along on most of these trips? Aunt Helen, of course. Retired and in her late seventies (and still in her apartment on West 77th Street), she was taken in by my group, who adored her, especially when she would pass out candies from the depths of her purse before a show would begin.

* * * *

Now with almost fifty years of theatre behind me, I continue to see as much as I can whenever I can, though certain attitudes of mine have changed. Much as great theatre energizes me, bad theatre depresses me. At a movie you can always eat your popcorn or Junior Mints and laugh inappropriately if you like. Why not? No one onscreen will know.

There were days when even if the view from up in the cheap seats made it difficult to see, I could still smell a stinker. Even when a show was truly painful to sit through, I sat. That's all changed today. If something is too excruciating to endure and there's an intermission, I head out into the street for air and recuperation. Then I'm gone.

But the biggest change of all is that I no longer sit in the cheap seats. Having the ability (most of the time) to afford seats closer to the stage, I'm not as happy if I'm too far away from the action anymore. In a simpler time, at simpler prices, when (I guess) I was a simpler kind of person, it was more than enough to be in a theatre. I didn't care where I was seated. Now I do.

Things change.

* * * *

On that note, in the four years since I began writing this book, I have had to face a fair share of change. Upheaval, really.

There was cancer surgery (completely successful, I'm happy to report) as well as the end of my twenty-seven-year marriage (amicable, which I'm also happy to report). As a result, after living in Los Angeles for thirty years I returned to New York City and the single life I left behind in my twenties. After settling in on the Upper West Side in January 2016, I flew out my best friend—my dog Dug. Three months later, I was informed out of nowhere that he had inoperable lung cancer. I was faced with the horrible task of putting him down. For anyone who has had to do this, my heart goes out to you. It was one of the most difficult things I have ever done.

Despite all of this, I continue to maintain a steady optimism, which is my nature. Hopefully my positivity will never change. Discovering new pleasures as well as rediscovering old ones invigorates me. That's part of my attraction to the theatre: finding new playwrights, actors, directors, designers—then following them on their journeys.

When I was growing up, Broadway was my refuge from the benign neglect of my parents and a home life that was anarchic and confusing. I was fortunate to find the comfort (and company) I desired among people of the theatre.

My return to New York has reconnected me with those who share the same feelings. Jason Alexander, a friend since we started in the business together in our early twenties, told me of his return to Broadway in 2015 after an absence of twenty-five years, succeeding Larry David in the play he wrote for himself, *Fish in the Dark*:

> *Having lived in Los Angeles for close to thirty years, it struck me that all the talk of a film community there was inherently false. When I returned to New York for only a limited run to do Larry's show, after such a long time away, it was so great to be reminded that there truly is a theatre community here.*
>
> *It's not just talk. It exists.*

Finishing this book in New York City is appropriate. It is where my story began. This town remains as welcoming to me as when I was eleven and making my weekly visitations. I am sustained by the warm feelings generated whenever I step inside a Broadway house—taking me back to a time when going to the theatre provided me with balance, hope and inspiration. There aren't many things that can deliver so consistently over such a long period. For that I will always be grateful.

In describing how the Broadway theatre gave her such pleasure, Julie Harris said:

> *You see so much talent here, it's just extraordinary. That is the excitement about creativity, that it never ends. It's constantly exciting us and reacquainting us with life and the past and future and the present. It's a never ending chain.* [3]

Which is why if I can manage to stick around for the next thirty years or so, there is little doubt that I will be that guy ever-so-slowly making his way into a theatre lobby, a cane in one hand and a ticket in the other.

ACKNOWLEDGEMENTS

To my children, Jeremy and Charlotte Fassler, who encouraged me throughout the years it took to write this book (with a special thank you to Jeremy for transcribing a number of interviews for me). They also need to be thanked for having lived with my Robert Preston obsession their whole lives, which prompted Charlotte to once say to me, "Face it, dad. You were in *love* with Robert Preston!"

I'm sure she was right.

To my parents, Dick and Sylvia Fassler, who presided over a rambunctious home (it wasn't easy) and, to the best of their abilities, raised six children. If I didn't require any more attention than my five brothers and sisters, I certainly commanded it. Their having never dissuaded me from following my heart's desire was a blessing. For that alone, thank you.

To Helen Brown, who took me to my first Broadway show because she knew how much it would mean to me. She lived to be close to one hundred and never stopped being anything but a kind and loving soul to me and to my siblings

I was fortunate to have two editors, Melanie Hogue and Alan Gomberg, who were invaluable in making sure everything in the book was proofed, vetted and intelligent. At least that was the goal.

Many thanks to Kimberly Brooks and all the people at Griffith Moon Publishing, who made the difficult task of getting this book ready for print seem the easiest thing in the world.

My special thanks to Jeff York for his commentary and creativity, as well as for providing such clever and humorous illustrations.

The encouragement and advice of the following people meant the world to me. Many, many thanks to: Michael Bernardi, Dave Boone, Scott Carter, Miles Chapin, Ted Chapin, Suzi Dietz, Caitlin Donohue, Paul Dooley, Larry Eichenfield, Lori Eichenfield, Allen Fassler, Robert Fassler, David Frankel, Susan Frankel, Ron Goldberg, Laurie Goodman, Janis Hirsch, Ernest Holzman, Terry Holzman, Winnie Holzman, Linda Howard, Peter Hunt, Tom Jones, Doug Kesten, Howard Kirsch, Julie Larson, Laurie Lebedin, Lou Lebedin, Loren Lester, Bob Malone, Sandy Malone, Jeffrey Marcus, John McKinney, Mark Nelson, Molly Newman, Cornelia Reed, Isabel Richardson, Peter Riegert, Elliot Rosenstein, Jo-anne Schneider, Don Spetner, Bob Swift, Carol Swift and Ken Winston.

To all those kind enough to speak or correspond with me, and whose contributions helped craft these stories, I humbly thank:

Jerry Adler, Jane Alexander, Jason Alexander, Joe Allen, Maureen An-derman, Emanuel Azenberg, Bob Balaban, Alec Baldwin, Gary Beach, Albert Brooks, Arvin Brown, Robert Curtis Brown, Maxwell Caulfield, Ted Chapin, Bryan Cranston, John Cullum, John Cunningham, William Daniels, Dan Da Silva, Ed Dixon, Harvey Evans, Peter Filichia, Peter Fre-chette, Penny Fuller, David Garfield, Anita Gillette, John Glover, Ran-dy Graff, Allan Gruet, Joseph Hardy, Sheldon Harnick, George Hearn, Paul Hecht, Adam Heller, Peter Hunt, Željko Ivanek, Timothy Jerome, James Earl Jones, James Karen, Stacy Keach, John Lahr, Nathan Lane, Paul Libin, Tom Ligon, Hal Linden, Lynne Lipton, John Lithgow, Peter MacKenzie, Alan Mandell, Leila Martin, Roberta Maxwell, Michael Mc-Guire, Bette Midler, Caroline Mignini, Robert Morse, Charlotte Moore, Christopher Murney, James Naughton, Austin Pendleton, Lonny Price, Harold Prince, Adam Redfield, Lynda Redfield, Clive Revill, Frank Rich, Peter Riegert, Stephen Root, Paul Sand, Chris Sarandon, Susan Schul-man, Carole Schwartz, Joan Scott, Jane Scovell, Thomas Shepard, Edwin Sherin, Alisa Solomon, Stephen Sondheim, Dale Soules, Brent Spiner, Clifford Stevens, Ric Stoneback, Lani Sundsten, Joel Thurm, John Till-inger, Steven Weber, Tony Walton and Sherman Yellen.

And to those I spoke with who are no longer with us, eternal grat-itude to John McMartin, Fritz Weaver, Biff Liff, Doris Roberts, Dick Latessa, Elizabeth Wilson and Mike Nichols, whose graciousness and generosity with the extra time he spent with me brought Nathan Lane's comment about him to mind: "He's like God, but more charming."

And a very special thank you to my devoted friend Ken Howard, who passed away before he could read this completed book, but whose encouragement on the chapters he read kept me going.

* * * *

When I began this process it was fitting that the first person with whom I had a conversation was William Daniels. We met on a rainy November afternoon in 2012 at Art's Deli in Sherman Oaks, California ("Where Every Sandwich is a Work of Art").

I had admired him for so many years. With a career that may well be the longest running of any of the one hundred artists I interviewed, I felt a bit daunted going in. Daniels first began in the business nearly eighty years ago, as a dancer with his two sisters—on the radio.

"My mother was Mama Rose in *Gypsy*," he told me.

I first met him in 1987 when I did a guest shot on *St. Elsewhere,* the NBC series that, besides John Adams, gave him his most fulfilling role. We corresponded a little after that and, when it was time to delve into this book in earnest, he was the first person to whom I reached out.

I could not have made a more perfect choice. Funny and forthcoming with his stories, he gave me the confidence that not only did I possess what it took to conduct a professional interview, but that this was going to be an exciting and worthwhile project.

Finally, a special thank you to Margaret Nagle, my best friend for thirty years. May the friendship continue.

ENDNOTES

Preface: "The Genesis" - *I Do! I Do!*
[1] William Goldman, *The Season* (New York: Harcourt Brace, 1969), 17.

Chapter 1: "The Hit" – *Fiddler on the Roof*
[1] *Palm Springs Arts Paper*, "Sheldon Harnick: At 90, legendary lyricist still looks forward," May 14, 2014.
[2] BBC World News Service, "Fiddler on the Roof's 50 Years of Musical Success," by Vincent Dowd, July 26, 2014.
[3] *New York Times*, "Looking Back to the Early Stages of 'Fiddler on the Roof,'" by Michael Paulson, March 28, 2015.
[4] Otis L. Guernsey Jr., *Broadway Song and Story*, (New York: Dodd, Mead & Company, 1986), 127.
[5] *New York Post*, "Theater: Mostel as Tevye in 'Fiddler on the Roof,'" by Richard Watts, September 23, 1964.
[6] Jared Brown, *Zero Mostel*, (New York: Macmillan Publishing Company, 1989), 230.
[7] Otis L. Guernsey Jr., *Broadway Song and Story*, (New York: Dodd, Mead & Company, 1986), 123.
[8] Frank Rich with Lisa Aronson, *The Theatre Art of Boris Aronson*, (New York: Alfred A. Knopf, 1987), 176.
[9] *Seattle Times*, "Harvey Fierstein finds himself in 'Fiddler on the Roof' role," May 22, 2010.
[10] Texas Performing Arts Broadway Talk Back podcast, Austin, Texas, March 4, 2010.
[11] Barbara Isenberg, *Tradition! The Highly Improbably, Ultimately Tri-*

umphant Broadway-to-Hollywood Story of Fiddler on the Roof, the World's Most Beloved Musical, (New York: St. Martin's Press, 2014), 9.

[12] Fresh Air with Terry Gross, "At 90, 'Fiddler' Lyricist Tells His Story," broadcast April 30, 2014.

[13] Interview with Herschel Bernardi, American Jewish Committee, Oral History Library, NYC, 1984.

[14] *Boston Globe*, "A Barn theater in Plymouth stars in a revival," by Stephanie McFeeters, July 23, 2015.

[15] *Los Angeles Times*, "Now it Really is a Tradition," by Barbara Isenberg, August 31, 2004.

[16] Harold Prince, *Contradictions: Notes on Twenty-Six Years in the Theatre*, (New York: Dodd Mead, 1974), 109.

[17] *New York Times*, "Michael C. Bernardi Channels His Father for a Day as Tevye in 'Fiddler', by Michael Paulson, August 22, 2016.

[18] Interview with Herschel Bernardi, American Jewish Committee, Oral History Library, NYC, 1984.

Chapter 2: "The Street"

[1] James Wolcott, *Lucking Out: My Life Getting Down and Semi-Dirty in the Seventies,* (New York: Doubleday, 2011), 56.

[2] *New York Post*, "'Here Lies Love' Seeks Happy Home," by Michael Riedel, August 14, 2013.

[3] *New York Magazine*, "Times Square: The City's Id, Now as Always," by Adam Sternbergh, October 4, 2015.

[4] *New York Times Magazine*, "Can Broadway Move?", by Walter Kerr, June 3, 1973

Chapter 3: "The Drama" – *The Great White Hope*

[1] *New York Times*, "The Winner..." by Walter Kerr, October 13, 1968

[2] *TCG Magazine*, "The Good Fight," by Nelson Pressley, 2006

[3] Ibid

[4] *Later with Bob Costas*, interview with Jane Alexander, April 1, 1996

[5] James Earl Jones, Penelope Niven, *Voices and Silences*, (New York: MacMillian, 1993), 188.

[6] *New York Times*, "Theater: Howard Sackler's 'The Great White Hope,'" by Clive Barnes, October 4, 1968

[7] Allen Jeffreys, ABC-TV, New York Theatre Critics Reviews, (New York: Critics Theatre Reviews, Inc. Vol. XXXIX, Number 27), October 4, 1968

[8] Greer Johnson, *Cue Magazine,* 1968

[9] James Earl Jones, Penelope Niven, *Voices and Silences,* (New York: Mac-Millian, 1993), 201-202.

[10] *Later with Bob Costas,* interview with Jane Alexander, April 1, 1996.

[11] *TCG Magazine,* "The Good Fight," by Nelson Pressley, 2006.

[12] Ibid.

[13] *New York Times,* "Can Broadway Move," by Walter Kerr, June 3, 1973

Chapter 4: "The Favorite"

[1] *Washington Post,* "Actress Julie Harris's Toughest Lines," by Chip Crews, February 12, 2005.

[2] *Washington Post,* "Julie Harris, Esteemed Film and Stage Actress Who Won Five Tony Awards, Dies at 87,"by Terence McArdle and Martin Weil, August 25, 2013.

[3] *New York Times,* "Julie Harris at 65: Gossamer and Grit," by Maureen Dowd, March 31, 1991.

[4] Playbill.com, "Julie Harris, Leading Actress of the American Theatre, Dies at 87," by Robert Simonson, August 24, 2013.

[5] Ibid.

[6] Seniorwomen.com, "Julie Harris—Too Good to be True?" by Rose Madeline Mula, August 9, 2000.

[7] *Los Angeles Times,* "An Appreciation: Julie Harris, Broadway Saint," by Charles McNulty, August 25, 2013.

[8] Downtownexpress.com, "For Julie Harris, Who Has Not Lived in Vain," by Jerry Tallmer, Vol. 19, Issue 26, Nov. 2006.

[9] Playbill.com, "Julie Harris, Leading Actress of the American Theatre, Dies at 87," by Robert Simonson, August 24, 2013.

[10] Elia Kazan, *Elia Kazan: A Life,* (New York: Alfred A. Knopf, 1988), 538.

[11] Walter Kerr, *Journey to the Center of the Theatre,* (New York: Alfred A. Knopf, 1979), 221.

[12] *New York Times,* "Julie Harris at 65: Gossamer and Grit," by Maureen Dowd, March 31, 1991.

[13] *Broadway: The Golden Age,* a film by Rick McKay, interview with Julie Harris, DADA Films, Inc. 2004.

[14] *The Charlie Rose Program,* Interview with Judi Dench and Maggie Smith, February 15, 2002.

15 *Laguna Beach Coastline News,* "Actress Opens Playhouse 80th Anniversary Season with a Reprise of 'The Belle of Amherst,'" by Aimee Greenberg, September 3, 2000.

16 *New York Herald Tribune,* review by Walter Kerr, November, 15, 1965.

17 *New York Times,* "Miss Harris," by Joan Barthel, November 7, 1965.

18 *People Magazine,* "Interview with Stella Adler," by Pope Brock, July 7, 1989.

19 Julie Harris and Barry Tarshis, *Julie Harris Talks to Young Actors,* (New York: Lotharp, Lee and Shepard Company, 1971), 82.

20 *Independent UK,* "Was Paul Newman's Acting Career Limited by his Good Looks?", March 25, 2010.

21 *New York Times,* "Stage View; When These Two Chat, an Era Is Speaking," by Ben Brantley, September 14, 1997.

22 *Hartford Courant,* "Julie Harris' Last Performance on Stage at Monomoy Theater on Cape Cod," by Frank Rizzo, August 25, 2013.

23 Ibid.

24 *New York Times,* "Julie Harris at 65: Gossamer and Grit," by Maureen Dowd, March 31, 1991.

25 Steve Capra, *Theater Voices,* (Oxford, UK: Scarecrow Press, 2004), 22.

26 Theatremania.com, "Stage Queen Julie Harris," by Lynda Sturner, May 16, 2000.

27 Ibid.

28 Jackson R. Bryer and Richard A. Davison, *The Actor's Art,* (New York: Lotharp, Lee and Shepard Company, 1971), 101.

29 Julie Harris and Barry Tarshis, *Julie Harris Talks to Young Actors,* (New Jersey: Rutgers University Press, 2001), 101.

30 *Los Angeles Times,* "Sharing the Soul of the Poet," by Jan Breslauer, September 3, 2000.

31 Julie Harris and Barry Tarshis, *Julie Harris Talks to Young Actors,* (New York: Lotharp, Lee and Shepard Company, 1971), 147.

32 Lin-Manuel Miranda in conversation with Blake Ross, September 29, 2015.

33 *New York Times,* "Stage View; When These Two Chat, an Era Is Speaking," by Ben Brantley, September 14, 1997.

34 *Huffington Post,* "A Public Farewell to Julie Harris," by Alec Baldwin, August 30, 2013.

35 Ibid.

Chapter 5: "The Obsession" – *1776*

[1] MasterworksBroadway.com, "It's a Masterpiece, I Say," by Peter Filichia, August 5, 2014.

[2] Myrna Katz Frommer and Harvey Frommer, *It Happened on Broadway*, (New York: Harcourt Brace & Company1998), 42.

[3] *Hollywood Reporter*, August 6, 2015.

[4] *Wall Street Journal*, Terry Teachout.

[5] *New York Daily News*, Joe Dziemianowicz.

[6] *New York Times*, David Brooks.

[7] *Entertainment Weekly*, Jason Clark.

[8] *Newsday*, George Oppenheimer.

[9] *New York Times*, Clive Barnes.

[10] *New York Post*, Richard Watts.

[11] *Journal of Commerce*, Ethel Colby.

[12] DC Theatre Scene, "Critic John Lahr's Theatrical Joy Ride," by Jonathan Mandell, September 23, 2015, http://dctheatrescene.com/2015/09/23/critic-john-lahrs-theatrical-joy-ride/

[13] New York City's Advertising Week—a talk with Lin-Manuel Miranda and *Playbill* Editor in Chief Blake Ross, September 29, 2015.

[14] *Playbill Magazine,* "The Legacy of 1776: A Conversation with William Daniels and Lin-Manuel Miranda," by Matt Weinstock, March 2016.

[15] Sirius Satellite Radio "Town Hall," recorded May 16, 2016.

Chapter 6: "The Touchstone"

[1] *Women's Wear Daily*, "Theatre," by Martin Gottfried, January 4, 1972.

[2] *The Nation*, by Harold Clurman, January 4, 1972.

[3] *New York Times*, Stage: Joe Orton's Loot directed by Tillinger, February 19, 1986.

[4] *Fairfield Citizen News*, "Joseph Maher," by Sue Kreisman Siegel, May 7, 1986.

[5] Maureen Hogan, text of remarks at Joseph Maher's memorial service, New York City, 1998.

[6] *New York Times*, "Broadway," by John Corry, March 30, 1979.

[7] *Hampstead Highgate Express*, "Not One to Shrink from Orton," by Mark Cook, November 30. 1990.

[8] *Fairfield Citizen News*, "Joseph Maher," by Sue Kreisman Siegel, May

7, 1986.

[9] *Daily Breeze/News Pilot*, "Maher and Orton," by Sandra Kreiswirth, July 10, 1987.

[10] *New York Times*, "Joseph Maher, Versatile Character Actor, Is Dead at 64," by Peter Applebome, July 21, 1998.

Chapter 7: "The Thriller" – *Child's Play*

[1] *New York Times*, "Theater: Robert Marasco's 'Child's Play' Opens," by Clive Barnes, February 18, 1970.

[2] *Time Magazine*, "The Beast of Broadway," March 25, 1966.

Chapter 8: "The Professional"

[1] *Dartmouth Alumni Magazine*, "The Actor Who Knew Too Much," by Ty Burr, July-August, 2012.

[2] *TCM Magazine*, August, 2013.

[3] *New York Daily News*, "41 Tears Later, 'The Front Page' is Again the Best Show in Town," by John Chapman, May 12, 1969.

[4] Harold J. Kennedy, *No Pickle, No Performance*, (New York: Berkley Books, 1977), 147.

[5] *New York Times*, "'Ryan Sees Something of Himself in O'Neill's People," by George Gent, April 5, 1971.

[6] Ibid.

[7] Franklin Jarlett, *Robert Ryan: A Biography and Critical Filmography*, North Carolina, McFarland & Co., Jefferson, 1990), 165.

[8] *Conversations at the Cinematheque: Remembering Robert Ryan,* text by Jeffrey Burbank, interview with Alan K. Rode and Lisa Ryan, November 11, 2009.

[9] *Newsweek*, by Paul D. Zimmerman, November 12, 1973.

[10] *Chicago Sun-Times*, December 10, 1973.

[11] Pauline Kael, *1001 Nights at the Movies*, (New York: Holt, Rinehart & Winston, 1982), 268.

[12] *Dartmouth Alumni Magazine*, "The Actor Who Knew Too Much," by Ty Burr, July-August, 2012.

[13] *TCM Magazine*, November, 2014.

Chapter 9: "The Near Miss" – *The Rothschilds*

[1] Jessica Hillman, *Echoes of the Holocaust on the American Musical Stage*,

(North
Carolina: McFarland, 2012), 127.

[2] Philip Lambert, *To Broadway, To Life!: The Musical Theater of Bock and Harnick*, (New York: Oxford University Press, 2010), 240.

[3] *New York Times,* "'The Rothschilds' Arrives with Style," by Clive Barnes, October 20, 1970.

[4] *WABC-TV,* review by John Schubeck, New York Theatre Critics Reviews, (New York: Critics Theatre Reviews, Inc. Vol. XXXI, Number 26), October 19, 1970

[5] Philip Lambert, *To Broadway, To Life!: The Musical Theater of Bock and Harnick*, (New York: Oxford University Press, 2010), 241.

Chapter 10: "The Workhorse"

[1] Kenneth Turan and Joseph Papp, *Free for All,* (New York: Doubleday, 2009), 382.

[2] *Paris Review,* "Neil Simon, The Art of Theater No. 10," interviewed by James Lipton, issue 1995, Winter 1992

[3] Maureen Stapleton and Jane Scovell, *A Hell of a Life,* (New York: Simon & Schuster, 1995), 231.

[4] *The Actor's Art*, by Jackson R. Bryer and Richard A. Davison, (New York: Lotharp, Lee and Shepard Company, 1971), 127-28.

[5] Maureen Stapleton and Jane Scovell, *A Hell of a Life,* (New York: Simon & Schuster, 1995), 196.

[6] Ibid, 94.

[7] Neil Simon, *Rewrites*, (New York: Simon & Schuster, 1996), 317.

[8] Ibid, 318

[9] Harold Clurman (edited by Marjorie Loggia & Glenn Young), *The Collected Works of Harold Clurman,* (New York: Applause Theatre and Cinema Books, 1994), 761.

[10] Maureen Stapleton and Jane Scovell, *A Hell of a Life,* (New York: Simon & Schuster, 1995), 24.

[11] Ibid, 30.

[12] *Guardian*, "Maureen Stapleton: Star Whose Fiery Eyes Lent her Conviction in Passionate Roles," by Ronald Bergan, March 14, 2006.

[13] Tennessee Williams, *Memoirs*, (New York: Doubleday, 1975), 161-162.

[14] Maureen Stapleton and Jane Scovell, *A Hell of a Life,* (New York: Simon & Schuster, 1995), 245.

[15] *Saratogian News*, "Actress Maureen Stapleton remembered for her lifelong love of Troy," by Andrew Beam, October 18, 2012.

[16] Maureen Stapleton and Jane Scovell, *A Hell of a Life*, (New York: Simon & Schuster, 1995), 207.

[17] Ibid, 30.

[18] Robert Simonson, *The Gentleman Press Agent* (New York: Applause Theatre & Cinema Books, 2010), 29.

[19] Piper Laurie, *Learning to Live Out Loud*, (New York: Penguin Random House, 2011), 239.

[20] Lillian Ross and Helen Ross, *The Player: a Profile of an Art*, (New York: Simon & Schuster, 1962), 301-02.

Chapter 11: "The Bomb" – *Dude*

[1] *New York Post*, "Broadway's Poster Boy," by Barbara Hoffman, January 29, 2012

[2] Ibid.

[3] Ethan Mordden *One More Kiss: the Broadway Musical in the 1970s*, by, (New York: Palgrave MacMillan, 2003) 12.

[4] *Time Magazine*, "Trash Basket," by T. E. Kalem, October 23, 1972.

[5] *The New York Times*, "Dude, an $800,000 Disaster… Where Did We Go Wrong?", by Patricia Bosworth, October 22, 1972.

[6] Ibid.

[7] *Newsweek*, "Bombs Away," review by Jack Kroll, October 30, 1972.

[8] WNBC-TV, Edwin Newman. New York Theatre Critics Reviews, (New York: Critics Theatre Reviews, Inc. Vol. XXX, Number 25), October 30, 1969

[9] *New York Times*, "Stage: Neglected Suburban Housewife," by Clive Barnes, October 31, 1969

[10] *New York Times*, "Dude, an $800,000 Disaster… Where Did We Go Wrong?", by Patricia Bosworth, October 22, 1972.

[11] *Newsweek*, "Bombs Away," review by Jack Kroll, October 30, 1972.

[12] *Miami Herald*, Meg Laughlin interview with Joe Allen, January, 1999.

Chapter 12: "The Natural"

[1] Broadwayworld.com, "He's Still Here: A Chat with Broadway's John McMartin," by Joseph F. Panarell, August 26, 2006.

Chapter 13: "The Critic"

[1] http://www.independent.co.uk/arts-entertainment/arts-gone-to-ground-in-the-sixties-he-was-a-superstar-the-hamlet-of-his-generation-a-dark-and-1489914.html.

[2] Ibid.

Chapter 14: "The Finale"

[1] *New York Times*, "Oliver Hailey, 60, Author of Plays and Scripts," January 24, 1994.

[2] Ibid.

[3] Jackson R. Bryer and Richard A. Davison, *The Actor's Art*, (New York: Lotharp, Lee and Shepard Company, 1971), 106.

THE FIRST 200 SHOWS

1. *I Do! I Do!*
2. *You're a Good Man, Charlie Brown*
   (the original Off-Broadway version.)
3. *Fiddler on the Roof*
4. *Red, White and Maddox*
5. *Hello, Dolly!*
6. *The Great White Hope*
7. *1776*
8. *Cop-Out*
9. *George M!*
10. *The Inner Journey* *
11. *Zorba*
12. *The Man in the Glass Booth*
13. *Hair*
14. *The Front Page*
15. *Man of La Mancha*
16. *The Year Boston Won the Pennant*
17. *Hamlet*
18. *Hadrian VII*
19. *The Miser*
20. *In the Matter of J. Robert Oppenheimer*

* *Many shows I saw, such as* The Inner Journey, *played Lincoln Center's Forum Theatre, later renamed the Mitzi Newhouse. Though technically not a Broadway house due to its 299-seat capacity, everything I saw there was of Broadway caliber with top-flight actors and, as such, has always been a part of the count on this list.*

21.   *Promises, Promises!*

22.   *Plaza Suite*

23.   *Oklahoma!*

24.   *Mame*

25.   *Play it Again, Sam*

26.   *Forty Carats*

27.   *Little Murders*

28.   *Cabaret*

29.   *Indians*

30.   *A Patriot for Me*

31.   *Butterflies Are Free*

32.   *The Penny Wars*

33.   *Three Men on a Horse*

34.   *Angela*

35.   *The Time of Your Life*

36.   *Our Town*

37.   *Buck White*

38.   *The Mundy Scheme*

39.   *La Strada*

40.   *The Increased Difficulty of Concentration*

41.   *Love is a Time of Day*

42.   *Private Lives*

43.   *Jimmy*

44.   *Coco*

45.   *No Place to Be Somebody*

46.   *Sheep on the Runway*

47.   *Brightower*

48.   *Gantry*

49.   *Camino Real*

50.   *Child's Play*

51.   *Paris is Out*

52.   *Norman, Is That You?*

53.   *Georgy*

54.   *Last of the Red Hot Lovers*

55.   *Minnie's Boys*

56.   *The Chinese and Dr. Fish*

57. *Purlie*
58. *Blood, Red, Roses*
59. *Operation Sidewinder*
60. *Look to the Lilies*
61. *Harvey*
62. *Candida*
63. *Cry for Us All*
64. *Borstal Boy*
65. *Inquest*
66. *Park*
67. *The Boy Friend*
68. *Company*
69. *Landscape and Silence*
70. *The Engagement Baby*
71. *Beggar on Horseback*
72. *Applause*
73. *Charley's Aunt*
74. *Hello, Dolly! (9th Dolly, Ethel Merman)*
75. *Othello*
76. *The Me Nobody Knows*
77. *Bob and Ray*
78. *Conduct Unbecoming*
79. *Les Blancs*
80. *Not Now, Darling*
81. *Story Theatre*
82. *The Good Woman of Setzuan*
83. *The Rothschilds*
84. *Hay Fever*
85. *The Candy Apple*
86. *Sleuth*
87. *The Gingerbread Lady*
88. *Two by Two*
89. *Home*
90. *Four on a Garden*
91. *The Playboy of the Western World*
92. *Ari*
93. *The Sign in Sidney Brustein's Window*

94.   *Happy Birthday, Wanda June*
95.   *The Birthday Party*
96.   *The School for Wives*
97.   *No, No, Nanette*
98.   *An Enemy of the People*
99.   *And Miss Reardon Drinks a Little*
100. *Father's Day*
101. *The Philanthropist*
102. *All Over*
103. *A Midsummer Night's Dream*
104. *How the Other Half Loves*
105. *Follies*
106. *Abelard and Heloise*
107. *Scenes from American Life*
108. *1776 (second visit… then stopped counting)*
109. *70 Girls 70*
110. *Long Day's Journey Into Night*
111. *Frank Merriwell*
112. *Captain Brassbound's Conversion*
113. *Scratch*
114. *Earl of Ruston*
115. *Metamorphoses*
116. *Pictures in the Hallway*
117. *Antigone*
118. *70 Girls 70 (final performance)*
119. *Applause (one and only time I saw a show from the lighting booth)*
120. *Lenny*
121. *You're a Good Man, Charlie Brown (first Broadway production)*
122. *Play Strindberg*
123. *The Trial of the Catonsville Nine*
124. *Man of La Mancha (final performance)*
125. *Fiddler on the Roof (longest running musical performance)*
126. *Grease*
127. *Solitaire, Double Solitaire*
128. *The Incomparable Max*
129. *Ain't Supposed to Die a Natural Death*
130. *On the Town*

131. *Unlikely Heroes*
132. *The Grass Harp*
133. *Twigs*
134. *The Prisoner of Second Avenue*
135. *People Are Living There*
136. *Mary Stuart*
137. *Old Times*
138. *Inner City*
139. *1776 (final performance)*
140. *Memphis Store Bought Teeth (Off-Bway, forgotten, but oh, that title!)*
141. *Fun City*
142. *Applause (2nd cast, Anne Baxter)*
143. *Jesus Christ Superstar*
144. *There's One in Every Marriage*
145. *Narrow Road to the Deep North*
146. *The Ride Across Lake Constance*
147. *Vivat! Vivat Regina!*
148. *Wise Child*
149. *The Love Suicide at Schofield Barracks*
150. *Nightwatch*
151. *Twigs (Actors Fund Performance)*
152. *Moonchildren*
153. *Sticks and Bones*
154. *Children! Children!*
155. *The Country Girl*
156. *The Selling of the President*
157. *Two Gentlemen of Verona*
158. *Voices*
159. *A Funny Thing Happened on the Way to the Forum*
160. *Sugar*
161. *Twelfth Night*
162. *Elizabeth I*
163. *Promenade All*
164. *Tough to Get Help*
165. *All the Girls Came Out to Play*
166. *The Crucible*
167. *Lost in the Stars*

ABOUT THE AUTHOR

Ron Fassler is a writer, actor and director who made his professional acting debut in 1979 at the Cincinnati Playhouse and most recently appeared in 2015's *Trumbo* with Bryan Cranston. Among the directors with whom he has worked are Mike Nichols, Clint Eastwood, Christopher Guest and Jay Roach. His dozens of TV shows, cartoons and commercials include portrayals of doctors, lawyers, journalists, game show hosts, police captains, police snitches and the voice of a talking toilet bowl. *Up in the Cheap Seats* is his first book.

www.ronfassler.org

CPSIA information can be obtained
at www.ICGtesting.com
Printed in the USA
BVHW071427250122
627118BV00008B/138

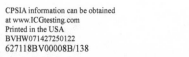

9 780999 315392